HONOR IN POLITICAL AND MORAL PHILOSOPHY

HONOR IN POLITICAL AND MORAL PHILOSOPHY

Peter Olsthoorn

SUNY PRESS

Published by State University of New York Press, Albany

For information, contact State University of New York Press, Albany, NY
www.sunypress.edu

Production, Diane Ganeles
Marketing, Anne M. Valentine

Library of Congress Cataloging-in-Publication Data

Olsthoorn, Peter.
  Honor in political and moral philosophy / Peter Olsthoorn.
      pages cm
  Includes bibliographical references and index.
  ISBN 978-1-4384-5546-4 (paperback : alk. paper)
  ISBN 978-1-4384-5547-1 (hardcover : alk. paper) 1. Honor.
2. Honor—Political aspects. I. Title.
  BJ1533.H8O57 2015
  179'.9—dc23   2014014918

10 9 8 7 6 5 4 3 2 1

Contents

Preface and Acknowledgements   vii

Introduction   1

1. Honor as a Social Motive   15

2. Democratic Honor and the Quiet Virtues   32

3. Defining the Honor Group: Loyalty and Distance   73

4. Internalizing Honor: Integrity   105

5. Denying Honor: Respect and Humiliation   133

Conclusion   155

Notes   161
References   195
Index   213

Preface and Acknowledgments

The role of honor in political and moral philosophy was already the topic of my dissertation (written in Dutch), and since then I have returned to the subject in several articles, book chapters, and papers, yet, the idea for writing this book on honor did not occur to me until working on *Military Ethics and Virtues: An Interdisciplinary Approach for the 21st Century*, which was published by Routledge in 2010. The purpose of that work was to bring scholarly discussions about some specific virtues to the current debate in military ethics on military virtues. As a result, it discussed a number of virtues, such as honor, courage, and loyalty, which do not always get a lot of attention nowadays, but are still relevant, also outside the military. Yet, looking back, honor was the underlying theme of most of the chapters, and working on that book made me realize once more that some of the old arguments for honor, brought forward by thinkers from Cicero and Sallust to Bentham and Mill, are still compelling. The aim of this book is to convince the reader of the same.

Some parts of this book draw on the just mentioned *Military Ethics and Virtues*, and I am grateful that Routledge permitted me to reuse some material. All the older material has been rewritten, updated, and expanded. I am also very much indebted to Twan Hendricks, Daniel Demetriou, and the two anonymous reviewers of SUNY Press for their useful comments on earlier versions of the manuscript. Many thanks also to Michael Rinella at SUNY Press and Diane Ganeles, Anne M. Valentine, and Lori Cavanaugh for their support during the publication process. Finally, I would like to thank the Netherlands Defence Academy for the collegial support while writing this book.

Introduction

Joseph Conrad's novel *Lord Jim*, published on the brink of the twentieth century, tells the story of Jim, his lost honor, and a failed attempt to win it back. The story takes off when Jim, a sailor with an honest appearance who chose for a life on the sea after a course of "light holiday literature," starts working as chief mate of the rusty steamer *Patna*. Although Jim and the rest of the crew realize that their ship is far from seaworthy, they nonetheless expect it to carry them, along with eight hundred or so pilgrims, from East Asia to Mecca. When the *Patna* starts taking in water and appears to be sinking rapidly, the crew decides to abandon ship—and the sleeping pilgrims with it. Although Jim had always aspired to be a hero and lives "in his mind the sea-life of light literature" (Chapter 1), he too jumps ship in a moment of weakness, joining the other three crew members who had already left some moments earlier in a lifeboat. The four reach land—and find out that the pilgrims had done so too. The vessel had miraculously stayed afloat and when the pilgrims, who had been rescued by a French gunboat, tell their side of the story this differs considerably from the account that the crew had provided, namely that they had not had the time and means to do more for their human cargo.[1] The captain and the two engineers find ways to steer clear of prosecution, but Jim does not. In fact, he does not want to flee, "from no man—from not a single man on earth" (Chapter 6). But according to one of the assessors, the immaculate Captain Brierly, not evading trial is not a sign of courage; in a case like this it is a sign of having no sense of dignity.

The hearing attracts a lot of attention, and even in the remotest seaports Jim comes to be known as a man who broke the code of honor, as someone not to be trusted, as a man "with a soft spot." It is because of

1

this unhappy episode, and because his tainted reputation keeps coming up, that he follows the well-meant advice to make a new start. After an intermezzo as a water-clerk, work without "a spark of glamour," he sets himself up as a trader in far-away Patusan, where he earns a position of trust—he becomes *Tuan* (Lord) Jim—among the local population. But his successes bring him no fame, as Patusan is shut off from an indifferent world by thirty miles of forest, and "the noise of the white surf along the coast overpowered the voice of fame" (Chapter 22). That does not preclude his past from haunting him again when a pirating rogue named Brown (*Gentleman* Brown, as he calls himself)—a man who is everything Jim does not want to be—suggests that there is common ground between them: Brown asks Jim whether he himself does not understand that when "it came to saving one's life in the dark, one didn't care who else went—three, thirty, three hundred people" (Chapter 42). Jim's judgment errs again when he misapprehends Brown's intentions, a mistake that costs the lives of several members of the local population, including Jim's best friend Dain Waris. In an attempt to redeem himself, Jim this time chooses death, and in doing so for a second time betrays those who have put their trust in him; above all, he has failed to see how the wife he found among the inlanders needs him. In the words of the narrator of the story, the sailor Charles Marlow, Jim went "away from a living woman to celebrate his pitiless wedding with a shadowy ideal of conduct" (Chapter 45).

A Quaint Survival?

Conrad's *Lord Jim* centers on a number of virtues, such as loyalty, courage, integrity, and, especially, honor, which all have in common that they, with the possible exception of integrity, have a somewhat old-fashioned ring to them. In the case of honor that marginal position today is easily explained by the fact that honor (but loyalty to some extent too) is a very inauthentic virtue, somewhat at odds with the ideals of autonomy and authenticity, valued by most people in our day (and no doubt in Conrad's day as well, although perhaps to a lesser degree). It is probably not only because of Conrad's own background—he was a sailor until his late thirties—that the story is located in a maritime setting, and thus somewhat peripheral to society at large, where different virtues hold sway. The theme of Conrad's novel, lost honor, even seems to stand in need of defense: seventeen years after its publication Conrad wrote a foreword, defending the book against a complaint by one reader who thought the story was "all so morbid." The response Conrad came up with, after an hour of anxious thought, was that

> such a consciousness [of lost honor] may be wrong, or it may be right, or it may be condemned as artificial; and perhaps, my Jim is not a type of wide commonness. But I can safely assure my readers that he is not the product of coldly perverted thinking (*Author's note to 1917 edition*).

But if we grant Conrad that Jim is not a result of "coldly perverted thinking," is it then also true that, as Conrad put it, Jim is perhaps "not a type of wide commonness?"

On first sight, someone so concerned about his honor might seem a singular character, at least in our time. According to intellectual historian Quentin Skinner, only some "quaint survivals" of honor are left today, such as the academic *cum laude* and *summa cum laude* (1978, 101). According to another author, sociologist Peter Berger, the notion of honor has become obsolete altogether (1984), while the term itself, writes anthropologist Julian Pitt-Rivers, "has acquired some archaic overtones" (1974, 39). Nowadays we like to think that we are not too concerned, and also that we should not be too concerned, about how our conduct might appear to others; we are, as we think we should be, primarily motivated by how it looks in our *own* eyes, and face and reputation are no longer considered to be of overriding importance. Many of us, at least in Western countries, accordingly hold that we, different from our distant ancestors, live in a guilt culture rather than in a shame culture, and it is generally seen as a leap forward in our moral development that our actions are only considered morally good to the extent that they are undertaken for the right reasons; good conduct should not be a result of, for instance, peer pressure, the fear of punishment, or the concern for reputation, nor of the wish for praise, esteem, and approbation. At the same time it is evident that many people are still concerned about (and influenced by) how others think of them, but this is in general seen as regrettably falling short of the ideals of autonomy and authenticity. Most modern political and moral philosophy mirrors (and to some extent feeds) these ideals. But even though honor has evidently lost much of its appeal, especially as a guide in matters of morality, the assumption underlying this book is that Jim is in fact a common type, and that

[handwritten margin notes: "Demise of reputation"; "Loosening external codes of moral conduct"; "Sociological claim"]

there is probably more of him in us than we care to acknowledge. Jim, as Conrad put it—one time in his foreword and quit a number of times, by means of his narrator Marlow, in the novel—is "one of us."

Yet, even if it is in all likelihood still a common motivator, there are, although there has been a notable increase in attention in recent years, still only a limited number of books on honor. Six fairly recent examples are Kwame Anthony Appiah's *The Honor Code* (2010), James Bowman's *Honor: A History* (2006), Sharon Krause's *Liberalism with Honor* (2002), Alexander Welsh's *What is Honor? A Question of Moral Imperatives* (2008), William Lad Sessions' *Honor for Us* (2010), and Robert Oprisko's *Honor: A Phenomenology* (2012).[2] Appiah's *The Honor Code* has received deserved praise for its description of honor as a driver of moral change, but does not go very deeply into the theoretical and historical background of its subject, honor and honor codes. Also, with its attention for the role of honor in four concrete cases that are culturally far away from most readers (dueling in Britain, footbinding in China, slavery in the British Empire, and honor killings in modern-day Pakistan), it is on the whole very different from this book, which argues that honor is something relevant outside such exotic contexts as well. Krause's book, staying somewhat closer to home, is an important work on honor in political theory, but Krause's focus on a possible role for honor in U.S. politics limits the scope of her book somewhat. The books of Bowman and Welsh focus not only on the role of honor in political and moral philosophy, but also pay a lot of attention to the place honor has in popular culture (especially Bowman) and literature (Shakespeare for instance, in the case of Welsh's book). In fact, Bowman's book does not say (and does not pretend to say) a lot on the role of honor in political and moral philosophy. Welsh's book does, but is different from this book in that its main focus is on the shape honor took during the Enlightenment, with the result that it is for the most part about honor as an internal quality, and has less to say on honor as public recognition (as is also the case, incidentally, in the work on honor of Krause and Appiah). As to all the shapes and forms honor can take: the last two books mentioned, that of Sessions and Oprisko, do a great job in explaining the distinctions between different meanings of the word honor. Both books differ from this book in that they are mainly conceptual, perhaps lacking somewhat in historical background and illustration.

In light of its presumed obsolescence it is not very surprising that the scholarly literature on honor is overall still relatively scarce, and it is the purpose of this book to contribute to our understanding of this

somewhat neglected subject. To do so, relatively many examples from
war (especially in the chapter on how honor groups are defined) and
literature will be used; in extremis and in fiction things tend to become
a lot clearer. War seems to be a setting in which notions such as honor
and loyalty still play an important role, and in many ways it forms an
excellent laboratory for studying the workings of these two phenomena. As to fiction: it is remarkable in how many novels written before,
say, the twentieth century honor and reputation, and related emotions
as shame and humiliation, are important themes—Theodor Fontane's
Effi Briest, Stendhal's *The Red and the Black*, and Thomas Hardy's *Tess
of the D'Urbervilles* are just a few obvious cases in point (as is of course
Lord Jim). Books that also remind us that, in spite of the disappearance
of honor from political and moral philosophy (and to a lesser extent also
from modern literature), we still have to find our own position as to how
much weight we want to, or have to, attach to how others judge our doings, and to what extent, if at all, we are willing to change our conduct
to bring it into conformity with those judgments.

As to that last point, until not too long ago many moral philosophers
and political theorists held the view that people cannot be expected to
do what is right without at least some reward in the form of reputational
gain. Authors such as Marcus Tullius Cicero, John Locke, David Hume,
Adam Smith, and John Stuart Mill did not so much dispute that we
can be brought to accept the principles of justice on an abstract level,
but noted that in concrete instances our strong passions, our partiality
to ourselves, and our inability to be a good judge of our conduct, often
prevent us from both seeing and acting on what is just and virtuous, and
that (external) honor, in the sense of public recognition, is a necessary
incentive to both make us see and actually do what is right. Although
they held that we generally act in accordance with what justice and common decency demand, they also thought that our reason for doing so is
more often a concern for our honor and reputation than a concern for the
greater good, and that this should not be held against us.

Today, many authors have a more demanding view, and tend to hold
that we are to be just from a love of justice, not from a fear of losing
face. The question whether this demand is realistic has been a recurring
theme from Plato's tale of Gyges' ring to, for instance, H. G. Wells' *The
Invisible Man* (1897) and Paul Verhoeven's movie *Hollow Man* (2000),
although often molded into the question what someone would do if he
or she were invisible, and the correcting gaze of bystanders no longer
fulfills its function (also the situation Jim was in when he, in the pitch

dark, jumped from the Patna). Both Gyges and the main characters of the novel and the movie, scientists Griffin and Sebastian Caine respectively, do a convincing job proving the truth of John Locke's words from the seventeenth century:

> View but an army at the sacking of a town, and see what observation or sense of moral principles, or what touch of conscience for all the outrages they do. Robberies, murders, rapes, are the sports of men set at liberty from punishment and censure (*An Essay Concerning Human Understanding* I.ii.9).

Locke believed that man has no innate moral principles (*Essay* I.iii.13), and he therefore saw a role for a form of conventional ethics that we today tend to consider morally dubious: in practice people usually behave well, but this is often mainly because they are sensitive to peer pressure and concerned about how their behavior looks in the eyes of others.

The visibility that such conventional ethics depends on is also its weakest point: morality is potentially reduced to a matter of not being caught—not unlike the outside of the Patna was painted to hide its rust. As Marlow asks (with a "disconcerted smile") an elderly French third lieutenant who did his part in the rescuing of the Patna and who held that, since man is born a coward, honor (seen by him as the concern for how our conduct will look in the eyes of others) is a necessary incentive for courage: "Couldn't it reduce itself to not being found out?" (Chapter 13). Although the Frenchman considers that question "too fine" and much above him, it is most likely because of what Marlow hints at here that most ethicists and moral philosophers today are not too upset that the conventional ethics of honor and shame have given way to more demanding forms of ethics that give central place to the notion of autonomy. As said, we generally expect people to do the right thing from a love of justice or virtue, and not from a fear of losing face.

Yet, even though we tend to think that a moral action should stem from morally worthy motives to deserve that predicate, in real life this ideal might be too demanding; what ought to motivate people according to most modern political and moral philosophy is not always the same as what makes them tick in practice. The question then is if we can close the gap between the spheres of *is* and *ought* by appealing to motives that are to some extent self-regarding. Although many people will think that a virtuous act undertaken for a reward hardly deserves to be called moral, this might not be such an odd suggestion. Which brings us back to what Locke already suggested, namely that most people can be induced to conform to the rules of justice and even to act for the greater good, although for a motive that is not completely altruistic, when an appeal is made to their honor.

Honor as Public Recognition

This somewhat archaic sounding notion of honor is best understood by, first of all, contrasting it with the more modern notions of conscience and dignity. The latter differs from honor, something not everyone shares in and without meaning when equally distributed, in the important aspect that it is inclusive and lacks gradation (see also Margalit 1996, 43), with the noteworthy exception that we can lose our dignity by behaving too reprehensibly.[3] Although this loss of dignity is something we would wish to avoid, dignity does not have a function in steering our conduct in the way that honor and conscience have, and it should therefore not concern us here (although we will return to it briefly in Chapter 5). In other aspects, especially as a guide in matters of morality, honor has given place to conscience. Since it presupposes moral autonomy this notion of conscience is, particularly in its popular (and very un-Lockean) understanding as an inner voice, much more demanding than honor—it might for instance require someone to go against social norms.

The most important difference, then, between conscience and honor is that the latter, contrary to conscience, has an important external component as it concerns both the value that someone allocates to himself *and* the value others place on him. Charles H. Cooley, an American sociologist from the early twentieth century who wrote about a "reflected or looking-glass self," captures this nicely in his often-quoted definition of honor as

> a finer kind of self-respect. It is used to mean either something one feels regarding himself, or something that other people think and feel regarding him, and so illustrates by the accepted use of language the fact that the private and social aspects of self are inseparable. One's honor, as he feels it, and his honor in the sense of honorable repute, as he conceives it to exist in the minds of others whose opinions he cares for, are two aspects of the same thing. No one can permanently maintain a standard of honor if he does not conceive of some other mind or minds as sharing and corroborating this standard (1922, 184).

Honor as external

According to the already mentioned anthropologist Pitt-Rivers, some-one's honor is "the value in his own eyes, but also in the eyes of his society. It is his estimation of his own worth, his *claim* to pride, but it is also the acknowledgement of that claim, his excellence recognized by society, his *right* to pride" (1974, 21; see also Cooley 1922, 238).

This popular bipartite theory of honor (F. H. Stewart 1994, 19) might be too straightforward, though. Pieter Spierenburg distinguishes an extra level in the introduction to his edited volume on honor and violence: "Honor has at least three layers: a person's own feeling of self-worth, this person's assessment of his or her worth in the eyes of others, and the actual opinion of others about her or him" (1998, 2).[4] The first two layers Spierenburg mentions together make up what we could call the internal element of honor, consisting of two rather different things: how we value ourselves, and how we think others value us. One could say that that latter aspect is in fact somewhat of an intermediate element that forms a bridge between the internal and the external element of honor, as our assessment of our worth in the eyes of others is basically external honor internalized. To complicate things even further, we will see that most authors of old who considered honor important as a moral guide pointed out that we are not only concerned about how others value us, but that we are equally anxious about how others would value us *if they were fully informed*. It is this aspect of honor, internalized but de-pending on the imaginary view of all-knowing others, that we see back in Adam Smith's remark that man is not only endowed "with a desire of being approved of, but with a desire of being what ought to be approved of" (*Theory* III.2.7). We will return to this later.

What all these bipartite and tripartite definitions have in common is that they show that it is only in his or her relationships with others that it becomes clear whether someone is a man or woman of honor. In his book on honor, Alexander Welsh appropriately remarked, with regard to Pitt-Rivers definition of honor as someone's value "in his own eyes, but also in the eyes of his society," that the reverse order might in fact be more in place (2008, 9). Although Jim's heroic self-image remained by and large intact after his jump from the Patna, he could no longer maintain that he was a man of honor after the rest of the world stopped seeing him like one. That too suggests that the internal element of honor depends more on how we imagine that others see us than on our estima-tion of our own worth.

For the external element of honor—our value in the eyes of soci-ety—moral philosophers of earlier days distinguished essentially two functions. First of all, the articulated opinions of others may be of help in finding out what is the proper thing to do. Secondly, and probably more important, for many people the desire to be well thought of forms an important incentive to actually do what is right. Honor often functions as a reward for making the right choice between higher interests and self-interest—Jim for instance felt shame, the emotion most closely related to honor, because he fell short in light of the ideal set by the "light literature" he had read.[5]

That it was his not living up to an ideal that caused Jim to feel shame suggests that honor and shame have more to do with character and virtues than with rules and duties, and there is in fact a clear agreement in the secondary literature that shame is often the result of falling short of an ideal, or of the "self as I want to be" (Giddens 1991, 68). To give just one example, according to psychologists Fossum and Mason, "from the shame perspective, a person feels qualitatively different from other human beings, not really a full-fledged member of the human race" (1966, 22).[6] Guilt, on the other hand, is the emotion related to the notion of conscience, and follows on the transgression of a rule. It therefore asks for reparation (Lindsay-Hartz et al. 1995, 289). As John Rawls summed up the difference, "in general, guilt, resentment, and indignation invoke the concept of right, whereas shame, contempt, and derision appeal to the concept of goodness" (*A Theory of Justice* §73; see also Lynd 1958, 22; Cairns 1993, 18, 20; Sennett 2003, 115). In this view pride and shame are the emotions of the hero, while guilt is the emotion of the saint (Rawls *Theory* §72). Others have nuanced this distinction somewhat. Classicist Douglas L. Cairns, for instance, wrote in his book on honor and shame in Greek literature, *Aidos*, that "it would be wrong to focus too closely on the supposed distinction between failure and transgression; any transgression of a boundary is a failure to observe it, and a failure to achieve a goal can be a transgression of an interdiction" (1993, 20).

Nonetheless, the difference between conscience and guilt on the one hand, and honor and shame on the other, seems to be a real and significant one. Although honor can reinforce rules and virtues alike and as a consequence does not fit very well into the duty-based ethics versus virtue ethics dichotomy (see also Krause 2002, 52), honor is not especially apt to promote obedience to the law and the following of rules; it seems much better suited to further the practicing of virtues that are not backed by legal sanctions yet are important in the private lives of people and for the functioning of society as a whole. Examples

Honor
os
extrat
legal

are self-command, benevolence, and propriety, and it is probably no co-incidence that modern political theory, silent on honor, also does not say a lot about these virtues (self-command, for instance, is dealt with by Rawls in about six lines when he discusses the supererogatory virtues in section 72 of *A Theory of Justice*), whereas earlier authors, say from Aristotle to David Hume and Adam Smith, elaborated on all three quite extensively. Although most of these authors also mentioned familiar notions such as justice, obedience to the law, and respect for property as main beneficiaries of the concern for reputation, they at the same time worked with a broad conception of virtue, staying aloof from the exclusive focus on justice sometimes present in modern political theory. On a more general plane they thought that honor could advance the public interest, not only justice per se. In this function of being a spur to displaying virtuous behavior, honor sometimes comes in more dramatic appearances: in its ultimate form it involves the choice between life and death. As Leo Braudy put it in *From Chivalry to Terrorism*: "Historically, it is the concept of honor that mediates between individual character and outside forces, as well as the body that wants to survive and the mind that seeks other goals, including a glorious death" (2003, 49). The honorable choice is often, although not always (Jim wrongly chose life when the Patna appeared to be sinking, but later, in Patusan, he wrongly chose death), the choice against life, and honor is the reward for making the right choice. "It's a matter of honor that the master is the last to leave. Nothing less will do in this profession," said the chairman of the Swedish Maritime Officer's Association after the arrest of Captain Francesco Schettino for abandoning his passengers when his ship, the Costa Concordia, sank on 13 January 2012—a case that reminds a lot of Jim's jump from the Patna.[7]

It is in all likelihood mainly this idea of it being a reward for virtuous behavior, more than the fact that in the past honor often endorsed rather eccentric and contra productive behavior (dueling, for instance), that brought discredit upon the notion of honor in modern times. If autonomy is the ideal, then honor is somewhat suspect because of the two already mentioned functions it fulfills; the heteronomous nature of honor shows both in the fact that the opinions of others have a role in determining what is right and in the fact that it often functions as a reward after having made the right choice, in general, as said, being a choice between the general interest and the interests of others on the one side, and self-interest on the other. Honor makes it that one chooses to give priority to the former, although partly for reasons belonging to the realm of the latter.

This conception of honor as something with an important external component differs from a more contemporary usage of the term that emphasizes the internal aspect of honor, and has more to do with what Pitt-Rivers called our value in our own eyes than with our value in the eyes of society. The term honor is today often used to denote something that is more a personal quality or virtue, as for instance is the case when we say that someone has a sense of honor (see also F. H. Stewart 1994, 44–53), than something with an important external element as well.[8] A good example of this is the West Point honor code ("a cadet will not lie, cheat or steal, nor tolerate those who do"). Cadets are expected to live by this code because they have internalized it, not because they are concerned about what others might think of them when they breach it. Honor is here synonymous with integrity or, even more general, being ethical, and in fact it seems that if the term is used nowadays (the West Point honor code and the well-known West Point credo "Duty, honor, country" might indicate that the term is used more often in the United States than in, for instance, Europe), honor is increasingly taken to mean something close to integrity (subject of Chapter 4). Integrity, however, is a lot more demanding than the notion of honor as thinkers from Cicero to Smith conceived it, and more or less on the same plane as conscience, as both integrity and conscience presuppose moral autonomy.

Such definitions that see honor as an internally felt duty are in line with our wish to rely on our conscience to inform us on what is the right course of action, and our belief that knowing what is just ought to be enough motivation in itself to act upon it (see Sessions 2010 and Oprisko 2012 for the different meanings of the word honor). Appiah writes that "a person of honor cares first of all not about being respected but about being *worthy* of respect" (2010, 16), but especially in a chapter on the role of honor in dueling that seems to be overstating the case a bit. Although the conception of honor as an internal quality has the advantage over external honor that it cannot be reduced to a matter of "not being found out," we might lose sight of one of the essential characteristics of honor if we no longer see it as something that ultimately depends on how others see us, and that cannot exist without a public. The emphasis in this book is therefore on honor in its inauthentic form, that is, on external honor or, in other words, on honor as public recognition (see Krause 2002 for honor codes and for honor as a "quality of character").

Clearly, it is in particular because of its external element that honor as public recognition, central to this book, is less than altruistic. But although nowadays most people tend to see honor as a self-regarding motive, it would be incorrect to see it as a purely selfish drive; honor is a notion that just cannot be categorized as either an altruistic or an egoistic motivation. In the end, it is a social motive. And even though the more demanding notion of conscience, not only aware of our actions but also of the underlying motivation, is clearly on a par with the way most people see themselves, it could be argued that even today, without deep roots in our present-day vocabulary, the older notion of honor as a reward for virtuous behavior can still be of use because it is *less* demanding. Yet if it is true that we need honor as a reward, this would mean that we are still on a lesser level of moral development, at least from the point of view of most political and moral philosophers. So, how bad is it to be on this allegedly suboptimal plane? Not that bad, it will be argued in the following chapters. Drawing on moral philosophy from Cicero to Amartya Sen this book argues that honor, despite its limited role in our moral language, still has a role as a heuristic tool and an incentive to do what is right.

Overview of this Book

But is it really a good idea to use honor to motivate people to, for instance, choose a course of action that would benefit others, or the public cause, more than it would benefit their own interest? Doesn't that boil down to substituting one self-regarding motive for another? To answer these questions, but even more to get a better understanding of what honor exactly is (as many people might have lost sight of that), and of what the pros and cons of the motive of honor are, the next chapter delves relatively deep into the early, aristocratic notion of honor as found in the works of, among others, Sallust, Plutarch, and Cicero, who all held that honor is a necessary incentive for virtuous behavior, and even something worth dying for. But this chapter also pays attention to the Stoic and Epicurean views on honor, which somewhat resemble today's prevailing view that sees honor as something artificial, and even dangerous, and thus not as a legitimate motive at all.

After that, in Chapter 2, we turn to its successive conversion into a more modern, egalitarian form as envisaged by later thinkers, from John Locke and Bernard Mandeville to Michael Walzer. This chapter also addresses some of the serious drawbacks of the honor ethic in its traditional shape, which mainly stem from the exclusiveness of honor and its being something external, and tries to identify some solutions to these problems. These problems and solutions will be elaborated on further in the subsequent chapters, which will focus on three virtues closely related to honor: loyalty, integrity, and respect.

Chapter 3 deals with the question how honor groups are defined, and does so by exploring the virtue of loyalty. It addresses the problem that the number of people whose opinions we see as relevant to our honor and reputation tends to be limited, and that we are inclined to give priority to the interests of that limited number of people. Using war and utilitarianism as examples, a very particularistic activity and an especially universalist strand of thought respectively, this chapter not only argues that it is doubtful whether loyalty is really a virtue, since it can serve both good and bad causes alike, but also that a lot depends on the form it takes: loyalty to one's own honor group (which can range from the primary group to the nation), loyalty to a principle (such as justice), or, somewhat in between, loyalty to a profession. Although most people tend to stress the first form, it could be argued that loyalty should be somewhat less exclusive and particularistic than that; loyalty to principle and (a little less principled) professional loyalty are examples of such more encompassing forms of loyalty.

The subsequent Chapter 4 is all about a special form of loyalty, namely to one's own principles, which often goes under the name of integrity. Although integrity seems to be on a higher moral level than honor, as it cannot be reduced to a matter of not being found out, it comes with its own set of drawbacks. Integrity is overwhelmingly vague, and in its most common meaning inherently subjective, while the motivation behind sticking to one's own principles can be quite self-serving, more about maintaining one's own morals and a certain self-image than about its possible beneficiaries. So while many people today consider integrity an essential virtue and a prerequisite to be able to look at themselves in the mirror, the notion of integrity as upholding personal values and principles is in fact a rather problematic one. The chapter ends with the conclusion that insofar as the virtue of integrity could have a benevolent role in theory, that role can in practice better be played by other virtues, for example respect.

Not coincidentally the subject of Chapter 5 is respect, which can be seen as the democratic descendant of the notion of honor. Although respect misses some of the drawbacks of honor and costs nothing, it seems to be in short supply nonetheless. The older notion of honor clearly plays a role here: as honor is predominantly a group phenomenon, it basically limits respect to members of that group, something that has a possible downside in a lack of respect for the honor and dignity of outsiders. For illustration the chapter addresses the question as to what extent a real or perceived lack of respect being shown can be said to induce people to resort to terrorism, as some recent authors seem to fear. This chapter is followed by a short conclusion.

1

Honor as a Social Motive

Although the view that virtues such as justice and courage need honor as a reward goes back a long way, it was worked out most systematically by various Roman authors who did not only discern something noble in the longing for honor and a name that never dies, but also ascribed an important function to it. For instance, the Roman historian Gaius Sallust wrote in the first century BC that the greatness of Rome was a result of the competition for glory between those young men who, destined to lead by birth and education, entered the battlefield with a burning desire to beat their peers by being the first to slay an opponent (*Catilinae Coniuratio* 1–2, 7). Nearly two millennia later, Colonel Ardant Du Picq stated in his *Battle Studies* that, where the Greeks mainly pondered on the ideal depth of the phalanx, the in military affairs much more successful Romans addressed the question of what makes men fight, and that they had found the answer in making use of the soldier's sense of honor and shame (1947, 50–5). Although Du Picq is not entirely fair to the Greeks here,[1] it is true that they were in general less inclined to the view that virtue needs a reward. Plato, for instance, wrote in *The Republic* that

> good men will not consent to govern for cash or honors. They do not want to be called mercenary for exacting a cash payment for the work of government, or thieves for making money on the side; and they will not work for honors, for they aren't ambitious (347b).

Although Plato stated in the concluding sections of *The Republic* that being just will be rewarded in this life with a good name (613), that reward is not presented as a helpful, let alone necessary, encouragement to virtue; a good man will persist in being good even if he gains a reputation for wickedness by it. Plato took a somewhat different position when he tried to sketch a more feasible ideal in his *Laws*; in that work he wrote about name and reputation as being necessary incentives, and the penalty of public disgracing as an effective disincentive (738, 740d, 754e-5a, 764a, 784d, 926d).

Although in general more practically minded than Plato, Aristotle wrote in the *Nicomachean Ethics* that reason keeps good men on the path of virtue and that they therefore do not really need their sense of shame—a good man would be ashamed if he did something shameful, however, as he is not shameless (1095b, 1128b). On first sight, this view that reason suffices to keep a good man good might seem at odds with the fact that in the same book Aristotle described honor as being the most important of the secondary goods, and not to be disdained (1123b). Finding a right position towards honor is in fact an important theme in the *Nicomachean Ethics*, where it is dealt with under the headings of magnanimity (for the great men) and ambition (for the rest of us). Magnanimity, wrote Aristotle, is about finding a mean between vanity and boastfulness on the one hand, and being overly modest on the other. Basically, the virtue of magnanimity, and the two accompanying vices of vanity and pusillanimity, are all about estimating one's own worth properly, and claiming due honor for it. The person who is too humble fails here just as much as the boaster does. One could even argue that the overly humble person is more to blame because his diffidence will bar him from an active life that, in the case of a man of virtue, would serve the public cause (*Nicomachean Ethics* 1123a–1125a). Ambition, more relevant to most people, is about finding the (unnamed) mean between seeking honor too much (and that goes under the name ambition) and too little (unambitiousness), and about seeking honor from the right sources and in the right way (*Nicomachean Ethics* 1125b). Yet, in the end Aristotle's account of honor is rather unenthusiastic, and entirely consistent with his dismissal of shame: the man of virtue only accepts honor because there is nothing greater to bestow upon virtue, and it only gives him moderate pleasure. He definitely does not need it as a spur to virtue (*Nicomachean Ethics* 1124a).

[handwritten marginalia: Poor reading of Aristotle]

[handwritten note at bottom: Insufficient dismissal of Greeks. What about Homer, Thucydides, and Xenophon?]

Honor and the Romans

Most Roman authors were much more outspoken on the good effects of honor than that: they thought that almost no one is willing to act for the greater good unless there is honor to be earned. Virtuous acts should therefore be seen and, more important, praised at length. Sallust, who sought fame as a man of letters only after other paths to glory (such as politics and the military) were blocked to him at a time (i.e., after the civil war that brought Julius Caesar to power) when, as he saw it, honor was no longer given to the deserving (*Bellum Iugurthinum* 3–4), opened his account of the conspiracy of Catiline with the statement that

> every man who wishes to rise superior to the lower animals should strive his hardest to avoid living all his days in silent obscurity, like the beasts of the field, creatures which go with their faces to the ground and the slaves of their bellies (*Catilinae Coniuratio* 1).

Other Roman historians held similar views, as did some Roman philosophers, most notably Marcus Tullius Cicero. The latter, besides a philosopher also a lawyer and statesman, is without a doubt the best-known and most subtle representative of the Roman honor ethic, and, until not too long ago, a very influential one, more influential for instance than the Greek philosophers that we today tend to hold in higher regard. In fact, Cicero's *On Duty* has been called (alongside Plutarch's *Parallel Lives*) the book most influential on the modern world (Strachan-Davidson 1894, 369; see also Long 2008, 56).

In Cicero's works we find a form of conventional ethics that is, albeit less demanding, as moral and as sophisticated as modern accounts of morality that give center stage to the notion of autonomy. A notion we can safely assume Cicero would have thought unattainable: although the view on honor that underlies the ideal of autonomy—honor is neither needed as an incentive, nor as a heuristic device to discover what is just—has come to be the dominant view only quite recently, it has always had its adherents. Opposing the honor ethic, writes Charles Taylor, there was for instance "the celebrated and influential counter-position put forward by Plato. Virtue is no longer to be found in public life (. . .). The higher life is that ruled by reason, and reason itself is defined in terms of a vision of order in the cosmos and in the soul" (1992a, 20). In Greek and

Roman antiquity varieties of this counter-position were defended by the Platonists, the Cynics, the Epicureans, and the Stoics (see also Taylor 1992a, 20). Cicero especially opposed the latter two schools, which both tried to convince their respective audiences that honor was definitely not worth pursuing, as it brings more ill than good.

To begin with the Epicureans (their ideas were spread among the Romans through the poet Lucretius' *De Rerum Natura*): they held that happiness and peace of mind are the two most valuable things in life. Our Sisyphus-like struggle for honor and glory puts those very things at risk, since failure clearly brings pain, while success only brings the envy of others. Equanimity (and with that a god-like life) can only be attained if we do away with our unwarranted fears, above all that of death, it being the principal source of the ambition for a name that lasts after one's demise (Lucretius *De Rerum Natura* III 59). The Epicureans were always keen to ridicule that wish for an eternal fame—why bother about one's standing when no longer around to enjoy it? But in Cicero's view, more polemic than truthful—Cicero must have read the work of Lucretius, but misrepresented the Epicurean moral philosophy as hedonistic all the same—Epicurean philosophy was mistaken in seeing man as essentially living for himself, and even self-seeking.[2] Although convinced of its being misguided, Cicero feared the consequences of people trying to live by Epicureanism nonetheless, neglecting their duties to the state.[3]

The Stoics were equally hostile to the notion of honor. Partly because of reasons similar to those the Epicureans held, and partly out of a more demanding view of man that held that people potentially love virtue, and should be able to act accordingly. That this potential is often not realized is because our natural, good inclinations seldom win out over the prejudices of society, which value money, power, and glory over virtue. That we in general listen to the murmuring around us is the main cause of our falling short of the Stoic benchmark, which states that an act undertaken in exchange for a reward, for instance honor or fame, is not virtuous in any way—below the level of perfect virtue everything is equally bad. Imagining that a Cato or Scipio is present might help someone on his path to virtue, yet virtue is only truly attained when being one's own witness suffices, Seneca wrote to his friend Lucilius (*On Reformation*).

According to Cicero the Stoic definition of virtue was unworkable and even dangerously strict, as it takes away the incentive for trying to be virtuous from those who are not without faults, but mean well (*De*

Finibus IV.21, 55, 63–8, 75–7; *Pro Murena* 61–5). Although it is conceivable that someone perfectly wise acts virtuously for the sake of virtue, just like the Stoics wanted to see it, such individuals are very rare—Cicero claimed he had never met one (*Tusculanae Disputationes* II.51). For the not so wise some feedback from peers might, in combination with a concern for reputation, be of help (see for instance *Tusculanae Disputationes* II.47–50). So where Epicurean philosophy asks too little, Stoic philosophy asks too much, while Cicero himself was proud that he wrote about what the Stoics called "mean duties," a level of morality that falls short of perfection yet is within reach for the average person (*De Officiis* III.14–17). Even such a less demanding philosophy is of no use, though, for those who fall below that average level; thieves and cut-throats have to be constrained by "chains and prison walls" (*De Officiis* III.73). It is a good thing that such nihilists form only a small minority. As Rome "had no central peacekeeping force" (Barton 2001, 18) the beneficial effects of chains and prison walls were bound to be limited. Rome could only flourish as long as honor, shame, and a fear of disgrace governed its citizens (Barton 2001, 23).

Fortunately most Romans remained convinced, despite the influence of Epicurean and Stoic thought, that honor was the highest good for men, and something with an existence in reality. Cicero therefore thought that honor could provide a middle ground between the alleged hedonism of Epicureanism and the strictness of the Stoics.[4] Virtuous persons are in general far from indifferent to praise, and this should not be held against them because of the two functions, already mentioned in the introduction, that honor performs. First of all, our concern for how others see us can help us to actually *see* what the virtuous way to behave is:

> We observe others and from a glance of the eyes, from a contracting or relaxing of the brows, from an air of sadness, from an outburst of joy, from a laugh, from speech, from silence, from a raising of a lowering of the voice, and the like, we shall easily judge which of our actions is proper, and which is out of accord with duty and nature (*De Officiis* I.146).

Also, since we detect faults more easily in others than in ourselves, it is wise to study others to find out what is unbecoming (*De Officiis* I.146). We do well, finally, to seek advice from men of learning and practical wisdom for guidance; not unlike painters, sculptors, and poets, we should consult the judgments of others to find out what to do and what to leave undone, and what to improve or alter (*De Officiis* I.147).

Secondly, the concern for reputation motivates to also *behave* virtuously; although most people are in general not selfish, we cannot expect them to perform their duties from a sense of duty alone. In one of his pleas Cicero stated that "magnanimity looks for no other recognition of its toils and dangers save praise and glory; once rob it of that, gentlemen, and in this brief and transitory pilgrimage of life what further incentive have we to high endeavour" (*Pro Archia Poeta* 28). What's more, "deep in every noble heart dwells a power which plies night and day the good of glory, and bids us see to it that the remembrance of our names should not pass away with life, but should endure coeval with all the ages of the future" (*Pro Archia Poeta* 29).[5] According to Leo Braudy, especially Cicero's later speeches became "more and more filled with allusions to the central importance of the urge to fame as a motivation to public service" (1986, 78). But honor forms not only a spur to virtue, it also keeps us from doing the wrong things; Cicero thought that the censure from our peers is a punishment we cannot run away from and, more important, that no one is insensible enough to put up with the blame of others—that is a burden too heavy to bear.

What confuses matters a bit regarding this second function—honor as an incentive to do the right thing—is that Cicero paid tribute to the exacting Stoic position (and described himself as being Stoic) on some instances in his philosophical work. Cicero took a strict and Stoic stance, for example, when he attacked Epicureanism in *De Finibus* (II.52–3), or in *De Re Publica* (I.27), defending the Platonic position that military commands and consulships should be undertaken from a sense of duty, not for profit or glory, and also in *De Officiis*, arguing that what is morally right is "worth the seeking for its own sake" (III.33). Referring to the tale of Gyges, Cicero stated there that good men "aim to secure not secrecy but the right" (III.38). What is *honestum*, that is, worthy of honor, still deserves honor when no one honors it (*De Officiis* I.14; *De Finibus* II.48; see also Moore 2002, 370).

But on the whole, it is the position that honor is legitimate and necessary motivator that he took most often, also in his philosophical treatises. In the first book of his *Tusculanae Disputationes* he for instance wrote:

Again, in this commonwealth of ours, with what thought in their minds do we suppose such an army of illustrious men have lost their lives for the commonwealth? Was it that their name should be restricted to the narrow limits of their life? No one would ever have exposed himself to death for his country without good hope of immortality (I.32).

And, in the second book:

Nature has made us, as I have said before—it must often be repeated—enthusiastic seekers after honor, and once we have caught, as it were, some glimpse of its radiance, there is nothing we are not prepared to bear and go through in order to secure it. It is from this rush, this impulse from our soul towards true renown and reputation that the dangers of battle are encountered; brave men do not feel wounds in the line of battle, or if they feel them prefer death rather than move one step from the post that honor has appointed (II.58).

Cicero thought that no one will put aside his or her own interests for the greater good if there is no fame or honor to be earned. He believed this applied to all, citizens and soldiers alike; we should not believe people who claim to be insensitive to fame and glory (*De Officiis* I.71). Something that of course not only holds true for the average and uneducated, but also for philosophers, even the Stoics and Epicureans: "Do they not inscribe their names upon the actual books they write about contempt of fame?" (*Tusculanae Disputationes* I.34).

Although it might appear a little ironic in light of his sometimes ambiguous position on the relation between honor and virtue, Cicero emphasized that in his opinion "philosophers (. . .) must be judged not by isolated utterances, but by uninterrupted consistency" (*Tusculanae Disputationes* V.31). Hannah Arendt, however, has argued (writing about Marx) that "fundamental and flagrant contradictions rarely occur in second-rate writers; in the work of great authors they lead into the very centre of their work" (1958, 104–5), and that might also be the case with Cicero's wavering position on honor. As to the question which is Cicero's most "true" position on honor, the Stoic one he now and then espoused in his philosophical work or the more enthusiastic one present in both his pleas and his philosophy, we should keep in mind that Cicero was not a philosopher's philosopher, but a practically minded author who wanted to be relevant, setting a standard that was achievable for most people. He certainly did not subscribe to the Aristotelian view, referred to in the above, that shame is not a virtue because a mature person can be expected to never do actions one should be ashamed of (Aristotle *Nicomachean Ethics* 1095b, 1128b).

True and False Honor

Yet, although recognizing that virtue needs a reward, Cicero at the same time insisted that recognition for public service should be sufficient re-muneration for a statesman or a general, and that seeking wealth as a reward for toils endured is, in fact, corrupt. Cicero cited examples from Roman history of commanders who brought enormous spoils into the treasury, but kept for themselves nothing except "the glory of an im-mortal name" (*De Officiis* II.76). In Plutarch we read how Coriolanus, although selfish in his desire for recognition, earlier in his career won admiration for declining the one-tenth share in war booty that was of-fered to him (*Coriolanus* 10). Later, Cato Major would act similarly, as he wanted to compete in bravery with the bravest, and not in greed with the greediest (Plutarch *Cato the Elder* 10). For his own rescuing of the republic from the hands of Catiline and his fellow conspirators, Cicero asked, in his speech to the people of December 3, 63 BC,

> no reward for my valour, no signal mark of distinction, no mon-ument in my honour except that this day be remembered for all time. It is in your hearts that I wish to have set all my triumphs, all the decorations of distinction, the monuments of fame, the tokens of praise (*In Catilinam* III.26).

In his speech to the senate he asked nothing, "except that you remem-ber this occasion and the whole of my consulship" (*In Catilinam* IV.23). Although this might have been modest requests in Cicero's own eyes, Plutarch wrote that most Romans after a while "grew tired of hearing him continually praising himself" (*Cicero* 24).

Reading Plutarch's biographies of Roman statesmen and command-ers suggests that all great Romans experienced some difficulties find-ing the correct attitude towards fame and recognition, with the more austere Romans of the earlier centuries of the republic doing a better job at it than their successors. Roman history contains some telling ex-amples of ambitious noblemen, such as Coriolanus, Catiline, and, most notably, Caesar, who brought the republic close to disaster by putting their own personal glory above state interest, taking up weapons against their fellow citizens in their quest for recognition. More a moralist than a historian, Plutarch portrayed Caesar, but also Coriolanus, Catiline, Marius, Sulla, Pompey, and Mark Antony, to serve as warnings of what can happen if the longing for honor and glory is not checked by wisdom and some zeal for the public cause. It is not a coincidence that in the end most of these men (Marius and Sulla are the exceptions) died violent deaths. Plutarch ends his *Life of Caesar* with the remark that Caesar, when he died, had not much more than "a glory which had awakened envy on the part of his fellow citizens" (69).

Recounting such examples from the past, as Plutarch and Cicero were in the habit of doing, served more purposes than just illustrating one's point; as most Roman authors they thought that examples, both the good ones and the bad ones, can also contribute something to character formation:

> For, if you turn your thoughts back to early history, you will see that the character of our most prominent men has been reproduced in the whole state; whatever change took place in the lives of the prominent men has also taken place in the whole people (Cicero *De Legibus* III 31; see also Aristotle *Nicomachean Ethics* 1103b).

In the Roman view, people do not get the government they deserve, as the saying now goes, but vice versa: politicians get the people they deserve by the example they set. According to Cicero, for instance, "every state is such as its ruler's character will make it" (*De Re Publica* I.47).[6] It is therefore important that the censors "shall allow no one guilty of dishonourable conduct to remain in the senate" (*De Legibus* III. 7), so that "the senatorial order shall be free from dishonour, and shall be a model for the rest of the citizens" (*De Legibus* III.10).

Although it was in his view the only reason to high endeavor in life, a necessary check on our behavior, and an indispensable tool to find out what is just at the same time, Cicero did see that a lack of moderation in the pursuit of fame and glory can be dangerous. He warned that the pursuit of honor can also work against the common good: the higher our ambition, the more easily our desire for recognition can tempt us to act unjustly (*De Officiis* I.26, 65; see also Barton 2001, 27, 54–5). Many Romans were more willing to part with their money or life than sacrifice the slightest amount of personal glory in the interest of the state (*De Officiis* I.84).

Like many philosophers of the past, Cicero therefore distinguished between true and false glory, and held that true glory should serve the public cause, not merely some personal end (*Tusculanae Disputationes* III.3–4). He described true glory as

> the agreed approval of good men, the unbiased verdict of judges deciding honestly the question of pre-eminent merit; it gives back to virtue the echo of her voice; and as it generally attends upon duties rightly performed it is not to be disdained by good men (*Tusculanae Disputationes* III.3–4).

Because false glory—mere public reputation—looks very similar to true glory, some people, despite having "some noble ambitions," are "misled in their quest of the best," and bring about the ruin of their country or themselves (*Tusculanae Disputationes* III.3–4). In Cicero's view

> true and philosophic greatness of spirit regards the moral good-ness to which nature most aspires as consisting in deeds, not in fame, and prefers to be first in reality rather than in name. And we must approve of this view; for he who depends upon the caprice of the ignorant rabble cannot be numbered among the great (*De Officiis* I.65).

Or, as Aristotle stated it before him: the rightfully proud man despises honor from ordinary people, given on trivial grounds (*Nicomachean Ethics* 1124a). Honor does not consist of the applause of the masses, and especially when we are doing well, we should not listen to flatter-ers suggesting that we are entitled to praise when we actually are not. Such flattery might lead to the worst kind of blunders (*De Officiis* I.91). Honor and fame are not the same (see also Bowman 2006, 273–9; Welsh 2008, 1–4).

But while this idea of honor as the agreed approval of good men, and serving a greater good, tackles some of the drawbacks of honor, Cicero at the same time feared that this was too demanding. Great ambitions in general spring up in "the greatest souls and brilliant geniuses" (*De Officiis* I.26), and Cicero thought that taking the moral high ground could bring us "on very slippery ground; for scarcely can the man be found who has passed through trials and encountered dangers and does not then wish for glory as a reward for his achievements" (*De Officiis* I.65). But as he did not subscribe to the Stoic belief that there is no relation at all between honor and virtue, our wish for honor and glory as a reward was not necessarily problematic in Cicero's view; that undeserved praise gives us little pleasure shows that honor and virtue are closely connected (*De Legibus* I.32). So Cicero could write quite unproblematically that

> the man who concludes that the soul is mortal may yet attempt
> deeds that will not die, not from a thirst for fame, of which he
> will have no enjoyment, but from a thirst for virtue, which of
> necessity secures fame, even if it be not its object (*Tusculanae
> Disputationes* I.91).

[handwritten margin note: ✳ How does this relate to his claim on p.??]

Mere "pretence" and "empty show," on the other hand, will not suffice to secure glory; the short cut to glory, Cicero cited Socrates, "is to strive to be what you wish to be thought to be" (*De Officiis* II.43). Cicero held that it was because of "the similarity between moral worth and renown" that "those who are publicly honoured are considered happy, while those who do not attain fame are thought miserable" (*De Legibus* I.32).

Cicero argued elsewhere that the wisdom of the statesman brings fame and is therefore preferable to the wisdom of the philosopher (*De Re Publica* III.6). And it is for good reasons that we laud the statesman more than the philosopher, seeing that "the existence of virtue depends entirely upon its use," and that "its noblest use is the government of the state" (*De Re Publica*, I.2). Such an active life leaves enough time to philosophize (*De Officiis* I.19). But in the end Cicero's urging to not neglect one's duties to the public cause proved to no avail. In Sallust we read how the competition for honor that had made Rome flourish, gave way first to ambition, a fault that, according to Sallust, still comes close to being a virtue, and later avarice, weakening man's moral fiber and in the end causing the ruin of the Roman republic (*Catilinae Coniuratio* 10). Cicero himself noted that "the moral sense of today is demoralized and depraved by our worship of wealth" (*De Officiis* II.71; see also *Pro Publio Quinctio* 93).

That Plutarch emphasized no less than three times that Caesar was more afraid of pale and lean (and hence virtuous) men, such as Brutus, than of fat and luxurious men (*Caesar* 62; *Brutus* 8; *Mark Antony* 11) is also a sign that times were changing for the worse. That Caesar feared the virtuous more than the wicked suggests, besides ill intent on his part, that it was personal glory he was after. In a way it is ironic that Cicero was to witness how unchecked hunger for glory caused the end of the Roman republic (and Cicero's life) when Caesar started a civil war because of perceived offences to his *dignitas*. Political theorist William A. Galston seems therefore to have been quite right when he wrote that vanity

> can never be satisfied with the honor and recognition of one or a few men, for every man who goes his own way or refuses to honor the vain man is a direct threat to his self-esteem. Vanity feeds on, indeed requires, new conquests, for in a curious way the men who bow down cease to be taken seriously, their esteem ceases to be esteemed. The vain man thus looks for larger and larger worlds to conquer and ends up by desiring universal recognition (1975, 238).

The Stoic and Epicurean view that peace, and especially peace of mind, is to be valued most in life would become more popular during the tumultuous days that followed the collapse of the republic. More than before, the competition for honor and glory was seen as endangering those very values.

Aristocratic Honor Criticized: Honor is a Form of Vanity

The end of the Roman republic did not bring an end to the honor ethic, however. The notion of honor still played an important role, for instance, in the code of chivalry of the Middle Ages, although it took a different form. In theory chivalry heavily depended on Christian notions of perfection (see for instance Matthew 5: 48) and purity of intention (Matthew 6:1–6 and 16–18) that were even more strict, and hostile to honor, than Stoicism was. According to Hannah Arendt,

> the one activity taught by Jesus in word and deed is the activity of goodness, and goodness obviously harbors a tendency to hide from being heard or seen. (. . .) The moment a good work becomes known and public, it loses its specific character of goodness, of being done for nothing but goodness' sake. When goodness appears openly, it is no longer goodness (1958, 74).

An otherwise good act that is seen by others is, because of that fact alone, not truly good.

But the Christian ideal actually raises the bar considerably higher than Arendt thought, seeing that even being conscious of one's own good deed, and possibly feeling good about it, already diminishes the goodness of that deed. A humble Christian, Avishai Margalit writes,

> is supposed to pay no regard to himself while being constantly preoccupied with himself, especially with the purity of his own motives. This seems to be a logical impossibility. In contrast, the Stoic "internal" man is supposed to ignore the outside social world—not an easy task, but not a logical impossibility (1996, 26).

In reality, chivalry often resembled the individualistic striving for honor as depicted by Homer (Huizinga 1982, 61). As the Polish philosopher Maria Ossowska put it: "Although the Church tried to make the knight subservient to its aims, the moral code of the knight was in disagreement with the teachings of the church. Pride was extolled instead of humility, vengeance was urged for every real or imaginary insult" (1971, 138). The Christian and bellicose elements came together in a favorite pastime of the mediaeval knight, the crusade, while another popular diversion, the tournament, provided the knight with a public to show his valor (although some public was present during medieval battles too). When in the late Middle Ages war began to resemble what we call guerilla tactics, the mediaeval form of honor began to dwindle. The canon eventually sealed the fate of chivalry (Huizinga 1982, 100).

[handwritten margin note: Inadequate dismissal of Christian honor]

In the Renaissance the rediscovery of classical thought gave the ethics of honor a new impulse; in 1341 Petrarca declared honor to be the highest good for a man of letters, starting the development of an ideology prescribing that the young should be educated to be enthusiastic seekers after honor (Q. Skinner 1978, 100–1). At the end of the sixteenth century, Francis Bacon, one of the founders of modern science, could still write that "there is an honour (. . .), which may be ranked among the greatest, which happens rarely: That is, of such as sacrifice themselves, to death or dangers, for the good of their country: As was M. Regulus and the two Decii" (*Of Honor and Reputation*). Honor even aspires to death, Bacon wrote elsewhere (*On Death*). With his belief that honor is a legitimate and necessary reward for virtue, Bacon stood in his moral writings still with both feet in the tradition developed by Romans like Cicero, as did many of his contemporaries.

The Renaissance ideal stayed very much alive until in the seventeenth century "with his bristling code of honour and his continual thirst for glory, the typical hero of the Renaissance began to appear slightly comical in his willful disregard for the natural instinct of self-preservation" (Q. Skinner 1978, 101). In that century Thomas Hobbes, who in his *Leviathan* had tried to establish a science of man modeled after the natural sciences, stated that people are mainly driven by self-interest, thus reducing honor to an important yet selfish (and dangerous) motive that is hard to distinguish from vanity.[7] According to Charles Taylor this "withering critique," denouncing the goals of the honor ethic "as vainglory and vanity, as the fruits of an almost childish presumption" proved successful in undermining the ethic of honor (1992a, 214; see also Johnson Bagby 2009). Although he locates that critique in the work of Hobbes, Pascal, La Rochefoucauld, and Molière, Taylor also points out that "the negative arguments in these writers are not new. Plato himself was suspicious of the honour ethic, as concerned with mere appearances. The Stoics rejected it; and it was denounced by Augustine as the exaltation of the desire for power" (1992a, 214). Yet, as said, it was not until the seventeenth century that this "rival theory about the universality of self-interest" did so well that for the first time many people stopped believing in the reality of honor (Q. Skinner 1978, 101).

This rival theory was so successful that less than a century after Hobbes the contemporary view of honor as something with no apparent relationship with virtue was foreshadowed in the work of Montesquieu, who saw honor as the principle of monarchies, a form of government wherein virtue gave way to honor, defined ("philosophically false," as Montesquieu himself admitted) as preferences, rank, distinction, and the like, leading to fine actions nonetheless. The principle of virtue governs in democracies, their flourishing or falling depending on its citizen's caliber of virtue (*Esprit des Lois* I.iii.1–7). Again a century later, less than two centuries after Hobbes, Alexis de Tocqueville famously described, in *Democracy in America*, modern individualism as "a calm and considered feeling which deposes each citizen to isolate himself from the mass of his fellows and withdraw into the circle of family and friends" (1969, 506). This is a complete turnabout from the days of Cicero and Sallust; the relatively safe private sphere was now deemed more important than the public realm, the domain in which a name could be made, not in the least by exploits in war. What happened was, again in the words of Taylor,

> what Nietzsche called a "transvaluation of values." The new highest good is not only erected as a standard by which other, ordinary goods are judged but often radically alters our view of

their value, in some cases taking what was previously an ideal and branding it a temptation. Such was the fate of the warrior honour ethic at the hands of Plato, and later of Augustine, and later still in the eyes of the modern ethic of ordinary life (1992a, 65).

Nevertheless, in Tocqueville's view "that which our ancestors called honor was really only one of its forms" (1969, 623), and those who, as Montesquieu did, held that there is no place for honor in democracies, mistook what was only a species, in Montesquieu's case the honor of the court, for the genus. According to Tocqueville, although at one point stating that only "some scattered notions" of the aristocratic notion of honor had survived in democratic America (1969, 620–1), honor still performs its function in modern society, although with rules less odd and less numerous, and its workings less visible.

Conclusion

As an astute observer of the difference between aristocratic and democratic honor, Tocqueville noted that in democratic times the rules of honor are not only less far removed from common sense, but also less specific. As a consequence, they are bound to lose something of their force; democratic honor is less compelling than aristocratic honor because it is less peculiar. Although, according to Tocqueville, a democratic people has needs "which give rise to common opinions concerning honor," these opinions never present themselves "with equal intensity to the mind of every citizen; the law of honor exists, but it is often left without interpreters" (1969, 624). With such an indefinite law of honor, less understood than the prescripts of old and accordingly hard to apply, public opinion, "the natural and supreme interpreter of the law of honor, not seeing clearly to which side to incline in the distribution of praise and blame, always hesitates in giving judgment" (Tocqueville 1969, 625). That in democratic societies (by which term Tocqueville basically meant egalitarian societies and not per se societies ruled by the people) the rules of honor are somewhat unclear—but also less martial and violent, and more gentle and productive—is in itself a relatively small price to pay for the providential fact that democratic honor, analogous to the shift from the Roman ranking concept of *dignitas* to the more egalitarian notion of dignity, is less hierarchical and more inclusive than Cicero's aristocratic notion of honor.

Essentially, democratic honor and its indefiniteness are the by-products of a more egalitarian society. Aristocratic honor concerned mainly those who were by birth destined to lead, and who therefore had a stake in specific rules and a rather violent conception of honor since that helped them to maintain their privileged position, whereas in a democracy, with its citizens less keen on eccentric conventions, it is the action itself that is praiseworthy or blameworthy; who performs it (or suffers from it) is irrelevant (Tocqueville 1969, 617; see also Walzer 1983, 251, 267). In other words, while in aristocratic society descent was very important, something that made honor based on merit close to impossible, democratic honor is based on desert. Or so it should be; in the real world, peculiarities—traces of more hierarchical notions—remain (Tocqueville 1969, 618). That notwithstanding, in democratic societies the rules of honor tend to stay close to "notions of right and wrong that are common to all the world," and do not resemble the "very exotic notions" that honor endorsed in earlier times (1969, 616).

A bit more particularistic, although in tune with the present (which somewhat clouds its particularity to us), is that in Tocqueville's days honor was supposed to advance the productive virtues, and not so much for instance military valor or courage in dueling, whereas such things as idleness were something public opinion should discourage: "all those quiet virtues which tend to regularity in the body social and which favor trade are sure to be held in special honor by this people, and to neglect them will bring one into public contempt" (Tocqueville 1969, 621). The admiration for these, in Tocqueville's terms, "quiet virtues" was at the expense of the esteem for the "turbulent" ones (the latter probably resemble what Adam Smith called the awful virtues in *The Theory of Moral Sentiments*) that bring glory but also trouble to a society. Emile Durkheim would in *The Division of Labor in Society* observe that "the praiseworthy man of former times is only a dilettante to us" (1964, 42). And, writes Durkheim, "we refuse to give dilettantism any moral value; we rather see perfection in the man seeking, not to be complete, but to produce; who has a restricted task, and devotes himself to it; who does his duty, accomplishes his work" (1964, 42). That in a democracy citizens are more disposed to admire the gentle and quiet virtues is of course because that is what benefits them, and society, most. These changes, as a more recent author put it,

> did not just mean the reduction or removal of the element of force from the prevalent concept of honor. The change also had

What about vassals?

a positive side, in the sense that something else took the place of force. Thus, by the seventeenth century, economic solidity was a major supplementary source of honor for men (Spierenburg 1998, 6).

This affirmation of ordinary life, which brought about the admiration for the productive and useful virtues, was bound to have a negative effect on the valuation of the, almost by definition unproductive, soldierly virtues. Immanuel Kant, who held that wars were the result of aristocrats fighting for personal honor and glory, had gone as far as stating, in his *Perpetual Peace: A Philosophical Sketch*, that putting the power in the hands of the people would make war a phenomenon of the past because ordinary citizens would only lose by it—a thought that still lies at the basis of the democratic peace theory in the study of international relations.

And indeed, according to Tocqueville, especially "martial valor is little esteemed" in the democratic era (1969, 620–2), while Hume already had pointed out that

> heroism, or military glory, is much admired by the generality of mankind. They consider it as the most sublime kind of merit. Men of cool reflection are not so sanguine in their praises of it. The infinite confusions and disorder, which it has caused in the world, diminish much of its merit in their eyes (*A Treatise of Human Nature* III.iii.ii).

Adam Smith held that officers of war, and "the whole army and navy, are unproductive labourers" (*An Inquiry into the Nature and Causes of the Wealth of Nations* II.3.2), and that war itself is a very destructive activity. For the rest, Hume and Smith did not mention war and the soldierly virtues nearly as often as for instance Cicero or Sallust had done. In our day Smith's observations are echoed by, for instance, Francis Fukuyama who remarked that the "struggle for recognition has shifted from the military to the economic realm, where it has the socially beneficial effect of creating rather than destroying wealth" (1995, 7). It seems that honor in the modern era should spur us to industrious lives. This more democratic and productive form of honor had gotten its intellectual footing in the political and moral philosophy in the two centuries or so that preceded that of Tocqueville.

2

Democratic Honor and
the Quiet Virtues

In the work of some moral philosophers from the eighteenth century, who often drew heavily from Cicero, we see less of honor in the more dramatic form that Hobbes had ridiculed. That was the form of honor that had lent legitimacy to the stratification of feudal society: in that worldview the nobles (i.e., those notable) ruled society because they were willing to die for their honor, whereas the lower classes, fearing death and pain more than disgrace, supposedly were not (we find an echo of the aristocratic, more bellicose attitude in the unofficial U.S. Marines credo "death before dishonor," a motto somewhat similar to the Ghurkha motto "it's better do die than to be a coward"). In the seventeenth and eighteenth century that all had changed, and honor was now to promote the quiet and peaceful virtues Tocqueville spoke of. The role of honor in the political and moral philosophy of that time is an important one, more important at least than the familiar idea of "an unbroken tradition of liberalism," from Locke to Mill, suggests (Winch 1978, 184). Instead of stressing the modern aspects of these authors, as we do when we use the term liberals or classical liberals for them, it may therefore be better to turn our back on the present in our attempt to understand them (Winch 1978, 184). Doing so shows that these thinkers took inspiration from antiquity, predominantly the Romans, and in general, "like the culture around them, drew their intellectual sustenance from Rome rather than from Greece—from Roman Stoics, Roman Epicureans, and Roman Eclectics" (Gay 1973, 94).

Peter Gay writes in his work on the Enlightenment that of these Roman authors Cicero was the "real favourite" (1973, 98), and although Cicero shared his eminent position with Lucretius (1973, 98) it was his work that influenced the philosophers of that period most (1973, 105). According to Gay, "Cicero's reputation in the Enlightenment is hard to appreciate today: nothing illustrates our distance from the eighteenth century better than this" (1973, 106; see also Hayek 1985, 122). To illustrate, David Hume, whose moral philosophy certainly drew on that of Cicero, wrote in his *An Enquiry concerning the Human Understanding* from 1748 that "the fame of Cicero flourishes at present; but that of Aristotle is utterly decayed" (sect. I). Hume himself was not at all unhappy with that state of affairs (Gay 1973, 105). Hume preferred Cicero also over the Christian writers, and had Cicero's *De Officiis* in his mind when working on his own *Treatise*, as he wrote in a letter to Hutcheson (cited in Jones 1982, 10–11).[1]

That this role of honor in, and the influence of Cicero on, eighteenth-century moral philosophy is somewhat neglected is, in the words of Quentin Skinner, presumably because of our tendency to write a "history of philosophy conceived in terms of our own philosophical criteria and interests" (1988, 292n16). Authors of long ago, writes Skinner, are too often read as contemporaries with answers to the perennial questions we still struggle with, or as precursors of modern notions as democracy, the free market, and so on—this tendency has come to be known as the Whig interpretation of history.[2] We tend to think, for instance, that "Machiavelli 'anticipated' or had 'insight' into theories of the modern state; and 'insightful,' 'perceptive' Aristotle 'anticipated' nearly everyone" (Condren 1985, 70). Likewise, "Hobbes, for example, becomes the 'originator of modernity' and, along with Spinoza, the 'founder of liberalism'" (Gunnell 1986, 109).

In reality, Aristotle, Machiavelli, Hobbes, and Spinoza were of course not laying the foundations for notions that would become fashionable centuries later, but mainly reacted to their contemporaries and forerunners, many of which have since long sunken into anonymity. According to Skinner, "no agent can eventually be said to have meant or done something which he could never be brought to accept as a correct description of what he had meant or done" (1988, 48). Historian John Pocock wrote that "a good test of the value of a piece of history expressed in highly abstract terms is to ask whether its abstractions correspond to realities actually experienced, to things which some identifiable Alcibiades really did or suffered" (1962, 188). Or, as another author put it, *Antigonè* is not about the right of self-expression (Saxonhouse 1993, 21). Likewise, it is rather pointless to blame William James for the fact that "he, like all psychologists before Freud, does not deal with the unconsciousness" (Fine 1986, 33).[3] "We must learn to do our thinking for ourselves" instead of falling back to thinkers of the past, as Skinner sums it up (1988, 66). According to Pocock, moved by "the passion of sympathy, not proprietorship" (1980, 139), the normative political philosopher too "will need to know how to think historically and that his thought will need a historicist dimension" (1980, 158).

On the other hand, one could argue that in the end approach of Skinner and Pocock is perhaps a bit too hostile "to the normative concerns of political theory" (Saxonhouse 1993, 15), and many of us, notwithstanding Skinner's plea not to do so, do in fact

Not sure why this debate is included

> turn to political theory for enlightenment about our condition in the contemporary world, for guidance about the normative choices that we as political creatures confront, for a sense of who we as political actors are or can be, for the conversations we must have about the meaning of political life (Saxonhouse 1993, 6).[4]

While there might be a point here, those who want to re-engage with the tradition of authors writing on honor have to answer the question which authors and theories to turn to. Although more or less agreeing on the functions honor can fulfill, different authors differed both on what honor should endorse and to whom the rules of honor should apply.

Regarding the authors and theories central to this and the preceding chapter there seems, not unexpected, to be more than merely time which separates us from Cicero's aristocratic notion of honor outlined in the above, while there might be plenty we can still relate to in the work of later authors who wrote on the subject of honor (in general somewhat more consistently than Cicero), closer to us in both time and outlook. *Justification of authors* Authors such as Locke, Mandeville, Hume, and Smith gave a distinctively modern turn to the notion of honor, and made it into something less hierarchical, and a little more internalized; the main reason their texts interest us here. Although we have to avoid reading these texts as if they were written by our contemporaries, studying them "represents a leap of faith that these works will repay our efforts" (Saxonhouse 1993, 22).

The Art of Governing Men

Locke is at present best known for his writing about concepts with a contemporary ring, such as the rule of law and the freedom of government interference in our private lives (notions that stem from his *Second*

Treatise on Government). But in his less known *Some Thoughts Concerning Education*, published a few years later, he wrote that the freedom citizens enjoy should be kept within due limits by making use of their concern for their name and reputation. That makes the latter book not so much a work on education as, as Nathan Tarcov phrased it in *Locke's Education for Liberty* (1984), on "the art of governing men"—a skill that makes extensive use of the love of praise and a good reputation, as well as the fear of disgrace. Locke held that "if thou can once get into children a love of credit, and an apprehension of shame and disgrace, you have put into them the true principle, which will constantly work, and incline them to the right" (*Thoughts* §55), and that children "find a pleasure in being esteemed, and valued, especially by their parents, and those whom they depend on" (*Thoughts* §56). This sensitivity for praise and blame is "the great secret of education," and works for children and adults alike (*Thoughts* §55, 56). Locke was of the opinion that this did not lessen the freedom of the citizen: who acts from a concern for reputation still acts freely and from something within (*Thoughts* §42; see also Tarcov 1984).

Nowadays, if we say that someone acts from "something within" we normally mean that he or she follows an inborn moral principle. Not so for Locke, who wrote in *An Essay Concerning Human Understanding* that "principles of action indeed there are lodged in men's appetites, but these are so far from being innate moral principles that, if they were left to their full swing, they would carry men to the over-turning of all morality" (I.iii.13). Our only inborn principles are the selfish longing for happiness and the equally selfish fear of pain, and both have to be checked "by rewards and punishments that will overbalance the satisfaction anyone shall propose to himself in the breach of law" (*Essay* I.iii.13). Among the punishments we should take into account, there is first that of God, consisting of a long and painful stay in hell; as we seldom think of this punishment, its influence is little. Equally limited is the influence of legal sanctions, since we often imagine that we can get away with our misbehavior. But there is one punishment we cannot escape, and that is the censure from our fellow citizens. More important, there is not

> one of ten thousand who is stiff and insensible enough to bear up under the constant dislike and condemnation of his own club. He must be of a strange and unusual constitution who can content himself to live in constant disgrace and disrepute with his own particular society. (. . .) This is a burden too heavy for human sufferance (*Essay* I.iii.12).

Locke therefore held, not unlike Cicero,

> that he who imagines commendation and disgrace not to be strong motives on men to accommodate themselves to the opinions and rules of those with whom they converse seems little skilled in the nature or history of mankind, the greatest part whereof he shall find to govern themselves chiefly, if not solely, by this law of fashion; and so they do that which keeps them in reputation with their company, little regard the laws of God or the magistrate. The penalties that attend the breach of God's laws some, nay, perhaps most men seldom seriously reflect on; and amongst those that do, many, whilst they break the law, entertain thoughts of future reconciliation and making their peace for such breaches. And as to the punishments due from the laws of the commonwealth, they frequently flatter themselves with the hopes of impunity. But no man escapes the punishment of their censure and dislike who offends against the fashion and opinion of the company he keeps and would recommend himself to (*Essay* I.iii.12).

But ought this be so?

We fear the opinions of others more than we fear hell or jail.

Where Locke's account of our concern for reputation is in all a positive one, not a long time later Bernard Mandeville, famous (and notorious) in his own time but now to some extent slipped back into relative anonymity, would take a much more skeptical position, although agreeing with Locke on the beneficial consequences of honor. Writing on the functions honor, pride, and reputation fulfill in society, Mandeville built a bad reputation for himself (which did not mortify him unduly) by arguing that vanity was the minister of industry, in a somewhat blasphemous poem published in 1705 under the title *The Grumling Hive: or, Knaves Turn'd Honest.* Two volumes of elucidation, published under the more famous title *Fable of the Bees: or, Private Vices, Publick Benefits,* only added to his notoriety. In the first of these two volumes Mandeville, a much more explicit debunker of the notion of honor than for instance Hobbes was, wrote that honor is a "chimera without truth or being, an invention of moralists and politicians, and signifies a certain principle of virtue not related to religion, found in some men that keeps them close to their duty and engagements whatever they be" (*Fable* vol. I 216).

Although Mandeville stressed its great instrumental value here (as it is the one thing that makes people behave), he at the same time pointed

out that honor is something fundamentally artificial. As he liked to do:
on the subject of the breed of men honor is found in, we read for instance
that

> The excellency of this principle [of honor] is, that the vulgar are
> destitute of it, and it is only to be met with in people of the bet-
> ter sort, as some oranges have kernels, and others not, though
> the outside be the same. In great families it is like the gout,
> generally counted hereditary, and all Lords children are born
> with it. In some that never felt anything of it, it is acquired by
> conversation and reading (especially of romances), in others by
> preferment; but there is nothing that encourages the growth of
> it more than a sword, and upon the first wearing of one, some
> people have felt considerable shoots of it in four and twenty
> hours (*Fable* vol. I 217).

Although such men of honor will disagree, Mandeville held that our
true nature is in every respect self-seeking.

But even the most egoistic individuals soon find out that seeking
direct gratification of their appetites brings worlds of troubles, and to
be able

> to indulge their own appetites with less disturbance, they agreed
> with the rest to call everything, which, without regard to the
> public, man should commit to gratify any of his appetites, vice;
> if in that action there could be observed the least prospect, that
> it might either be injurious to any of the society, or even render
> himself less serviceable to others: and to give the name of virtue
> every performance, by which man, contrary to the impulse of
> nature, should endeavour the benefit of others, or the conquest
> of his own passions out of a rational ambition of being good
> (*Fable* vol. I 34).

That empty endorsement of everyday morality does not have to stop
anyone from satisfying his or her desires in more covert manners that
are less harmful to society. In the case of sexual desires, for example,
one can do so by marrying the object of one's lust (*Fable* vol. I 63–4).
More in general, it seemed to Mandeville that "the man that gratifies
his appetites after the manner the custom of the country allows of, has
no censure to fear" (*Fable* vol. I 65). Elsewhere, we read that "to be at

once well-bred and sincere, is no less than a contradiction" (*Fable* vol. I 201).

Not that Mandeville thought that the world would be a better place if people were genuinely good and altruistic—poverty and boredom would await us. Mandeville therefore rhymed: "So vice is beneficial found/When it's by justice lopt and bound" (*Fable* vol. I 24). It was for polemical reasons only that Mandeville nonetheless stuck with the moralist's (Christian or Stoic) equation of altruism with virtue, and of everything in the slightest degree motivated by self-serving reasons with vice. This equation of virtue with altruism enabled him to show how we all lack in virtue, at least according to his strict definition, but this same definition also made it possible for Mandeville to argue with some plausibility that it is our vices, more specifically our self-regarding drives, that make societies prosper.[5] Those who claim to possess it might profess the contrary, but honor was in Mandeville's view nothing more than an instance of such a self-regarding drive.

Mandeville would have disagreed with Smith's remark, quoted above, that man also wants to be worthy of approval (*Theory* III.2.7). According to Mandeville, it is only the desire to be actually approved of that motivates us, and to a large extent honor is a matter of not being found out. He for that reason mockingly stated that "the reason why there are so few men of real virtue, and so many of real honour, is, because all the recompense a man has of a virtuous action, is the pleasure of doing it, which most people reckon but poor pay" (*Fable* vol. I 246). Insofar as honor is concerned, it is this grimmer view that sets Mandeville apart from authors such as Cicero and Smith. Yet, despite being essentially selfish (regarding intentions), honor was in Mandeville's opinion also a socially useful motive (regarding consequences), in the real world indispensable as a check on man's behavior. In fact, its invention has been a lot more beneficial to society than the invention of virtue, which, Mandeville explained elsewhere, predated the invention of honor by many centuries (*An Enquiry into the Origin of Honour and the Usefulness of Christianity in War* 15). Honor is, in this view, just another proof of the truth of the subheading of the *Fable of the Bees*, namely: *Private Vices, Public Benefits*.

So although Mandeville, like the Stoics, denied the reality of honor, he disagreed with them on a crucial point: he did not believe that people, despite all their pretenses to the contrary, would ever be capable of acting virtuously for the sake of virtue alone. Mandeville noted that there were other authors who shared his doubts about Stoicism and

have exploded those precepts as impracticable, called their notions romantic, and endeavoured to prove that what these Stoics
asserted of themselves exceeded all human force and possibility,
and that therefore the virtues they boasted of could be nothing but haughty pretence, full of arrogance and hypocrisy (*Fable*
vol. I 161).

But "notwithstanding these censures, the serious part of the world, and
the generality of wise men that have lived ever since to this day, agree
with the Stoics in the most material points" (*Fable* vol. I 161). As for
Mandeville himself, he admitted that he knew the Stoic teachings as
well as Seneca did, but was not so sure about how "philosophically" he
would react if someone "made the least motion of spitting in my face"
(*Fable* vol. I 163). Being a man of science, he was a physician specialized
in nervous diseases, Mandeville prided himself (just as Hobbes had done
before him) on being an author who did not present man to his readers
as he should be, but as he is. To no avail, he himself thought, because
people are prone to deceive both themselves and others:

> Ask not only the divines and moralists of every nation, but
> likewise all that are rich and powerful, about real pleasure, and
> they'll tell you, with the Stoics that there can be no true felicity
> in things mundane and corruptible: but then look upon their
> lives, and you find they take delight in no other (*Fable* vol. I 179).

The honor ethic expects us to put high value on ourselves and our repu-
tations, whereas the Stoic ethic demands humility. Strictly speaking,
honor and humility require the same thing. Honor is based upon someone's "estimation of his own worth," (Pitt-Rivers 1974, 21), and so is humility, but the difference is that in the eyes of those who see humility as
a virtue we are, different from what we tend to think, just not worth that
much. This is especially so in Jewish and Christian views on humility,
which in that aspect are somewhat on a par with the Stoic view: "In both
Hebrew scripture and the New Testament, humility is a quality of spirit
aimed at combating the greatest and most debilitating form of human
sin: pride or vanity," writes Mark Button (2005, 842). But for most of us,
pride still comes a lot easier than humility.

To illustrate: in *An Enquiry into the Origin of Honour and the Usefulness of Christianity in War*, from 1732, Mandeville stressed that the
Christian ethics of his day, in his view comparable with the Stoic ethics

of former times, was useless in war because it was incapable of motivating soldiers to sacrifice their lives. In practice, every commander will therefore take recourse to the opposite honor ethic, and

> the men are praised and buoyed up in the high value they have for themselves: their officers call them gentlemen and fellow-soldiers; generals pull off their hats to them; and no artifice is neglected that can flatter their pride, or inspire them with the love of glory (*Enquiry* 161).

Nowhere has pride been more encouraged than in the army, and "never anything had been invented before, that was half so effective to create artificial courage among military men" (*Enquiry* 60). Although in Mandeville's view principally a self-regarding drive, honor is clearly something that can make people forget their real interests.

The first volume of the *Fable of the Bees* even contains some practical suggestions how to accomplish that feat in the case of soldiers. One makes a soldier courageous by inspiring "him with as much horror against shame, as nature has given him against death" (*Fable* vol. I 231). Once the notions of honour and shame are received among a society, it is in fact easy to make men fight; just "put feathers in their caps, and distinguish them from others (. . .) and every proud man will take up arms and fight himself to death" (*Fable* vol. I 233).[6] To induce their soldiers to overcome their natural fear of death, commanders flatter and praise the bold, reward the wounded, and honor the dead. High-sounding words about the justness of the cause, despising death and the bed of honor, together with uniforms and decorations, provide against little cost the courage money cannot buy. The strongest motive for courageous behavior is the desire not to be seen as a coward: "One man in an army is a check upon another, and a hundred of them that single and without witness would be all cowards, are for fear of incurring one another's contempt made valiant by being together" (*Fable* vol. I 233). But Mandeville himself saw honor definitely not as something worth dying for, and he cynically rhymed that "The soldiers that were forced to fight, If they survived, got *honour* by't" (*Fable* vol. I 6).

It was not only soldiers who were in Mandeville's view so sensitive to shame and flattery. Somewhat similar to Locke in *Some Thoughts Concerning Education* (§55), Mandeville wrote that "it is certain, that nothing (. . .) has a greater influence upon children, than the handle that is made of shame" (*Fable* vol. II 78), and that this fear of "shame might be greatly increased by an artful education, and be made superior even to that of death" (*Enquiry* 40). As to flattery: there is no one who can resist its "witchcraft" (*Fable* vol. I 37). That we are so sensitive to flattery is itself a result of the workings self-liking, which "excites in us the love of praise, and a desire to be applauded and thought well of by others, and stirs us up to good actions" (*Enquiry* 6), and of pride, "that natural faculty by which every mortal that has any understanding over-values, and imagines better things of himself than any impartial judge, thoroughly acquainted with all his qualities and circumstances, could allow him" (*Fable* vol. I 125). Basically, "the moral virtues are the political offspring which flattery begot upon pride" (*Fable* vol. I 37). Similar to Locke in *An Essay Concerning Human Understanding*, Mandeville wrote in the first dialogue of *An Enquiry into the Origin of Honour and the Usefulness of Christianity in War* that the effect of religion on our behavior is small and of little force.

[margin handwritten note: Religion has little effect on our behavior]

Yet although man was tamed by "the skilful management of wary politicians," flattery only works when "artfully performed" since only "children and fools will swallow personal praise" (*Fable* vol. I 37). Those who are somewhat cleverer "must be managed with greater circumspection; and the more general the flattery is, the less it is suspected by those it is levelled at" (*Fable* vol. I 37).[7] That the "well-bred gentleman places his greatest pride in the skill he has of covering it with dexterity" (*Fable* vol. I 136) probably forms an extra reason for circumspection in these matters. As Appiah writes three centuries later on the complex connection between pride and honor: "One difficulty for pride, then, is that modesty may be part of the honor code" (2010, 17).

Mandeville combined the classical preoccupation with honor with the modern view of man as self-seeking. He was influenced by the work of the humanist and theologian Desiderius Erasmus (born in the same city as Mandeville, Rotterdam) who, in *In Praise of Folly*, asked rhetorically about the invention of the arts and sciences:

> what sedentary, thoughtful men would have beat their brains in the search of new and unheard of mysteries, if not egged on by the bubbling hopes of credit and reputation? They think a little glittering flash of vain-glory is a sufficient reward for all their sweat, and toil, and tedious drudgery, while they that are supposedly more foolish, reap advantage of the others' labors.

According to F.B. Kaye, in his influential introduction to the 1924 Oxford University Press edition of the *Fable*, "Mandeville means by vice pretty much what Erasmus means by folly" (*Fable* vol. I p. cvii). Although certainly not neglected, Mandeville's work has not been the subject of much recent research, and perhaps that is partly because many consider Kaye's introduction to be the final word on Mandeville. Mandeville's continuous irony, satire, and at times cynicism, might form another explanation; it makes it difficult to establish what his "true" position was on a particular topic.

What is certain, however, is that his work influenced later moral philosophers such as David Hume and Adam Smith (see also Hayek 1985, 264)—although the latter would speak of "true glory" in a way Mandeville would never do. But Mandeville did not get the credit, and Smith thought that it was

> the great fallacy of Dr. Mandeville's book to represent every passion as wholly vicious, which is so in any degree and in any direction. It is thus that he treats everything as vanity which has any reference, either to what are, or to what ought to be the sentiments of others: and it is by means of this sophistry, that he establishes his favourite conclusion, that private vices are public benefits (*The Theory of Moral Sentiments* VII.ii.4.12).[8]

As Smith saw it, "some popular ascetic doctrines which had been current before his time, and which placed virtue in the entire extirpation and annihilation of all our passions, were the real foundation of this licentious system" (*Theory* VII.ii.4.13). But Smith concluded that "some of the articles, at least, must be just, and even those which are most overcharged must have had some foundation, otherwise the fraud would be detected even by that careless inspection which we are disposed to give" (*Theory* VII.ii.4.14), and that the *Fable* would not have made such an impact, "had it not bordered upon the truth" (*Theory* VII.ii.4.13).

Hume's Judicious Spectator

We have seen that Locke thought that the sensitivity for praise and blame was "the great secret of education," and the basis for the art of governing men. Yet a clear standard for the distribution of praise and blame is for the most part absent in his work, although Locke did sometimes hint at utility (and impartiality), for instance when he wrote that since nothing can be more natural than to encourage with esteem and reputation that wherein everyone finds his advantage, and to blame and discountenance the contrary, it is no wonder that esteem and discredit, virtue and vice, should in a great measure everywhere correspond with the unchangeable rule of right and wrong, which the law of God has established (*Essay* II.xxviii.11).

The standard of utility makes the honor ethic somewhat less particularistic, and would in the subsequent century play a more prominent role in the work of Mandeville, as we have just seen, but even more so in the moral philosophy of David Hume, which would prepare the ground for the utilitarianism of Jeremy Bentham and John Stuart Mill.

Hume held, for instance, that there is no higher praise than that revealed in the remark that something is *useful*:

> Can anything stronger be said in praise of a profession, such as merchandise or manufacture, than to observe the advantages which it procures to society; and is not a monk and inquisitor enraged when we treat his order as useless or pernicious to mankind? (. . .) In general, what praise is implied in the simple epithet "useful"! What reproach in the contrary! (*An Enquiry Concerning the Principles of Morals* II.ii).

Because they were so unproductive Hume explicitly rejected "the whole train of monkish virtues" (*Enquiry* IV.i). We can assume that, if asked, Hume would also have rejected the equally unproductive soldierly virtues on the same grounds.

But although this shift from unproductive to productive virtues might suggest otherwise, "Hume talks of mankind and the species feeling this or that, as though all men felt and thought like a civilized eighteenth-century gentlemen inspired by Cicero and the models of classical antiquity" (Forbes 1975, 109; see also Moore 2002, 366).[9] In fact, there are substantial similarities between Cicero and Hume. To point out an important one: analogous to the way Cicero opposed the Stoics, Hume opposed those who in his time held views comparable with the strict Stoic view, and he thought that morality was not served by the claim that only behavior that springs from a sense of duty was to be called moral. Although man is capable of forming "an idea of perfections much beyond what he has experience of in himself," it would be unwise, and rather discouraging, to make a "comparison between man and beings of the most perfect wisdom" (*Dignity or Meanness of Human Nature*).[10]

Hume noted in *A Treatise of Human Nature* that it is in theory indifferent to us whether someone tries to do good to us, to our neighbor, or to someone in China (III.iii.i). Provided that we adopt "some steady and general points of view"—the viewpoint of what Hume famously called the judicious spectator—we in general praise just acts because they contribute to the common good. But that only goes for our judgments concerning the conduct of others. It does not mean that we are also motivated to *act* in the public interest; on the whole our sympathy with the public interest is too weak to determine our conduct. That led Brian Barry to conclude that Hume had no convincing answer to the question why we, let alone a "sensible knave," should act honestly, other than that virtue should be its own reward (1989, 167). If that really were the only answer Hume gave, it would indeed be a rather unconvincing one, if only because he wrote in the same work that the original motive to the establishment of justice was not the love of justice, but self-interest (*Treatise* III.ii.ii).

Hume's real answer was that when we act justly, as we usually do, this is often not done from a concern for the public interest, but from a concern for our own reputation. According to Hume,

> there is nothing, which touches us more nearly than our reputation, and nothing on which our reputation more depends than our conduct, with relation to the property of others. For this reason, everyone, who has any regard to his character, or who intends to live on good terms with mankind, must fix an inviolable law to himself, never, by any temptation, to be induced to violate those principles, which are essential to a man of probity and honour (*Treatise* III.ii.ii).

As Forbes put it in his book on Hume's political philosophy: "Men seek approval and will for the most part fashion themselves and behave in such a way as to win it; they will act and feel and judge in accordance with the prevailing norms of their society" (1975, 107).[11]

Politicians and parents put this love of reputation to use in bolstering the esteem for justice, and inducing people to behave accordingly. Although the progress of the sentiments of justice is according to Hume "natural, and even necessary," it is also true that this progress is pushed "by the artifice of politicians, who, in order to govern men more easily, and preserve peace in human society, have endeavoured to produce an esteem for justice, and an abhorrence of injustice" (*Treatise* III.ii.ii). And "as public praise and blame increase our esteem for justice; so private education and instruction contribute to the same effect" (*Treatise* III.ii.ii).[12]

But Hume emphasized that this does not mean that the esteem for justice is an invention of politicians, as some philosophers have argued. Perhaps he was thinking of (and disagreeing with) Mandeville here, seeing that what Hume blamed these authors for is that they "have represented all moral distinctions as the effect of artifice and education, when skilful politicians endeavoured to restrain the turbulent passions of men, and make them operate to the public good, by the notions of honour and shame" (*Treatise* III.iii.i). Depicting honor as an invention of moralists and politicians, like Mandeville had done, is an exaggeration of the role of politicians: "if nature did not aid us in this particular, it would be in vain for politicians to talk of *honourable* or *dishonourable*, *praiseworthy* or *blameable*" (*Treatise* III.ii.ii). Also,

> had not men a natural sentiment of approbation and blame, it could never be excited by politicians; nor would the words laudable and praiseworthy, blameable and odious be any more intelligible, than if they were a language perfectly unknown to us, as we have already observed" (*Treatise* III.iii.i).

Nevertheless, where for Cicero both the strength of our love of honor, and what society deemed honorable, were constants, this was not how Hume saw it. For Cicero honor was a necessary incentive, but not so much something to manipulate with, while for Hume honor was an important instrument that should be cleverly put to use in a manner that advances the interests of society.

That the motivation behind just conduct is often not so noble was unimportant to Hume. Because he believed that otherwise good conduct, although motivated by somewhat self-regarding reasons like vanity, is the best we can hope for, he disagreed with those who, like the Stoics of earlier times, wanted man to be just for the sake of justice, not for the sake of his good name. In his essay *Of Moral Prejudices* we read that there is a

> grave philosophic endeavour after perfection, which, under pretext of reforming prejudices and errors, strikes at all the most

endearing sentiments of the heart, and all the most useful by-passes and instincts, which can govern a human creature. The *Stoics* were remarkable for this folly among the ancients; and I wish some of more venerable characters in latter times had not copied them too faithfully in this particular. The virtuous and tender sentiments, or prejudices, if you will, have suffered mightily by these reflections; while a sullen pride or contempt has prevailed in their stead, and has been esteemed the greatest wisdom; though, in reality it be the most egregious folly of all others.[13]

Hume felt that too many of his contemporaries copied the Stoics, whose philosophy he regarded as utterly unsound, and as having "a very bad effect on those, who indulge it" (*Of Moral Prejudices*; see for a similar opinion Bentham *An Introduction to the Principles of Morals and Legislation* XI.xvi). These indulgers might have self-serving motives to do so, finding an excuse in Stoicism for their natural indolence.[14]

Similar to Cicero, Hume thought that vanity and the love of fame were closely related to virtue (*Treatise* II.i.xi, II.ii.i), and are for that reason better not called vices. In his essay *Dignity or Meanness of Human Nature* Hume wrote that

Hume: vanity and virtue are very closely related

it has always been found, that the virtuous are far from being indifferent to praise; and therefore they have been represented as a set of vain-glorious men, who had nothing in view but the applauses of others. (. . .) But vanity is so closely allied to virtue, and to love the fame of laudable actions approaches so near the love of laudable actions for their own sake, that these passions are more capable of mixture, than any other kinds of affection; and it is almost impossible to have the latter without some degree of the former. (. . .) To love the glory of virtuous deeds is a sure proof of the love of virtue.

Vanity is therefore "rather to be esteemed a social passion, and a bond of union among men" (*Treatise* III.ii.ii), and "there are few persons, that are satisfied with their own character, or genius, or fortune, who are not desirous of showing themselves to the world, and of acquiring the love and approbation of mankind" (*Treatise* II.II.i). This close relation between vanity and virtue is what distinguishes vanity from, for instance, revenge and avarice; we are, writes Hume, rightfully suspicious of actions motivated by those emotions (*Dignity or Meanness of Human Nature*).

In *An Enquiry Concerning the Principles of Morals*, intended as a reworking of Cicero's *De Officiis* and the book Hume himself was most satisfied with (Moore 2002, 365–6), he wrote that the "desire of fame, reputation, or a character with others, is so far from being blameable, that it seems inseparable from virtue, genius, capacity, and a generous or noble disposition" (VIII). In the next section he concluded that the "love of fame" is a "spring of our constitution that brings a great addition of force to moral sentiment" (*Enquiry* concl.i). It is by the pursuit of a name and a reputation in the world that

> we bring our own deportment and conduct frequently in review
> and consider how they appear in the eyes of those who approach
> and regard us. This constant habit of surveying ourselves, as it
> were in reflection, keeps alive all the sentiments of right and
> wrong (*Enquiry* concl.i).

A habit that is "the surest guardian of every virtue" (*Enquiry* concl.i).

According to Hume, this love of fame rules with "uncontrolled authority in all generous minds, and is often the grand object of all their designs and undertakings" (*Enquiry* concl.i). Hume also thought that, "next to emulation, the greatest encourager of the noble arts is praise and glory" (*The Rise of Arts and Sciences*). In his short autobiography *My Own Life* he admitted his own "ruling passion" was the "love of literary fame" (in Hume's time "literary" included philosophy; Sabl 2006). This passion for fame is probably best kept hidden from the public view, though. It is to keep society tolerable, despite our tendency to think too highly of ourselves, that

> custom has established it as a rule, in common societies, that
> men should not indulge themselves in self-praise, or even speak
> much of themselves; and it is only among intimate friends or
> people of very manly behaviour, that one is allowed to do himself justice (*Enquiry* VIII).

Modesty is therefore "a quality immediately agreeable to others" (*Enquiry* VIII).

Smith's Impartial Spectator

Adam Smith elaborated further on many of the themes that Mandeville and Hume had addressed. In line with Mandeville, who held that "every individual values itself above its real worth" (*Fable* vol. II 134; see also vol. I 125), and Hume, who wrote that "men have, in general, a much greater propensity to overvalue than undervalue themselves" (*Enquiry* VIII), Smith started from the assumption that we lack self-knowledge: incapable of judging our own conduct objectively, we tend to esteem ourselves too highly. Imagining how a well-informed impartial spectator sees our conduct was according to Smith the only way to correct "the natural misrepresentations of self-love" (*Theory* III.3.4). It is for that reason that the Stoics recommended that "we should view ourselves, not in the light in which our own selfish passions are apt to place us, but in the light in which any other citizen of the world would view us" (Smith *Theory* III.3.11). Such an impartial spectator is not only aware of our conduct, but also of our motives. In fact, the virtuous man "almost becomes himself that impartial spectator, and scarce even feels but as that great arbiter of his conduct directs him to feel" (*Theory* III.3.25). But even though this notion of the impartial spectator appears countless times in his *The Theory of Moral Sentiments*, Smith is at present mostly remembered for his metaphor of an invisible hand that regulates free markets—the term invisible hand itself appears only a few times in his major works, however.

Although today primarily associated with modern economics, Smith's lectures on ethics "show him a Roman Eclectic in modern dress" (Gay 1973, 54–5), recommending "that we should follow the practice of the ancients" (Larmore 1987, 17). This eclectic was influenced by the work of Cicero, but also by that of Stoics such as Aurelius and Epictetus (see also Gay 1973, 54–5; Larmore 1987, 17).[15] In some aspects Smith's impartial spectator—for which Smith is thought to have found inspiration in the work of the Stoics (see for instance Raphael 2007)—indeed somewhat resembles the world citizen that, the Stoics thought, we should all aim to be, and in general Smith was more of a Stoic, and hence more austere and less concerned with what is useful, than his friend Hume. But to Smith the impartial spectator was not almighty, and it is here that we see the influence of Cicero. To function well, the impartial spectator in the breast "requires often to be awakened and put in mind of his duty, by the presence of the real spectator" (*Theory* III.3.38). In the end the praise and blame of our fellow citizens are "the only looking-glass by

which we can, in some measure, scrutinize the propriety of our own conduct" (*Theory* III.1.5)—here lies the origin of Charles Cooley's looking-
glass self (1922), mentioned earlier.

In a telling passage Smith quotes Cicero: "Many people despise
glory, who are yet most severely mortified by unjust reproach: and that is
most inconsistently" (*Theory* III.2.30-1; see also *De Officiis* I.71). Smith
added, though, that this inconsistency

> seems to be founded in the unalterable principles of human na-
> ture. The all-wise Author of Nature has, in this manner, taught
> man to respect the sentiments and judgments of his brethren;
> to be more or less pleased when they approve of his conduct,
> and to be more or less hurt when they disapprove of it (*Theory*
> III.2.30–1).

What's more, there are many situations in which it is difficult for him to
go against the confounding judgments of ignorant and weak men, and

> In such cases, this demigod within the breast appears, like the
> demigods of the poets, though partly of immortal, yet partly
> too of mortal extraction. When his judgments are steadily and
> firmly directed by the sense of praiseworthiness and blamewor-
> thiness, he seems to act suitably to his divine extraction: but
> when he suffers himself to be astonished and confounded by
> the judgments of ignorant and weak man, he discovers his con-
> nection with mortality, and appears to act suitably, rather to the
> human, than to the divine, part of his origin (*Theory* III.ii.32).

Our motives are often a mixture of the human and the divine element:
like Cicero and Hume, Smith held that virtue and the love of praise were
closely intermingled, and that "there is an affinity too between the desire
of becoming what is honourable and estimable, and the desire of honour
and esteem, between the love of virtue and the love of true glory" (*Theory*
VII.ii.4.10). Although a love of virtue for its own sake might seem more
pure than a love of glory, even in that love of virtue there is "some reference to the sentiments of others," because he who does not care about
the opinions of others, cares very much about how other *should* think of
him, and this is "the great and exalted motive of his conduct" (*Theory*
VII.ii.4.10). Earlier in the *Theory* Smith already wrote that virtue has "an
immediate reference to the sentiments of others. Virtue is not said to be

amiable or to be meritorious, because it is the object of its own love, or of its own gratitude; but because it excites those sentiments in other man" (*Theory* III.1.7). As to glory, Smith held that

> the desire of the esteem and admiration of other people, when for qualities and talents which are the natural and proper objects of esteem and admiration, is the real love of true glory; a passion which, if not the very best passion of human nature, is certainly one of the best (*Theory* VI.iii.46).

In the same section, in words similar to those of Locke, Mandeville, and Hume, Smith wrote that "the great secret of education is to direct vanity to proper objects."

Emerging theme

Smith, who considered his moral philosophy to be a descriptive activity rather than a normative one (Forman-Barzilai 2005, 191), realized that we are not always able to conform to the verdict of the impartial spectator. Especially when our passions and our partiality to ourselves overwhelm us, this may ask too much from us (*Theory* III.4.5–6). In these instances we should follow the "general rules" of society: somewhat similar to Cicero's remark that we should study others to find out what is unbecoming, Smith wrote that it is through "our continual observations upon the conduct of others" that we know that some actions could render us "the objects of universal disapprobation" (*Theory* III.4.7). We therefore lay down to ourselves, firstly, that as a general rule "all such actions are to be avoided, as tending to render us odious, contemptible, or punishable, the objects of all those sentiments for which we have the greatest dread and aversion." And, secondly, the general rule to perform those actions that are generally honored and rewarded, exciting the love, gratitude, and admiration of mankind we all desire (*Theory* III.4.7). Only with those general rules we are able to correct "the misrepresentations of self-love concerning what is fit and proper," while without such rules, "there is no man whose conduct can be much depended on" (*Theory* III.5.2).[16]

Despite the role Smith sees for general rules, and although he acknowledged that his impartial spectator needs real spectators to function, Smith's philosophy is more demanding than that of Cicero, Mandeville, or Hume. Although the impartial spectator is not an inner voice that is unique to someone, to the contrary, it nonetheless can be seen as a "consciencelike faculty" (Forman-Barzilai 2005, 195). And although honor, praise, and reputation were still important in the work of such later thinkers as Bentham and Mill, the work of Smith forms somewhat of a turning point, taking us in a new direction—although it would take another century and a half or so, the role honor had in political and moral philosophy was about to come to an end.

But having arrived at this point, it seems fitting to first pay attention to the evident downsides of an honor ethic. Since they in general gave honor a lot of thought, at least compared to most modern-day authors, it is no wonder that many pre-twentieth century philosophers, from Cicero and Seneca to Smith and Tocqueville, also had an eye for these shortcomings, and came up with some solutions too.

Problems with Honor

To start with the drawbacks: even the defenders of the honor ethic realized that if honor is reduced to a matter of "not being caught," everything is permitted when no one is around. According to Tocqueville, honor "is only effective in full view of the public, differing in that from sheer virtue, which feeds upon itself, contended with its own witness" (1969, 626). It seems that what is only known privately and is not out in the open does not even exist for those who are led by external honor only (Bowman 2006, 42-4; see also Margalit 1996, 131). A point proven by Gyges, Griffin, and Sebastian Caine. The view on morality present in Gyges' tale as Glaucon tells it in Plato's *Republic* (it is evidently not the Platonic/Socratic view on morality), Wells' novel (although to a lesser extent—Griffin is portrayed as a rather atypical person), and the Paul Verhoeven movie is basically the same as that of Mandeville: morality is all about pretense and artificiality, something that we abandon when we think ourselves unobserved. The question is to what extent Gyges, Griffin, and Caine are truly universal characters.

But if the view on human nature that they depict is true, similar problems might arise if there are too many witnesses around. According to Hume, "honour is a great check upon mankind: But where a considerable body of men act together, this check is, in a great measure, removed" (*On the Independency of Parliament*). Hume's fellow Scotchman Adam Ferguson wrote about commercial society that "it is here indeed, if ever, that man is sometimes found a detached and solitary being" (*An Essay on the History of Civil Society* I.iii). In Tocqueville's view, honor is less binding in a "constantly fluctuating crowd" (1969, 626). If we do not care for the opinion of those who witness our conduct because we do not know them, like they do not know us, an important check on our conduct disappears. Smith was for that reason concerned about the effects of modern industrial, urban society; especially the man of low condition is only taken notice of as long as he lives in his small rural village. But "as soon as he comes into a great city, he is sunk in obscurity and darkness. His conduct is observed and attended to by nobody, and he is therefore very likely to neglect it himself, and to abandon himself to every sort of low profligacy and vice" (*Wealth of Nations* V.i.g.12). A gentleman, on the other hand,

> is by his station the distinguished member of a great society, who attends to every part of his conduct, and who thereby obliges him to attend to every part of it himself (. . .). He dare not do anything which would disgrace him or discredit him in it (*Wealth of Nations* V.i.g.12).[17]

That same gentleman, staying far from what is vile and base, could err on the other side, however. Smith noted that

> place, that great object which divides the wives of alderman, is the end of half the labours of human life; and is the cause of all the tumult and bustle, all the rapine and injustice, which avarice and ambition have introduced into this world (*Theory* I.iii.2.8).

Smith shared with Cicero an ambiguous view on ambition; in line with the Stoic teachings, Smith held that happiness was in reach of everyone who contents himself with tranquility and enjoyment (B. Singer 2004, 47). Francis Bacon already wrote that "glorious men are the scorn of wise men; the admiration of fools; the idols of parasites; and the slaves of their own vaunts" (*Of Vain Glory*).

At the same time Smith saw that social climbing is the "great purpose of human life," and that "it is chiefly from this regard for the sentiments of others that we pursue richness and avoid poverty," seeing that our basic needs are met by the wages of "the meanest labourer" (*Theory* II.iii.28). In Smith's view, writes Donald Winch, ambition is mainly about "respect and admiration, the satisfaction of our desire to emulate those above us on the social ladder, and the gratification of our vanity and craving for social esteem" (1978, 91). On the credit side is that ambition motivates people to work hard, and it is therefore "a passion, which when it keeps within the bounds of prudence and justice, is always admired in the world, and has even sometimes a certain irregular greatness, which dazzles the imagination" (Smith *Theory* III.6.7). On the negative side is that, as Brian Singer writes, "the poor and middling classes, in the struggle for recognition, are willing to sacrifice their immediate happiness, in the pursuit of its tokens" (2004, 47).

Ambitious men that live by the individualistic honor ethic we see in the *Iliad* embodied in Achilles and Agamemnon, and aimed at personal aggrandizement before anything else, can, as Mandeville already pointed out, even manipulate their followers by appealing to *their* love of honor, putting pressure on people to do things definitely not in their own interest. In Julius Caesar's *De Bello Gallico*, for instance, we read how Caesar's being a witness on the battlefield motivated his men to a rather extreme degree (III.14, VII.62). Field Marshall Bernard Montgomery, resentful after General Eisenhower took over Ground Forces Command against Montgomery's wish, in his pursuance of personal glory according to some accounts took irresponsible risks with the failed Operation Market Garden, which should have brought him back to the top position yet in fact cost the lives of many soldiers. All in all, John G. Peristiany and Julian Pitt-Rivers stated in a foreword to their *Honor and Grace in Anthropology* (1992), honor probably caused more deaths than the plague.

Another drawback of honor is that it tends to reinforce existing inequalities in a society or organization, even in relatively democratic times. It is not that long ago that it was thought quite honorable for an officer to not pay his tailor, to flog a soldier, or to be drunk. But among equals not paying your gambling debts or not adequately responding to an insult was deemed very dishonorable. Even though these are (apart from the flogging) relatively innocent examples that can be remedied, such an exclusivist ethic of honor might also take more harmful and persistent forms. Although honor and virtue were closely related in his view, Smith also noted that the "disposition to admire, and almost worship, the rich and the powerful, and to despise, or, at least, to neglect persons of poor and mean condition" persisted into modernity. This was in Smith's opinion "the great and most universal cause of the corruption of our moral sentiments" (*Theory* I.iii.3.1). Like Cicero, Smith observed that the rich and powerful receive the respect and admiration "due only to wisdom and virtue," while their follies and vices are looked upon with some forgiveness. Our contemporary celebrity culture provides ample illustration of how respect and admiration are still not always distributed according to merit. The poor man, writes Smith, is meanwhile ashamed of his poverty, and feels that it either "places him out of the sight of mankind," or is looked upon with contempt. Whether overlooked or disapproved of, he is equally mortified: "as obscurity covers us from the daylight of honour and approbation, to feel that we are taken no notice of, necessarily damps the most agreeable hope, and disappoints the most keen desire, of human nature" (*Theory* I.iii.2.1; compare Hume *Treatise* II.ii.v.).

Although his personal background remains somewhat unclear (we are half-way through the story before we learn his last name, his first name remains untold), it is not unlikely that Griffin, the protagonist of *The Invisible Man* and aiming for world domination by establishing a reign of terror, was motivated in his struggle with mankind by the fact that he had been socially invisible when he ("almost an albino") was still physically visible. This social invisibility is, incidentally, the theme of Ralph Ellison's 1952 novel *Invisible Man*; its African-American protagonist was invisible because, as he put it in the opening lines, "people refuse to see me." In the final pages he realizes that he has always been "as transparent as air." Different from Griffin, he remains nameless throughout the story. Interestingly, and bringing us back to the point made at the beginning of this section, Ellison's socially invisible man realizes that he, although getting no respect and recognition (similar to Smith's "man of low condition"), has almost unlimited freedom in the big city: "How many days could you walk the streets of the big city without encountering anyone who knew you, and how many nights? You could actually make yourself anew" (Chapter 23). Although physically visible, he is in that sense in a position somewhat similar to that of Gyges and Wells' invisible man; the latter marveled at "all the wild and wonderful things" he "had now impunity to do" (Chapter 20). But Griffin's initial happiness did not last very long. After one miserable day in the streets of London,

> it seemed all disappointment. I went over the heads of the things a man reckons desirable. No doubt invisibility made it possible to get them, but it made it impossible to enjoy them when they are got. Ambition—what is the good of pride of place when you cannot appear there? (Chapter 23).

A final, more theoretical, objection is that, from the point of view of an ethicist at least, a good action undertaken for honor does not in every respect deserve the predicate moral. This is a point the Stoics put forward, and was considered a bit too strict by Cicero. But the Stoic position has always appealed to many, and we see it for instance in Montaigne's essay

Of Cato the Younger: "There are no longer virtuous actions extant; those actions that carry a show of virtue have yet nothing of its essence; by reason that profit, glory, fear, custom, and other suchlike foreign causes, put us on the way to produce them." As a sympathizer of the Stoic position, Montaigne was skeptical about Cicero's nuanced stance on honor: if Cicero "had dared, I think he could willingly have fallen into the excess that others did, that virtue itself was not to be coveted, but upon the account of the honor that always attends it" (*On Glory*). The advocates of honor have never satisfactorily resolved the objection that an act motivated by honor is not really a moral act, but in all probability this was never considered a problem by those who benefited from good behavior motivated by honor. Nor was this of great concern to them. As Richard Sennet put it, "so what, if men are spurred to produce great things in hopes of being praised?" (1977, 120). The more important question is of course whether it is possible to somehow improve on the points that are not merely of theoretical interest, and the obvious thing to do is to first look for suggestions in the work of the authors who also identified most of the shortcomings of honor.

Solutions

Most of the philosophers who considered honor a legitimate reward for virtue thought that honor should be internalized, at least to some extent, so that the actual presence of others is no longer needed, and the gaze of imaginary others will be sufficient enough for honor to function. Morality should not be a matter of not being caught. Smith, for instance, pointed out that applause from our peers should not mean much to us if we know that a better-informed impartial spectator, not only aware of our conduct but also of our intentions, would frown on us. Man not only wants praise, but also wants to be praiseworthy, and (as we briefly noted in the introduction) Smith held that "nature, accordingly, has endowed him, not only with a desire of being approved of, but with a desire of being what ought to be approved of; or of being what he himself approves of in other men" (*Theory* III.2.7). For Smith, the internal element of honor (if we can call it that; it is, as said, more of an intermediate element) was not so much our worth in our own eyes, something Cooley and Pitt-Rivers had included in their definition of honor, but external honor internalized: our estimation of how others value us, and, more important, of how they would value us if they were all-knowing. As Smith asked rhetorically: "What so great happiness as to be beloved, and to know that we deserve to be beloved?" (*Theory* III.1.7). We have seen that Smith (and Mandeville and Hume) had an opinion about how we tend to value ourselves—much too high, mainly—but that they did not see this value we put on ourselves as an element of honor. In fact, they saw the expressed opinions of others as a necessary check on our inherent tendency to overestimate ourselves.[18]

The idea of internalized honor somewhat resembles the solution of the ethicist that moral education should aim at reaching a higher level of moral development, that is, beyond the level of conventional ethics (see for instance Toner 2000, 165). Some might wonder how realistic this is. Yet, the idea of internalized honor does indicate that the honor ethic should be more than just a concern about how our behavior looks to others. If not, something like moral courage (more on that in the chapter on integrity), the type of courage that generally brings moral disapprobation, would never be attained. Bernard Williams describes in *Shame and Necessity* how even in paradigmatic shame cultures, such as the heroic society Homer depicted, shame was to a certain degree internalized, and that it is therefore a silly mistake "to suppose that the reactions of shame depend simply on being found out" (1993, 81; see for a different view Bowman 2006, 42–4).[19] Without shame being internalized the idea of a shame *culture* would make no sense (Williams 1993, 81–2).

The internalization of honor clearly makes the honor ethic more demanding, yet it is still much less demanding than an ethic based on autonomy; although abstracted and generalized, the internalized other "is potentially somebody rather than nobody, and somebody other than me" (Williams 1993, 84). As Smith has pointed out, the "man within" has to be woken up by real spectators now and then. Or, as Cooley put it, "the imagination, in time, loses the power to create an interlocutor who is not corroborated by any fresh experience" (1922, 95). It is this correction by fresh experience, Cooley thought, which stands between ambition and megalomania (see for similar views Cicero *De Officiis* I.91; Hume *Treatise* II.xi; Smith *Theory* III.iii.4). And although, according to Williams, the imagined other does not necessarily resemble the people who are geographically or psychologically closest to us (1993, 83–4), such a real spectator, or interlocutor, awakening the impartial spectator and putting a bound on megalomania, will in reality probably be near rather than far, meaning that ultimately the opinions of one's near and dear matter the most.

In the end, the notion of honor is itself devoid of predetermined content. One author has for that reason called honor a "higher-order

Honor depends on its content ✓

virtue" that encompasses other virtues that are relative to a group (Challans 2007, 88). Because honor is inherently particularistic, depending
on group norms that not everyone shares, honorable behavior and moral
behavior can never be equated. To what extent honor can work for the
good depends for a large part on the norms and values to which people
subscribe. Honor works out well as long as the values and norms of the
group are aligned with, or at least do not go directly against (as more
exotic honor codes tend to do) what justice and fairness demand (see also
Sessions 2010, 37–9). It is not without ground that Locke wrote that
"murders in duels, when fashion has made them honourable, are committed without remorse of conscience" (*Essay* I.ii.9).[20] To what degree
honorable behavior and moral behavior do overlap varies greatly from
group to group and depends on the eccentricity of the group norms (one
can speak consistently of the honor of thieves), although Tocqueville
suggested that in larger society this overlap is greater in modern times
than it was in older days.

Even though what honor actually is expected to sanction differs
considerably from culture to culture, and of course also from era to era,
it is clear that to perform well in helping us to see what is right the honor
ethic needs (and cannot exist without) some kind of a standard that lies
outside itself (but is internal to a group or society), for instance in the
form of a set of rules with do's and don'ts. Such a touchstone is not only
a prerequisite for honor to function; it seems likely that the articulation
of praise and blame—honoring and dishonoring—can contribute to its
formation, which would mean that what is considered praiseworthy and
blameworthy in a society can be steered to some degree. Appiah shows
in his book *The Honor Code* how something that was once thought honorable can be turned relatively quickly into something to laugh about,
as happened to the practice of dueling in Great Britain, or as something
backward, which was the fate of footbinding in China (2010, especially
51, 100, 162). In this chapter we have seen how aristocratic honor had
to give way to a more democratic conception of honor, and how the productive virtues became honorable at the expense of the bellicose virtues.
In fact, according to Steven Pinker war suffered a fate similar to that of
dueling: both activities were long seen as honorable, but eventually came
to be seen as something ridiculous, although for war this happened only
after World War I had ended (2011, 352).

This more democratic conception of honor does not alter that honor
is inherently inegalitarian. Defending the class-conscious Roman society, Cicero wrote that "when equal honour is given to the highest and the

lowest—for both types must exist in every nation—then this very fair-ness is most unfair" (*De Re Publica* I.53). As Spierenburg writes, "honor is exclusive by nature; it presupposes infamy or, at least, lesser honor. If all were honorable, no one would be really honorable" (1998, 11). Smith, however, would, for the reasons stated in the previous section (i.e., the poor being placed "out of the sight of mankind"), probably have favored a distribution of honor that was detached from the distribution of wealth (see for instance *Theory* I.iii.3.2–4), more according to merit, and with a stage for everyone, yet would not have thought it possible. And perhaps a more equal distribution of honor was unattainable in his day, possibly less hierarchical than Cicero's time yet considerably more than ours.

With today's more egalitarian ordering, Michael Walzer deems a redistribution of honor realizable (1983, 257). Honor as public recogni-tion could serve as compensation for work that is, although important and socially useful, not abundantly rewarded moneywise. But this only works if people can be brought to see this kind of work—not so much dishonored as disregarded—as honorable. This in turn depends on the possibility to detach honor at least to some degree from professional status and other social goods (Walzer 1983, 257). It is, Walzer writes, legitimate that professional status brings esteem, but not in the amount it gets nowadays, and he sees a role for "public honor" in educating "ordi-nary citizens to look beyond their prejudgments and to recognize desert wherever it is found, even among themselves" (1983, 266). Walzer thinks that such a redistribution can be reached without a "gigantic increase in social control" (1983, 257). Notwithstanding Walzer's optimism on this point, it is difficult to see how such a redistribution of honor can be achieved, as it means not just a—largely—equal distribution of honor and status, as Rawls proposed (Walzer considers an equal distribution of honor a "bad joke"), but something that would probably amount to a near complete turnaround of the existing distribution of these goods.

Nonetheless, with the honoring of the rich and powerful not having diminished since Smith's days, there is a message here. According to Appiah, "we should take care to avoid creating honor worlds and honor codes that grant so much standing to the successful that they imply a disrespect for the rest of us" (2010, 131). Without the somewhat freer appraisal Walzer calls for, giving precedence to desert over wealth, the aristocratic distribution of honor would in our day be replaced by a plutocratic instead of a meritocratic one. According to Thorstein Ve-blen, the economist who differed from many of his colleagues in that he held, in his famous *The Theory of the Leisure Class* from 1899, that people maximize their status, not their utility, this is already the case in modern society, where reputation rests on "pecuniary strength," and where "relative success, tested by an invidious pecuniary comparison with other men, becomes the conventional end of action" (1970, 40). A year before Conrad's *Lord Jim* was published, it was thus an economist who had to point out that honor in modern society was as important as it had been in barbaric tribes; the only thing that had changed was what was deemed honorable: the acquisition of wealth instead of performing successful acts of violence. Later economists would see less of a role for honor.

[handwritten: Affirmation of thesis]

The Disappearance of Honor: Economy

Charles Taylor wrote about the economic view of man that

> most people tend to accept the atomist-instrumentalist conception because it meets their experience: the experience of contemporary men in society who have formed an identity as individual agents, or in relation to some group, while looking on their political society as an environment in which their goals are attained or frustrated. We may judge that this fact of modern experience is the main reason for the popularity of the instrumentalist view (1980, 87).

For instance, according to one exponent of the atomist-instrumentalist view that Taylor criticizes, economist and Nobel laureate Gary S. Becker, "the rational choice model provides the most promising basis presently available for a unified approach to the analysis of the social world by scholars from different social sciences" (1996, 156). That, despite the popularity of this economic view of man, not all "decision units" realize that they are maximizing their self-interest is according to Becker "consistent with the emphasis on the subconscious in modern psychology" (1976, 7). Becker's colleague economist and Nobel laureate Milton Friedman thought that "positive economics is, or can be, an 'objective' science, in precisely the same sense as any of the physical sciences," although he acknowledged that "the fact that economics deals with the interrelations of human beings, and that the investigator is himself part of the subject matter" can bring some difficulties (1960, 4). Becker himself stated that "the economic approach is uniquely powerful because it can integrate a wide range of human behavior" (1976, 5), and is "applicable to all human behavior" (1976, 8).

Both Becker and Friedman stand in a positivist tradition that emphasizes the principle "that scientific results have to be 'replicable,' that everyone who puts himself in the position to make the relevant observations must come up with the same results" (Taylor 1980, 87). They are, in this aspect at least, heirs of Mill, who wrote in *A System of Logic* that, now the scientific method had brought success to the natural sciences, only the more complex "moral sciences" were "still abandoned to the uncertainties of vague and popular discussion"—a "blot on the face of science" (VI.I.i).[21] Mill's ideas (and that of authors like Auguste Comte and Herbert Spencer) about social science underlie behaviorism (Truman 1968, 542), Marxism (Hollis 1994, 11; Gordon 1991, 277, 297, 316), functionalism (Runciman 1969, 2), rational choice theory (Hollis 1994, 115–18), and modern utilitarianism (Gordon 1991, 248). To some extent, it also underlies the approach of Skinner and Pocock to the history of ideas, briefly outlined in the introduction of this chapter.

Not surprisingly, some economists see that "vague and popular discussion" as characteristic of the science of politics as well, and Friedman for one was happy to see the coming of "a fresh approach to political science that has come mainly from economists—Anthony Downs, James M. Buchanan, Gordon Tullock, George J. Stigler, and Gary S. Becker, who along with many others, have been doing exciting work in the economic analysis of politics" (Friedman and Friedman, 1980, p. ix–x). According to Buchanan and Tullock, for instance, political theorists wrongly assume "that the representative individual seeks not to maximize his own utility, but to find the 'public interest' or common good'" (1967, 20). According to the same authors, "the failure to separate positive analysis and normative ethical statements has been one of the major barriers to scientific progress in political theory. Rarely does one encounter so much confusion between 'what is' and 'what ought to be' as in this field of scholarship" (1967, 265). An early attempt to do better was that of economist turned political scientist Anthony Downs, whose first "testable proposition" in *An Economic Theory of Democracy* was that "party members have as their chief motivation the desire to obtain the intrinsic rewards of holding office; therefore they formulate policies as means to holding office rather than seeking office in order to carry out preconceived policies" (1957, 296). Colleague political scientist Robert Dahl noticed that "neither common experience nor systematic research seem to give much support to the hypothesis that people who engage in politics are primarily motivated by a concern for the public good" (1991, 5).[22]

According to Amartya Sen, however, yet another economist and Nobel laureate, this economic view of man has some serious shortcomings when it comes to understanding motivation—basically, it is much too narrow (2009, 184–93, especially 190 for a critique on Becker).[23] Although their "methodological individualism" is according to Buchanan and Tullock only a method and not an "an organizational norm" (1967 *preface*), such an economic view of man's motives can become self-fulfilling, not unlike Cicero's concern that Epicurean philosophy, although mistaken, could have adverse effects if people came to believe in it. Allan Bloom observed, somewhat analogous to Sen and Taylor, that

> if, for example, one sees only gain as a motive in men's actions, then it is easy to explain them. One simply abstracts from what is really there. After a while one notices nothing other than the postulated motives. To the extent that men begin to believe that there are no other motives in themselves. And when social policy is based on such a theory, finally one succeeds in producing men who fit the theory. When this is occurring or has occurred, what is most needed is the capacity to recover the original nature of man and his motives, to see what does not fit the theory (1987, 255).

Although Tocqueville already noticed that in his day people attributed their own behavior to self-interested motives, even when it was clear that more altruistic motives were at play, it nonetheless seems that this narrowness is a comparatively new phenomena. Writing less than a century before Tocqueville, and although considered a founding father of modern economic theory, for Adam Smith self-interest was still just one of many motivations (next to sympathy, generosity, and public spirit, to mention three other possibilities) people might have (Sen 2009, 185). Self-interest itself was, writes Winch, in Smith's view "not directed solely by pecuniary motives towards economic ends: honour, vanity, social esteem, love of ease, and love of domination figure alongside the more usual considerations of commercial gain as motives in economic as well as other pursuits" (1978, 167). As we have seen, Veblen still saw a role for such notions too. But "as greater rigor permeated the theory of consumer demand, variables like distinction, a good name, or benevolence were pushed further and further out of sight" of most of today's economists, according to the just mentioned Becker at least (1996, 163), who himself has a broader conception of self-interest, yet like many of his colleagues, and different from Smith, deems it impossible that someone acts from motives that are not self-regarding.[24]

The Disappearance of Honor: Autonomy

Economic view

↓

Devaluing honor

Although this economic view of man, which goes back to Hobbes and bears some distant similarity to Epicurean thought, has influenced our present-day views on honor (or, more precisely, has contributed something to our forgetting of it), our evaluation of honor for the larger part follows the views of the Stoics. According to the already mentioned Braudy, the Stoa's "vocal distrust of the urge to distinction in public life (. . .) and their paradoxical urge to a fame defined by turning away from recognition, are all in great part still with us, if only whenever we believe that anyone interested in public office is by definition not suited to it" (1986, 148). Many people today seem to share the Stoic suspicion that virtue and honor do not go hand in hand. With the Stoics we tend to think that people are to be virtuous from a love of virtue, not from a fear of losing face, and that a virtuous act undertaken for honor is not really a moral act—the term moral seems somewhat out of place in such a case.

Probably as a consequence of such suspicions, many feel that the present distribution of honor, status, respect, and reputation is unfair, and that these good things are often bestowed upon the wrong people. Social status goes to the rich and mighty, not to the deserving, and virtue is not a way to fame and glory, but precludes it. According to Alasdair MacIntyre, to quote one example,

> notoriously the cultivation of truthfulness, justice and courage, the world being what it contingently is, bar us from being rich or famous or powerful. (. . .) We should therefore expect that, if in a particular society the pursuit of external goods were to become dominant, the concept of the virtues might suffer first attrition and then perhaps something near total effacement, although simulacra might abound (1985, 196).

That reputation does not always follow virtue, and that people can gain glory without deserving it, was a concern for philosophers from Plato to Smith and an insight to Machiavelli, but has become a truism today (see also Walzer 1983, 257). Montaigne, who wrote that it is "chance that helps us to glory, according to its own temerity. I have often seen her go before merit, and often very much outstrip it" (*On Glory*), was an early adopter of this modern position (although the Stoics held a similar position).

Instead of seeing a role for honor, we have put our faith in conscience, and, as indicated in the introduction, the dominant view is that we, in contrast to our predecessors, live in a guilt culture, not a shame culture. Authors such as Eric Dodds (1951, 28–50) and Ruth Benedict (1967, 156–7) made this view popular (see also Cairns 1993, 27), and, as said, this shift from a shame culture to a guilt culture is generally seen as a moral improvement. Contrary to Cicero, Hume, Smith, and Mandeville, many modern authors label shame a "negative emotion," and emphasize its painful side, not the positive function shame can have or the sense of moral direction it can give (see also Tarnopolsky 2010).[25] And although still an object of study, in modern social science shame lacks the moral overtones it had in the work of Cicero and Smith. If man is "the product of society and culture" (Lasch 1979, 23), it is not the actor that deserves praise and blame but the environment that steers him.[26] In the view of the behaviourist B. F. Skinner, for example, "a permissive government is a government that leaves control to other sources" (1971, 97; see also 21 and 73). Charles Cooley asked his readers to free themselves from "metaphysical formulæ" and "to *see* the facts as they are," so that "some healthy understanding of the matter" becomes possible. That is difficult enough, since "the mechanical control of suggestion" is easily overlooked (1922, 55).

That "objective" view at least partly explains why the notion of honor, which unlike shame cannot be conceived without moral connotations, not only lost its place in political and moral philosophy, but also in the social sciences. But where many political and moral philosophers present autonomy as an ideal, social scientists tend to describe an altogether different reality. In *After Virtue* MacIntyre presents philosopher Jean-Paul Sartre and sociologist Erving Goffman (who elaborated Cooley's idea of a looking-glass self) as respective representatives of these two extreme, yet (or thus) influential, positions (1985, 32).[27] He has stated elsewhere that "the virtue of Hume's ethics, like that of Aristotle and unlike that of Kant, is that it seeks to preserve morality as something psychologically intelligible" (1969, 50).[28] It seems that this tradition of psychologically intelligible moral philosophy, extending from Aristotle to Hume, has been lost.

How has this come about? Although the ideal of moral autonomy goes back to the Stoics, in its modern form it probably has its source in (as also MacIntyre suggests) Kant's moral philosophy, which is rather different from, and certainly much more demanding than, ways of thinking in which honor was still seen as a legitimate motive. Put very briefly, the Kantian ideal somewhat resembles the Stoic ideal of perfect virtue in that it too holds that any action motivated by self-interest, and for Kant the concern for reputation fell under that heading, does not deserve to be called moral (see also Herman 1981, 364). Kant, as he himself said, did not care very much whether there was anyone who could live up to that ideal. Ethics should be free from all that is empirical and belongs to anthropology (*The Groundwork of the Metaphysics of Morals*, preface). In Kant's moral philosophy, today a lot more influential than that of Hume or Smith, "shame is on the bad sides of all the lines" (Williams 1993, 77). Although Kant took a much more realistic stance in some of his other writings, where he for instance wrote quite considered about honor and dueling (LaVaque-Manty 2006), it seems that since Kant many political and moral philosophers have concerned themselves less with empirical insights into human nature.

Rawls, for instance, stated in *Political Liberalism* that his moral psychology was not "originating in the science of human nature," because "beyond the lessons of historical experience and such bits of wisdom as not relying too much on scarce motives and abilities (say, altruism and high intelligence), there is not much to go on" (1993, 86–7).[29] Rawls deontological liberalism presupposes "no particular theory of human motivation" (Sandel 1982, 9). Yet, different from Kant (in his ethical writings, that is), Rawls, as a political philosopher, claims to write about real people and a society as it could be, making him liable to the accusation of basing his political philosophy on a faulty conception of human nature; one could argue that the premises of principles of justice should at the minimum "bear *some* resemblance to the conditions of creatures discernibly human" (Sandel 1982, 43).[30]

Most social scientists, for instance, count among their "bits of wisdom" (to use Rawls' words) that face and reputation are important factors in human behavior,[31] while some political and moral philosophers have suggested that honor still exists in the form of reputation, fame, praise, dignity, distinction, status, and, above all, respect and recognition (Walzer 1983, 252; see also Taylor 1994; Fukuyama 1995, 7; Margalit 1996, p. ix; Krause 2002; Miller 1993). According to Charles Taylor, for instance, the honor ethic "is still alive for some people today" (1992a, 20), and "the fierce competition for this kind of dignity is part of what animates democratic politics" (1992a, 25). Although some domains of modern life, such as politics, business, and sports, are difficult to understand without taking honor into account (see on politics and business Fukuyama 1993, 229, 233),[32] most modern philosophy somewhat underestimates this fact. Rawls' views on self-respect, shame, status, and moral development can serve as examples of that.

Of course, Rawls sees that approval is crucial for most people. In a key paragraph he writes that, although self-respect first of all "includes a person's sense of his own value," it also rests on "finding our own person and deeds appreciated and confirmed by others" (*Theory* §67). According to Rawls, this self-respect is perhaps the most important of the primary goods. That Rawls subsequently defines shame as the *loss* of self-respect (*Theory* §67), that is, the loss of a very important primary good that should be protected, not damaged, in a just society, means that for Rawls our need for approval can only be of limited value when it comes to steering our conduct. Insofar as he sees a role for shame, it is a restricted one: "someone is liable to moral shame when he prizes as excellences of his person those virtues that his plan of life requires and is framed to encourage" (*Theory* §67). Moral shame can thus be avoided by choosing a plan of life carefully. And even though self-respect depends on the appreciation and confirmation by others, which life plan we choose does not matter much for our self-respect because "for the purpose of justice [we are to] avoid any assessment of the relative value of one another's way of life" (*Theory* §67). Despite our need for approval, self-respect lies within everyone's reach.[33]

More serious than a lack of the virtues that one's plan of life requires is a deficiency of "general virtues," such as "self-command and its attendant excellences of strength, courage and self-control," which is a source of shame that you cannot avoid by just choosing your plan of life carefully (*Theory* §67). Not that Rawls sees an important role for shame here: as we noted earlier, Rawls pays little attention to self-command and its attendant virtues. For Rawls justice ranks higher than the teleological striving for the good, which is the domain of saints and heroes. The role of shame is therefore mainly restricted to the extras; "in particular, the moralities of supererogation provide the stage for shame" (*Theory* §73).

Having secured equal self-respect for everyone, Rawls does the same for status; although one might think that an egalitarian distribution of status would render it meaningless, Rawls holds that status inequalities, for instance based on differences in income, do not have to occur in a just society:

The account of self-respect as perhaps the main primary good has stressed the great significance of how we think others value us. But in a well-ordered society the need for status is met by the public recognition of just institutions, together with the full and diverse internal life of the many free communities of interests that equal liberty allows. The basis for self-esteem in a just society is not then one's income share but the publicly affirmed distribution of fundamental rights and liberties. And this distribution being equal, everyone has a similar and secure status when they meet to conduct the common affairs of the wider society (*Theory* §82).

Interesting here is that Rawls does not argue for the Stoic position that status should not concern us, but instead tries to provide everyone with equal status. Many authors think this is impossible. According to William Ian Miller, "Rawls ignores that the whole point of honor is to distinguish oneself from others (. . .). No distinction, no honor" (1993, 129). Margalit writes that "social honor given equally to everyone will be empty" (1996, 42). Other authors have made the same point.[34] According to Brian Barry, the strictly egalitarian division of status in Rawls' just society is a consequence of the opinion of Rawls that "inequalities of status are necessary neither as incentives nor as means to the fulfillment of socially desirable tasks. Therefore inequality of status will not occur in a just society" (Barry 1973, 47).

Rawls indeed argues that status ceases to be a necessary incentive as soon as the education for autonomy is completed, and it is especially in his account of moral development that we see the contemporary idea that people are to be just from a love of justice, not from a concern for their reputation. Rawls distinguishes two traditions, with two more or less opposing views on how moral sentiments are formed. The first is the empiricist tradition that we see in the work of, for instance, Hume and Sidgwick, and which holds that "the aim of moral training is to supply missing motives: the desire to do what is right for its own sake, and the desire not to do what is wrong" (*Theory* §69). Making good these defects "is achieved by the approbation and disapprobation of parents and others in authority" (*Theory* §69). The second tradition is that of, among others, Rousseau, Kant, and Piaget, and in their view "moral learning is not so much a matter of supplying missing motives as one of the free development of our innate intellectual and emotional capacities according to their natural bent" (*Theory* §69). Although Rawls does not want to "asses the relative merits of the two conceptions," and thinks it best to combine them in a natural way, he clearly sympathizes with the second tradition. Since Freud, writes Rawls, we know that "parents and others in authority are bound to be in various ways misguided and self-seeking in their use of praise and blame" (*Theory* §69).

Nonetheless, Rawls thinks that the fear of losing face can have a positive influence on someone's conduct during the earlier phases of his moral development, when the motive for complying with the principles of justice "springs largely from his ties of friendship and fellow feeling for others, and his concern for the approbation of the wider society," and "moral conduct is based in large part on wanting the approval of one's associates" (*Theory* §72). This is still reminiscent of Locke's ideas on education. But different from Locke, Rawls thinks that we, after some time, can reach the phase of moral autonomy:

> Once a morality of principles is accepted, however, moral attitudes are no longer connected solely with the well-being and approval of particular individuals and groups, but are shaped by a conception of right chosen irrespective of these contingencies. Our moral sentiments display an independence from the accidental circumstances of our world, the meaning of this independence being given by the description of the original position and its Kantian interpretation (*Theory* §72).

Although the opinions of others have a role in the earlier phases of moral development, in the end

> moral education is education for autonomy (. . .). It follows that in accepting [the principles of justice] on this basis we are not influenced primarily by tradition and authority, or the opinion of others. However necessary these agencies may be in order for us to reach complete understanding, we eventually come to hold a conception of right on reasonable grounds that we can set out independently for ourselves (*Theory* §80).

This ideal of educating for autonomy has been advocated outside political philosophy too. The best-known example in moral philosophy of the idea that education should be education for autonomy, Lawrence Kohlberg's three-level (and six-stage) model of moral development, is for instance rather similar to Rawls' outline of moral development.

According to this model, people are egoistic and calculating at the pre-conventional level, when the fear of punishment is the one thing that keeps them from misbehaving. Once at the conventional level, they are also sensitive for peer pressure (at the first stage of this level) and the norms of society (at the second stage), and concerned about their reputation. Adherence to universal principles, the second stage of the post-conventional level, is deemed the highest, principled stage (Kohlberg 1981), and embodies the Kantian and Rawlsian ideal—in fact, Kohlberg saw Rawls' "model of justice as a rational description of parts of our sixth stage" (1984, 272).

The rare individual that reaches this highest stage resembles the perfectly wise person Cicero said he had never met—Kohlberg mentions Gandhi and Martin Luther King as examples. In line with Cicero's, Mandeville's, and Hume's criticism of Stoicism, one could argue that most individuals are probably stuck at the second, conventional level—and perhaps the majority of them function at the first stage of this level, being more inclined to conform to the norms of their own group than to the norms of society. But if our motivations are on the conventional level, that would mean that, from the point of view of a present-day moral philosopher at least, we are still on a lesser level of moral development. Or, to use the words of Bernard Williams, from a Kantian perspective we are, not unlike the thinkers of antiquity and some of their intellectual heirs from the seventeenth and eighteenth century, still children "in a Piagetian tale of moral development" (1993, 77)—a remark Williams possibly directed at Rawls, who built his account of moral development partly on the works of Piaget (Rawls *Theory* 461n). But its somewhat utopian ambition seems not to have diminished Kohlberg's popularity (see for instance Rest 1986), and his work is another example of the modern emphasis on the importance of having the right motives; something that holds true not only for deontological, duty-based ethics, but also for most modern moral philosophy in general.

So the work of Kohlberg and Rawls illustrate a larger trend, namely the gradual demise of honor as a legitimate moral motive, and it seems safe to say that strands of thought stressing utility and autonomy have replaced the ethics of honor, at least in our moral language. In theory these two strands share, like Epicureanism and Stoicism, an animosity towards the ideal of honor, although in practice, as indicated before, the ideal of autonomy, as found in the work of the Stoics, Kant, and Rawls, is more hostile to the notion of honor than the very loose tradition, in this chapter represented by Hume (and later taken further by Bentham and Mill), that stresses utility; the latter is alien to honor only insofar as it sees man as essentially a maximizer of material gain. This is the form it appears to take in the work of some modern economists, although others, as said before, leave room for non-material goods, such as reputation, as commodities man can strive for (see for instance Becker 1996, 5, 163; Cowen and Sutter 1997). Our present-day understanding of ourselves, and of what it means to be moral, remains closer to the Stoic and Kantian stance, holding that virtue should be its own reward. This ideal of moral autonomy, now, might very well ask too much. It requires that moral rules are followed, not because they are imposed from the outside and backed by sanctions (such as the censure of others), but because one accepts them by choice, something that requires a universalist outlook that in all probability is missing in many people. Different from the honor ethic, it seems to assume that knowing what is the good thing to do is often sufficient to motivate people to actually do what is good.

It is not so much that actions ask too much, but that it asks nothing of universal moral significance, the precondition of honor

Conclusion

Although occasionally listed as a virtue, honor is in fact not a virtue at all; it is above all a reward for virtuous behavior. Put schematically, there are three different answers to the question whether, and to what extent, such a reward in the form of honor is a necessary and legitimate incentive, and underlying these different answers are three different views of human nature, held by three kinds of thinkers. Those who do not see a role for honor sometimes have a view of man that is hopeful and demanding at the same time, and tend to think that people potentially love virtue, and should be able to act accordingly. Thinkers and schools as diverse as Plato, the Stoics, Rousseau, and Kant, for instance, held the view that virtue should be its own reward, and as a general rule (albeit to different degrees) saw nothing in honor but vanity and a probable source of turmoil and envy. Others, such as to some extent the Epicureans as depicted by Cicero, yet a lot more so Hobbes, Mandeville, and of course many of today's economists and policymakers, have a more negative, economic view that is just as hostile to the notion of honor as it sees man as a maximizer of his own interest, and honor consequently as "foolish pride" (although for instance Mandeville saw an important function for it); honor is in this view certainly not something worth dying for.

Honor = reward for virtue

*

View of
human
nature

[Those who, in line with Locke's political philosophy, think that honor can fulfill an important function in "the art of governing men" occupy the middle ground between these two positions. They tend to have a conservative view on human nature, and do not believe that man has a natural tendency to be good, and to act virtuously. Hume, for instance, wrote that "in contriving any system of government, and fixing the several checks and controls of the constitution, every man ought to be supposed a knave, and to have no other end, in all his actions, than private interest," and it is by man's private interest that "we must govern him, and, by means of it, make him, notwithstanding his insatiable avarice and ambition, co-operate to public good" (*Of the Independency of Parliament*).[35] The same idea seems, incidentally (though not coincidentally—Madison turned to Hume's political essays for guidance when working on his contribution to the federalist papers), to lie behind the remark in the *Federalist Paper* no. 51 that "if men were angels, no government would be necessary" (Madison et al. 1987). At the same time, these authors also reject the economic view of man insofar as it sees him as necessarily self-seeking in a purely materialistic sense. Cicero, Hume, and Smith, among others, held this position that virtue is within reach of most people, but needs a reward. Especially in the motivational aspect, conscience appeared somewhat impotent to them.

All three positions have been maintained at different times by different authors, yet it is the first two positions that have gained ground. Traces of both Epicurean and Hobbesian philosophy are still present in the economical view of man, with the important difference that Epicures and Hobbes wanted to expose honor for what it, in their view, was (a fancy and a self-regarding drive respectively), whereas most of today's economists merely ignore it. But it is especially the Stoic/Kantian view of honor that we see in our contemporary moral outlook, discourse, and, more specifically, our ideals of autonomy and authenticity. Although it seems that in philosophy criticism of honor has been largely replaced by silence on the topic: whereas present-day sociology and psychology suggest that the quest for honor might not have disappeared, but still exists in the form of the need for recognition, respect, approval, and dignity, most political and moral philosophers, in general intellectually more indebted to Aristotle or Kant than to Cicero, have contrary to their predecessors not much to say on honor (see also Sessions 2010, p. x), and when they do write about it, they often hold that there is less room for honor in today's more egalitarian societies (see for instance Berger 1984,

Man must be
lulled into
public service

153; Finley 1993, 118; Taylor 1994, 27; Margalit 1996, 42–3; see for a different view Tocqueville 1969, 616–17).

As we have seen, the view that a social hierarchy with an essentially fixed distribution of honor is likely to hamper honor in its functioning is just as plausible. The shift to a more egalitarian conception of honor is in fact essential if honor is to have a role in today's world; we commonly associate honor with aristocratic times, but we can only have an open evaluation, a precondition for honor to function properly, in a democratic age (see also Krause 2002, 66–7). It is because of today's more egalitarian conditions that honor can perform its two roles (making people see, and motivating them to do, what is in the general interest) better in our day than in the past, thus making up for the ground lost by the rules of honor having become more indefinite in our time. The view that a concern for honor and reputation, put to use correctly, might still induce people to act for the greater good, if necessary against their immediate self-interest, is, however, pretty much absent today. If there is some truth in the above, it is all the more regrettable that most modern theorists have turned a blind eye on the topic.

Although one could argue that this discrepancy between theory and practice is of less concern for political theorists than for moral philosophers, as the former are in general more interested in what a just society would look like than in what motivates people to act justly, while the latter are concerned about motivation (and in general see justice as one among many values), one could equally argue, as for instance Rawls does, that "a complete theory of justice must include a motivational story" (Mendus 2002, 17). But we have seen that Rawls himself, although of the opinion that respect and status are important to us, did not see much of a role for honor here, and such unenthusiastic views on honor are widespread today—honor and reputation are generally considered to be on the wrong side of the line. Abandoning the requirement of having a moral motivation definitely falls short of the ideals put forward by Aristotle, Kant, and Kohlberg; from their point of view, settling for conventional ethics would mean settling for a "lesser" level of moral development. But that is, although it comes with some drawbacks, not necessarily a bad thing.[36]

As to the drawbacks of being on a lesser level of moral development; in the case of honor they seem to lie mainly in its exclusiveness (limiting the number of people who matter to someone) and in its being something external (which potentially reduces morality to not being caught).

A twofold movement, outward and inward, is needed to address these two shortcomings. To avoid that too much priority is given to the opinions and interests of those who are near and dear to us, it seems necessary that the boundaries that define the honor group should be drawn somewhat less restrictively than now often is the case. In the second place, but just as important: honor should be internalized to some extent, because otherwise it is indeed reduced to not being found out. The next two chapters, on loyalty and integrity, address the question whether, and if so, how, these two goals can be accomplished.

Two solutions for honor

3

Defining the Honor Group:
Loyalty and Distance

Although in democratic times productive virtues partially replaced the more bellicose virtues of earlier times, the democratization of honor also opened the door to national honor and nationalism. Honor, according to one author, became less of a personal (or family) attribute, and more a collective one, and this to the extent that by the start of the twentieth century "honor was tied to the nation" (Spierenburg 1998, 11–12).[1] Or, as Bowman put it, patriotism depends "on an idea of the whole nation as a single honor group" (2006, 5). Although it is likely that in aristocratic times the lower and middle classes had a concept of honor too, it is equally likely that the elite had no interest in it (Spierenburg 1998, 10; see also Barton 2001, 11–13, 75). The lower strata, on the other hand, "usually recognized middle- and upper-class persons as honorable, but this had little relevance for their own honor games (. . .). The definition of who was honorable and how much so largely took place within one's peer group" (Spierenburg 1998, 10). But society changed, and by the nineteenth century middle and higher classes shared a common honor code (Nye 1998). To illustrate: where an aristocratic warrior of old—say, a knight—would consider his opponent as belonging to the same honor group, but his lower born fellow countryman—say, his page—not, this is different for a modern soldier: a U.S. soldier in Iraq in 2003 would not consider an enemy combatant as belonging to the same honor group; his honor group would consist of, first of all, his fellow soldiers, and, second, his fellow countryman.

This idea of national honor might partly explain why in the twentieth century Western powers were sometimes reluctant to part with their colonies. Shortly after World War II, for instance, the Netherlands

73

made an ill-conceived attempt to keep the Dutch East Indies (Conrad had located his imaginary Patusan somewhere in that archipelago) as a colony by means of what were euphemistically called "police actions." The Dutch population and most of its politicians largely supported the operation, but it led to widespread international disapproval. With reason, given that the methods used included the summary execution of hundreds of insurgents and innocent civilians, torture, and the burning of villages and houses. At the time, this reminded some observers of the Nazi brutalities the Dutch had suffered in the preceding years. At present, we cannot but notice the similarities with a number of much more recent incidents in today's counter-insurgency operations.

Poncke Princen, a Dutch soldier who had been a Nazi prisoner in 1944–5, did not want to be part of it. He deserted in 1948 to join the guerrillas that fought for the independence he believed they were entitled to, as most of the world did. As a guerilla he at least on one occasion fired at his former comrades, and possibly killed one or more of them. Princen became an Indonesian national after the Dutch East Indies gained independence, and spent eight years in prison for his fight for human rights in the now independent country. The excesses in the former Indies, meanwhile, were not talked about in the Netherlands in the years after the war, and in the seventies Princen could still visit the Netherlands without attracting too much attention.[2] But in the 1990s, with most of the veterans having ended their working lives and having plenty of time to think, a second visit met with great resistance, with Princen receiving numerous death threats. That the Indonesian struggle for independence had been legitimate was no longer disputed by that time; what Princen's former colleagues blamed him for was his, in their view, flagrant disloyalty to his country and, especially, his comrades.

Almost six decades after Princen's desertion Joe Darby, the sergeant who in January 2004 went to the U.S. Army Criminal Investigation Command with the Abu Ghraib pictures, was shunned by many because his alleged disloyalty to his colleagues, and he even had to live in protective custody after Defense Secretary Donald Rumsfeld had made his name public. The harsh treatment that befalls whistleblowers like Darby and defectors like Princen (the same seems to hold, albeit to a lesser extent, for conscientious objectors) points to a special feature of disloyalty: disloyal persons are not only condemned because of the damage they cause, but also, and probably more so, for the disloyalty itself (see also S. Keller 2007, 216; Fletcher 1993). One could say that the colleagues of Darby and Princen perceived their actions as a breach of the minimal loyalty one owes the object of one's loyalty (Fletcher 1993, 40). The American Taliban John Walker Lindh, who in all likelihood did not join the Taliban to kill U.S. soldiers but was nonetheless sentenced to a 20-year sentence without parole, might be another case in point. Disloyalty adds insult to injury, hence the fact that "the worst epithets are reserved for the sin of betrayal" (Fletcher 1993, 41). Whistleblowers, for instance, are often penalized more than would seem proportional considering the harm they did, and this is probably because their lack of loyalty is seen as a betrayal of their own honor group (Bowman 2006, 4), which, in the case of whistleblowers, defectors, and conscientious objectors, can consist of immediate colleagues, the larger organization, and even the nation. Being disloyal is as a result often perceived as being dishonorable, and in all it appears to be a serious character flaw. But is it a flaw?

Is Loyalty a Virtue?

Loyalty is not on the ancient and medieval lists of virtues of for instance Plato or Aquinas. That does not mean that loyalty is a modern virtue (just think of God's jealous testing of Abraham's faithfulness, or Sophocles' play on conflicting loyalties *Antigone*), but that it is only since fairly recently that it goes under its own name. As is the case with honor, the existing literature on loyalty is rather scant (some exceptions are Ewin 1992; Fletcher 1993; Kaurin 2006; S. Keller 2007; Royce 1995; Wheeler 1973), and that might very well be for the reason that loyalty is a virtue that is rather hard to define. More important, the harder one tries to grasp its content, the more questionable it becomes whether it really always is a virtue. It is perhaps so in the private realm—being loyal to your spouse, for instance. With friends the situation already becomes more complex. How far, for example, should one go in protecting a friend who one knows is in the wrong? Outside that personal sphere things are even less clear. For instance, being loyal to king, country, or organization when all is well seems a bit easy, even gratuitous. It requires little virtue, and it seems unlikely that loyalty is nothing more than that. On the other hand, remaining loyal in difficult times is not praiseworthy either. Defending one's fellow countrymen, colleagues, or organization when it is clear that they are in the wrong is certainly not the moral thing to do. "Our country, right or wrong" cannot be right from a moral point of view (Primoratz 2008, 208). It is this unquestioning loyalty that Princen and Darby had lacked.

Yet, it seems that to a certain extent that is what loyalty is about: sticking with your group just because that is what it is, your group. In general, loyalty involves giving priority to the interests of its object, be it an individual, a group, or a country, even when reason dictates a different direction (Ewin 1992, 406; for a critique of this view see S. Keller 2007, 8–11). In this meaning loyalty "requires us to suspend our own independent judgment about its object," and "affects one's views of who merits what" (Ewin 1992, 403, 406, 411). Some might argue that such unreflective loyalty is not loyalty at all, but that seems too easy a way out (see also Ewin 1992, 404). One might even say that the opposite is more likely to hold true: someone who is cautious with his or her loyalties, weighing them carefully against other values, is not someone we would describe as having loyalty as a paramount attribute (S. Keller 2007, 158; see also Ewin 1992, 411). Although not all loyalty is blind loyalty, it does presuppose a certain near-sightedness.

So, if a virtue is a corrective disposition (Foot 2002, 8–12), then loyalty is clearly not always a virtue; loyalty is most likely a disposition, but whether it is a beneficial one differs from situation to situation. Miller calls it a gray virtue, one that can serve both good and bad causes alike (2000, 8). According to ethicist Stephen Coleman, loyalty is

> an instrumental virtue, in that loyalty is only good as a consequence of the effects that it brings about and not good in and of itself. This means that the character (or characteristics) of the person or object of loyalty will be extremely important in determining whether loyalty is in fact a virtue at all (2009, 110).

In addition, one can speak coherently about bad or misplaced loyalty, while it seems nonsensical to talk about bad or misplaced justice. Or, to be more precise, one could perhaps speak coherently about misplaced justice, but who does so clearly does not consider it to be justice. That misplaced loyalty is still considered loyalty might be another indication that loyalty is not a virtue under all circumstances (compare Ewin 1992, 415; S. Keller 2007).

Is, in the same way, disloyalty perhaps not always a vice? Whistleblowers appear to act disloyally but, provided they have the right reasons (like Darby had), are clearly justified in their whistleblowing (see also S. Keller 2007, 215). We therefore see a whistleblower who goes public for good reasons not as a disloyal person, that is, not as someone willing, or even tending, to betray, deceive, desert, or let down. It seems that having a disloyal character cannot be seen as anything else but a severe defect—to most people a disloyal Nazi will seem even more contemptible than a loyal one (see also Ewin 1992). Yet, can one consistently hold that acting disloyally is not always morally wrong, when being a disloyal person clearly is a bad thing? Is the conduct of the whistleblower disloyal in the first place?

Some of the confusion disappears if we do not see loyalty and disloyalty as opposites on the same dimension, as two excesses we have to find a mean between, but as two distinct continuums. Perhaps the opposite of acting loyal (and being a loyal person) is not disloyalty, but the absence of loyalty in someone's deeds and character, that is, the absence of the tendency to suspend judgment and to back a person or group unquestioningly. Someone never led by loyalty might be an unusual human being, but he or she is not per se morally flawed. Likewise, the opposite of disloyalty is not loyalty but not being disloyal, that is: not betraying the persons who have put their trust in you. Seen in that light, a whistleblower like Darby is not disloyal, but someone who is not led (astray) by loyalty, in this case to his colleagues and employer. A similar line of reasoning might also hold true for Mr. Princen, although his case also illustrates that it remains difficult to draw the distinctions; one could say that his refusal to take part in the police actions, and his subsequent desertion, testify of a healthy lack of loyalty, but was his shooting at former colleagues not disloyal?

Following a different line of argument, one could argue that whistleblowers are not only not disloyal, but may even qualify as loyal, although to a principle instead of to a group or organization. Although often treated as the same thing, it is very much the question whether loyalty to a person, group, or nation on the one hand, and loyalty to a principle on the other, are really two manifestations of the same phenomenon. To mention one important difference: loyalty to principle does not require the suspension of independent judgment, or the "willingness *not* to follow good judgment" (Ewin 1992, 412). From this point of view, it is mainly insofar as loyalty takes the form of loyalty to principle that it can be said to be a laudable trait, while loyalty in its more familiar meaning of loyalty to a group is, because of its inherent bias towards near and dear, in general not a moral quality.

Josiah Royce's conception of loyalty in *The Philosophy of Loyalty* from 1908, probably the best-known (and most well-disposed) philosophical treatment of the subject, bears quite some resemblance to loyalty to principle. Loyalty, writes Royce, is the devotion of a person to a cause, for instance of a captain of a ship to the requirements of his office. A loyal captain will, and this in contrast to Jim, be the "last man to leave the ship, and is ready if need be to go down with his ship" (1995, 9–10). In *Some Reflections on the Loss of the Titanic* Conrad relates the story of the Douro. When that ship sunk its crew, after having put all passengers in a life boat, "went down with her, literary without a murmur." The five crew members that accidentally survived were the men who were tasked with bringing the passengers into safety (Conrad 2007).[3] It is this kind of loyalty to a cause that is, according to Royce, "the heart of all the virtues, the central duty amongst all duties" (1995, p. xxiv).

This interpretation of loyalty as enthusiastic commitment to a cause clearly goes much further than the non-betrayal that minimal loyalty calls for; it seems to amount to a "fervent maximum," characterized by "affirmative attention and devotion" to someone or something, and in which loyalty "blurs the distance between subject and object" (Fletcher 1993, 40, 61). Although this might suggest that maximum loyalty is most often found among those who are loyal to a cause or principle, this is in reality not the case. As we will see, loyalty to a group (ranging from one's primary group to one's country) reaches that "fervent maximum" more easily than loyalty to a principle, especially if that group is one's honor group. It is also evident that the two forms of loyalty often collide. The claims that someone's loyalty to a group make upon him or her frequently go against the demands of loyalty to principle, a form which we might call justice since it often boils down to that (Rorty 1997).

Thin and Thick

One could say that these inevitable clashes between loyalty to principle and group loyalty are in fact conflicts between reason and emotion, on the assumption that justice is founded on reason, while loyalty to persons, groups, organizations, and countries is based on sentiment (Rorty 1997). That sharp distinction between reason and emotion gets somewhat fuzzy, by the way, if we follow Richard Rorty's view that conflicts between loyalty and justice are not so much conflicts between group loyalty and loyalty to principle as cases of conflicting group loyalties, namely between a small group that includes our friend (from the example above) that we want to protect, and a group large enough to include those affected by the wrongdoings of that same friend. According to Rorty, the fact that someone is the victim of our protecting our friend torments us only if we see that victim as one of us in some sense. Justice is in this view not a distinct virtue, but nothing more than loyalty to a very large group: that of all human beings (1997; for a critique see Pattyn 1997). Apart from that very specific form of group loyalty (and one could argue that loyalty to mankind somewhat resembles equal honor for everyone: the term loses its meaning), group loyalty is clearly "the sort of thing that one grows into rather than decides to have" (Ewin 1992, 408).

Some authors, most notably communitarians such as Michael Walzer, hold that these group loyalties represent forms of thick morality, and that those are not only stronger than, but also prior to, forms of thin morality such as justice. "In much communitarian writing," writes Simon Keller in his book on loyalty, the

> central claim is that loyalty is a central human need and, indeed, the foundation of moral agency. You need to be loyal, runs the suggestion, in order to understand or construct your very identity, and in order to have a plan for a moral life and the motivation to live it. The moral life is, or at least grows out of, the loyal life (2007, p. ix).

We derive universalist concepts such as justice from our particularistic loyalties, not the other way around, thinks Walzer (1994). And since they do not serve someone's particular interest and bear no mark of their particular origin, thin moralities such as justice are impersonal (Walzer 1994, 7). As a result, they are much feebler. To be just towards people outside one's own group is much more difficult than it is to be loyal to a (small) group of people we can identify with. This is all the more so in difficult circumstances, writes Rorty: "The tougher things get, the more ties of loyalty to those near at hand tighten and those to everyone else slacken" (1997, 139). Not surprisingly, Darby and Princen's former comrades felt utterly betrayed. What is surprising is that both men almost as a matter of fact preferred the thin morality of justice, or loyalty to principle, to loyalty to concrete groups or persons. Or, to follow Rorty, that the group they identified with was not limited to the soldiers who belonged to their honor group, but was large enough to include those who belonged to the other side too.

But Darby and Princen seem to be the exceptions to the rule, and for most of us it is in fact not that easy to see whether, and to what extent, we have a moral duty to help those who are unrelated to us, save for the rather thin tie of a shared humanity. That in the eyes of many people those moral obligations to strangers are at best limited, and that thick moralities thus generally prevail over universal principles as justice and fairness, is in line with what group loyalty is all about: giving priority to the interests of those who stand close to you. Both Walzer's distinction between thick and thin moralities and Rorty's idea of justice as loyalty to a very large group suggest that we mainly feel moral obligations to persons not so close to us—to those who do not belong to our honor group—to the degree that we are willing, or able, to see them as one of us nonetheless. That is nowhere clearer than in the example this chapter uses, war, and not in the least in the kind of wars Western militaries are more and more involved in: conflicts far from home, and at least partly fought for moral reasons.

Although it stands in rather stark contrast to the universalist ambitions behind many of such interventions, politicians and militaries in the West generally see casualties among the local population as less important than casualties among own military personnel or among Western civilians living in the country of deployment. Hence the emphasis on the evacuation of own nationals, maximum force protection, and relatively safe ways of delivering firepower, such as artillery and bombers (see also Shaw 2005, 79–88).[4] The general public, faced with the choice between the safety of its own society and that of faraway individuals, appears to accept this development.[5] At the moment, the use of armed unmanned aerial vehicles reduces the risks for their operators to about zero.[6]

Although insurgent forces are often responsible for the majority of civilian casualties, reducing risks for Western soldiers at the expense of the local population is nonetheless likely to fuel the resentment against the West, and to facilitate recruitment for both the insurgency and the terrorist groups Western troops are trying to fight.[7] A few years ago the Human Rights Watch on civilian casualties in Afghanistan reported that airstrikes that hit villages had "significant political impact, outraging public opinion in Afghanistan and undermining public confidence in both the Afghan government and its international backers" (Human Rights Watch 2008, 3). According to the NGO, the rising number of civilian losses increased the support for the Taliban, as "each civilian death for which US or NATO forces are perceived to be responsible increases hostility to the US and NATO forces" (Human Rights Watch 2008, 6). Although taking "tactical measures to reduce civilian deaths may at times put combatants at greater risk," it is a prerequisite for maintaining the support of the local population that the mission in Afghanistan depends on (Human Rights Watch 2008, 5).[8]

It might seem somewhat dubious to use such expediency-based arguments to convince militaries to use more caution, but Human Rights Watch does so for a reason. Although local civilians form a large part of those killed in today's conflicts, their deaths get relatively little attention at the home front, and there is consequently little societal pressure to induce militaries to see these victims as something to be avoided independently of what is in it for them. That these victims get relatively little attention is first because they, geographically and psychologically far removed from us, clearly do not belong to our honor group. Secondly, their deaths were, although perhaps foreseen, certainly not intended—civilian casualties are an unhappy side effect of otherwise good actions. One could say that the first reason (that nearness matters) is in general considered to be a fact of life that, some think, has to be accepted as such, while the second reason (the relevance of intention) seems to be a more principled one that is in line with some basic moral intuitions that most people share. Let us first take a closer look at that moral intuition that says that intentions matter.

Intentions

Although honor and group loyalty are clearly related, they differ in at least one important aspect. Where honor as reward for virtue presupposes a certain indifference regarding the purity of intentions and motives, loyalty is about doing things with the right state of mind. Legal philosopher George Fletcher writes in his book on loyalty that we judge someone disloyal if he or she lacks "fidelity of the heart, steadfastness of mind, constancy of character"—qualities that form "the marks of loyalty" (1993, 47). Disloyalty, one could say, is essentially a crime of the heart (Fletcher 1993, 47). We have already seen that according to Rorty loyalty is more based on sentiment than on reason (1997). Now, if it is true that loyalty to a group or individual is more of a virtue (and a lack of it a vice) in the private than in the public sphere, as we have noted earlier, isn't that because we value intentions, motives, and sentiment on the whole more in the private than in the public sphere? To give a common example of that: in general, we want our partner to be faithful out of a good intention, and not because cheating gives such a fuss when discovered. Without that good intention, we would not want to call our partner loyal. In the public sphere, on the other hand, consequences ought to count for more (see for instance Sennet 1977; Weber 1978).

That it was with the best of intentions that Jim decided to believe his lawless countryman Brown on his word (and thus let him walk instead of killing him) did not alter much how the residents of Patusan judged Jim's leadership when Brown subsequently killed several of their fellow tribesmen. That intentions are less relevant in the public sphere not only suggests that honor can be a legitimate motive in that sphere; it also implies that there is less room (and less need) for loyalty in the public realm. To illustrate, we can stick to our example of war.

Concerning intentions in war, some might argue, in line with the argument that intentions are less relevant in the public sphere, that in warfare it does not matter much whether for instance civilian casualties were intended or not, and that a war cannot be just if civilian casualties are among the foreseen (or foreseeable) consequences. This is the position of most contingent (or conditional) pacifists who, although not rejecting war under all circumstances, hold that the killing of innocent people is never pardonable.[9] Pacifism, clearly more a form of loyalty to principle than of loyalty to a group, is also in its less than absolute varieties still a very principled and therefore inevitably also very private stance, unsuited for, say, politicians who have to take the outcomes of their decisions into account too, not in the least the survival of their political community. Politicians therefore tend to opt for a more realistic approach, and insofar as they do so without actually falling into the extreme of realism (holding that in war there is no room for moral considerations) they can find guidance in the just war tradition, which claims to be an alternative for pacifism and realism alike.

Regarding the killing of civilians, unavoidable in war, just war theorists have, contra the pacifist position, always argued that it makes an important difference whether or not that taking of innocent life was intended. No doubt there is a great amount of truth in that, although it is not easy to say exactly why. In his critique on utilitarianism, Bernard Williams writes that it is mainly because we are much more responsible for our own acts than for the acts of others (1973, 99). Perhaps it is also because murdering goes directly against the goals one wants to further (Nagel 1986, 182), and is intrinsically bad on top of that (Nagel 1986, 183). This is the basic distinction between "what one does to people and what merely happens to them as a result of what one does" (Nagel 1972, 131). One could abbreviate this as the "relevance of intention to permissibility" (McMahan 2009), an idea that underlies the principle of double effect, which illustrates quite well the importance we attach to intentions. Different authors formulate this principle of double effect in different ways, but it basically states that although one is not to kill an innocent person intentionally, an action leading to a foreseen but unintended death (an unforeseen death is either a genuine accident or a case of negligence; see also Coady 2008, 135) is morally a different matter.[10] Intention is central to the principle, and Walzer has called it "the burden of the argument" (1992, 153). That we consider intentions important explains why terrorism, a concept that is perhaps "essentially contested" yet by most accounts does involve the intentional killing of innocent civilians (Primoratz 2004), is considered morally wrong, whereas air strikes that unintentionally kill civilians are often seen as morally permitted. Without the distinction between intended and unintended deaths a bomber pilot would be on the same moral level as a terrorist; not a conclusion many of us would want to accept (see for an exception McPherson 2007).

But although it is a widely shared moral intuition that intentions matter, at the same time most people will think it an anomaly that the same action, for instance bombing a munitions factory, with the same foreseen adverse effects, say a number of civilian casualties, can be permissible if the intention is to destroy that factory, but not if the intention is to kill civilians living nearby.[11] That seems rather peculiar, and Thomas Scanlon suggests that intentions are perhaps not relevant to permissibility in the way adherents of the principle of double effect think they are; although significant, they primarily tell us something about the morality of the agent's reasoning (2008, 28; see also McIntyre 2009; see for an alternative way out Quinn 1989). In this view, the agent's intention determines how we evaluate his or her moral judgment, while we weigh the consequences to decide on the permissibility of an act.

That last point brings us to a more practical matter: the double effect principle does not require much effort to actively minimize civilian casualties. "Simply not to intend the death of civilians is too easy" writes Walzer in *Just and Unjust Wars* (1992, 155; see also S. Lee 2004, 235; Plaw 2010, 6). Walzer holds that soldiers have a further "obligation to attend to the rights of civilians," and insists that "due care" should be taken (1992, 155–6). But simply making efforts to avoid civilian casualties is by itself not enough; a soldier has to do this "accepting costs to himself" (Walzer 1992, 155). Reminding of Conrad's Jim, and Royce's definition of loyalty, cited above, as the thing that makes the captain "the last man to leave the ship," Walzer writes that soldiers "stand to civilians like the crew of a liner to its passengers. They must risk their own lives for the sake of others" (1992, 305). This requirement of risk acceptance is of course rather demanding (more on that in the next section), and that is according to Walzer precisely why we want to see it: we "look for a sign of a positive commitment to save civilian lives" that says that "if saving civilian lives means risking soldiers' lives, the risk must be accepted" (1992, 156). Within due limits, of course (Walzer 1992, 156; for a critique regarding the due limits clause see Shaw 2005, 135).[12]

On first sight the due care provision, although phrased in the language of rights, testifies to a somewhat more consequentialist approach that has little to do with expediency, and a lot with taking the consequences to all parties concerned seriously. Yet, that Walzer speaks of a "we" that would like to see "a sign of positive commitment" suggests that it is still intentions perceived by *us*, not consequences suffered by *others*, that matter most. That Walzer writes, in a later essay, that the acceptance of risk is the best indication of "the seriousness of the intention to avoid harming civilians" (2004, 137) points in the same direction. So, although Walzer addresses the leniency of the principle of double effect, he stops short of actually putting the consequences to civilians to the fore; at the end of the day a sincere effort to avoid civilian casualties is deemed more important than whether that effort is successful. What's more, it leaves the more fundamental question unanswered: why intentions should matter *that much* is still far from evident.

That the distinction between intentional and unintentional killing is part of a rights-based ethic that stresses the importance of universal, categorically binding moral norms, in this case the prohibition on killing, might seem a plausible explanation. But it seems likely that intent is also considered relevant here because of the effect of doing and not-doing things with the right intention on the moral standing of agents: if they bring about something bad unintentionally instead of intentionally, we hold them less bad persons for it—as also Scanlon suggested. Ultimately intent is more about the actors, their ability to look themselves in the mirror, and even the saving of their souls, than about those who suffer the consequences. One of the purposes of the double effect doctrine was to reconcile the absolute prohibition on murder in Christianity, which on first sight leaves no other option than pacifism, with the fact that in practice now and then innocent people are killed as a consequence of acts of Christian soldiers (Anscombe 1961).[13] To some extent the doctrine of double effect is, just like pacifism, about maintaining integrity. One could say that this attention for the agent is a virtue ethics element in the distinction between intentional and unintentional killing. Whereas in duty-based ethics the focus is on the act, that is, on what is wrong, right, permitted, or obligatory, the emphasis in virtue ethics is on terms that describe the actor, such as good, laudable, and praiseworthy.[14]

For our example of war, more attention for the consequences would mean shifting "the burden of the argument" from intention to proportionality. As we have seen, some, like Scanlon, think that in reality it has always been proportionality and not intention that explains why we sometimes deem acts that have bad effects permissible nonetheless (see also McIntyre 2009). If true, this means that the acceptability of evil consequences does not depend on whether or not they were intended (which would of course still tell us something about the moral caliber of the actor), but on the importance of the end; it all depends on the stakes. Those who hold that it is not permitted to kill one person to save five others, take a different position if killing one saves a million lives. An example is Walzer's claim that bombing residential areas can be permissible in the case of a supreme emergency (1992, 251–62).

Now, proportionality is a "darkly permissive principle" (Walzer 2009), and chances are that under the pretext of military necessity the idea of civilian immunity is reduced to "a useless garment" (Slim 2007, 174). Necessity is a matter of interpretation, and that inherent ambiguity is something with "enormous consequences for civilians" (Slim 2007, 174). Evidently, it is not possible to come up with an objective principle here without reviving the much-criticised idea of the utilitarian calculus. Nonetheless, taking these "enormous consequences for civilians" into account without differentiating too much between intended and unintended casualties would improve things, at least to some extent. If we want to combine deontology and consequentialism in a workable way, for instance because both strands can lead to perverse outcomes in their undiluted form, such a limited consequentialism is a better option than the threshold deontology of Walzer and some other deontologists, who have to specify at what point exactly (presumably located somewhere between five saved lives and a million) consequentialist arguments take over (see also Alexander and Moore 2008). That does not imply that it can be permissible to intentionally kill some civilians to save a greater number of others—the absolute prohibition on murder can operate as a limitation on consequentialist reasoning (see also Nagel 1972; Heinze 2005, 179)—but that we should take unintended killings, as real as intended ones, more seriously.

Distance

One could argue at this point that many people today already take a fairly inclusive viewpoint (see also Pinker 2011, 952–4; Rorty 1997, 140; P. Singer 1997; Walzer 1994, 16). Perhaps thinking that there must be some truth in the utilitarian dogma that letting die is as bad as killing—Cicero already wrote that permitting harm is as unjust as doing harm (*De Officiis* I.23), and that devoting all your time to philosophy amounts to the first form of injustice (*De Officiis* I.28)—many politicians maintain that human rights, and the fulfillment of basic needs, should be secured for everyone. Although every individual counts as much as another in that political rhetoric, in many other respects he or she clearly still does not; in reality politicians and the general public tend to give priority to the interests of those near to them. In the previous section we concluded that proportionality is possibly more important than intention, but it seems that simple distance, physical or psychological, is in turn more important than both intention and proportionality. For instance, in war friendly fire casualties, unforeseen and unintended but very near, always have a huge impact. So, when politicians say that they take the consequences of their actions seriously, as they should, the question is always: consequences for whom? Where lies their loyalty if thin and thick conflict? And to what degree do *we* have a moral obligation to outsiders?

 Conclusion?

For sure, one could simply argue that we have far-reaching obligations to other people, far and near. If intentions are not as important as we tend to think, this leads more or less naturally to the conclusion that permitting harm to be done is as objectionable as doing harm (see also McMahan 2009). The distinction between doing harm and permitting harm to be done somewhat resembles the Kantian distinction between a perfect duty (the obligation not to kill, for instance) and an imperfect duty (the obligation to do what you reasonably can to prevent someone getting killed). But where Kant and the law think that perfect duties weigh heavier than imperfect ones (Sen 2009, 372–6), consequentialists hold that they count for about the same. Basing himself upon the utilitarian principle that everyone's life and happiness is of equal weight, Peter Singer for instance has influentially argued that we have a moral duty to prevent the suffering of others when we are in a situation that allows us to do so "without thereby sacrificing anything of comparable moral importance," that is, "without causing anything else comparably bad to happen, or doing something that is wrong in itself, or failing to promote some moral good, comparable in significance to the bad thing that we can prevent" (P. Singer 1972, 231). Singer's example is that of the people in East Bengal, many of whom died in November 1971 "from lack of food, shelter, and medical care," caused by "constant poverty, a cyclone, and a civil war" (P. Singer 1972, 229). If we can lessen the suffering in such situations by opting for a more sober lifestyle, donating what we thus save to those in need, we have a moral duty to do so. Distance is not a factor in this view; that some catastrophe happens far away does not exempt us from our moral duty to act (see also Parfit 1987).

Going considerably beyond Singer's claim that we should give up some of our surplus wealth, the eighteenth-century utilitarian William Godwin notoriously held that he would rather save Fénelon, the Archbishop of Cambray, from a burning house than his valet, and if the latter happened to be his brother or father this would have no bearing on the matter (*An Enquiry Concerning Political Justice, and Its Influence on General Virtue and Happiness* II.ii). Most of us will think that rescuing the bishop is in this case not only unnatural but also immoral, but from Godwin's point of view there is no reason to give priority to the interests of those close to us (or even ourselves) over the interests of others: "What magic is there in the pronoun 'my,' that should justify us in overturning the decisions of impartial truth?" (*Enquiry* II.ii). We have seen that group loyalty is all about giving priority to the interests of a group, country, or organization, and it is this aspect that some universalists consider morally dubious (Parfit 1987, 98). That we are more inclined to help our near and dear than unknown persons in far-away countries, even when the latter's predicament is much worse, is perhaps understandable and natural, but certainly not moral. Somewhat similar to Godwin, Igor Primoratz writes about patriotism that "the concern of the patriot is by definition selective; and the selection is performed by the word 'my.' But the word 'my' cannot, by itself, play the critical role in an argument showing that a line of action is morally valuable" (2008, 221). The idea of thick morality is in this view a form of common-sense morality that is morally flawed because we cannot consistently held that we have special obligations to those close to us that override our obligations to strangers, and self-defeating because if everyone gave priority to the interests of special others above those of strangers we would all end up less fortunate (Parfit 1987, 95–108, 444).

But Walzer has pointed out that we do not value "each and every person" in the same way when "solidarity collapses" (2004). That is in particular the case in the example of this chapter, war, where we see little willingness to take the consequences to all parties into account equally. Mandeville already wrote that when troops "are to enter upon action, to besiege large town, or ravage a rich country, it would be very impertinent to talk to them of Christian virtues; doing as they would be done by; loving their enemies, and extending their charity to all mankind" (*Enquiry* 161). So in war, writes Walzer, "cost/benefit analysis has always been highly particularistic and endlessly permissive for each particular. Commonly, what we are calculating is our benefit (which we exaggerate) and their cost (which we minimize or disregard entirely)" and in the end "no 'enemy life' has any positive value; we can attack anyone; even infant deaths bring pain and sorrow to adults and so undermine the enemy's resolve" (2004, 39).

Yet, notwithstanding his (later) views about the strength of thick moralities, Walzer thinks that in war rights and rules should prevail over group loyalty. The contradiction here is only apparent since, to Walzer, just war theory lies firmly within the domain of thin morality (Orend 2000, 32).[15] In real life thick moralities often win through. Research among American soldiers and marines in Iraq found that only a quarter of them were willing to risk their own safety to help a non-combatant in danger, with marines scoring marginally lower (Mental Health Advisory Team IV 2006). This might be an unavoidable consequence of stressing group loyalty, setting a premium on bonding over bridging. It is probably telling that, as we have seen, even an organization like Human Rights Watch thought it best to bring up the safety of Western troops in order to convince Western militaries to choose a more careful approach in Afghanistan.[16]

On the other hand, can we expect military personnel to run risks on behalf of strangers, while most of us do not feel an obligation to donate their surplus money to, say, hunger or malaria fighting organizations? Soldiers are not confronted with the choice between their own wish to lead a comfortable life and the right to life of those starving in faraway countries, but between one's own right to life and that of colleagues on the one hand, and that of a stranger on the other. To give priority to the safety of the latter is considerably more than what Singer asked for when he stated that we are to help strangers if that can be done "without thereby sacrificing anything of comparable moral importance," and it is not that clear if a soldier really has a moral obligation to run risks protecting outsiders. Some argue that soldiers have only fairly limited obligations to strangers, and that states do not have a right to ask their soldiers to take risks on behalf of non-nationals (Kasher and Yadlin

2005; Plaw 2010; see also Kasher and Yadlin 2009; Walzer and Margalit 2009; Øverland 2011).

The debate is theoretical: in practice, militaries and politicians rather transfer risks from their own soldiers to the local population than the other way around (Shaw 2005). Since civilian casualties are mostly an unintended and proportional side-effect this risk transfer generally remains within the limits of the principle of double effect (whether Walzer's due care requirement is met is a different matter), but it is none-theless rather sobering to see how little attention there is for the faraway and unintended victims of some of today's conflicts (Coker 2008, 18), especially when compared with the interest for the more visible victims of for instance the Abu Ghraib prison abuse and the Haditha killings in Iraq.[17] This lack of attention for the statistical victims of technical violence is of course a constant: the 400 victims of the 1968 massacre in the Vietnamese village of My Lai have become iconic, while American aerial bombardments on Vietnamese cities killed tens of thousands of civilians who were soon forgotten. Today, that seems to be the fate of the estimated 100,000 civilians who since March 2003 have died in Iraq as a result of the war.[18] However regrettable, this is in line with the ethic of honor in at least two aspects: we are mainly concerned about what happens to members of our honor group, and, as we have noted earlier, it also seems that what is not seen does not really exist in the honor ethic to begin with.

The Greatest Happiness for the Greatest Number

Not surprisingly, some see the role intentions and distance play in our moral judgment as two manifestations of a flawed common sense moral-ity, and subscribe to the strand of thought known as utilitarianism in its paradigmatic form and consequentialism in its more modern varieties. Under any name, it is an ethic that is rather unreceptive to the notion of loyalty, and hence often also to war, which has been said to be the greatest sin of loyalty (Fletcher 1993, 151). As to whether our obliga-tions should extend to complete strangers too, utilitarians think that neither intentions nor (physical or psychological) distance should have much of a role in these matters. Classical utilitarianism holds that we should base our judgment of whether an act is morally right or wrong (and hence also whether it should be done or not) upon the foreseen consequences. In this aspect utilitarianism differs from virtue ethics and duty-based ethics, which both stress the importance of acting from the right motivations and intentions, implying that good consequences alone do not make an action good.

One might therefore think that utilitarianism is a suitable philosophy for those who work in the public interest. As Robert E. Goodin writes in his defense of utilitarianism as a public philosophy:

> perhaps it is novel nowadays to look at utilitarianism as essentially a public philosophy. If so, the novelty is itself wholly new. In earlier times it was much more of a commonplace to suggest that utilitarianism constitutes a solution to public rather than personal moral problems, to defend it as a public philosophy rather than as a personal moral code (1995, 11–12; for a different view, see Williams 1973).

To what extent intentions matter depends on the context, and the anomalies in the distinction between intentional and unintentional killing, and in our tendency to give priority to the interests of those who are near and dear to us, suggest that in the public sphere the focus should be on weighing the consequences to all parties concerned, while an ethic that emphasizes the importance of good intentions and motives is less suited for those who hold public office. This in keeping with Weber's well-known distinction in *Politik als Beruf* between *Gesinnungsethik* and *Verantwortungsethik*, that is, between an deontological ethic that is about maintaining purity of intention and integrity (this is the ethic of the pacifist, which is only consequentialist in that it does not differentiate much between intended and unintended civilian casualties), and the more consequentialist ethic of the politician who also considers the foreseeable results of an action (some consequentialists are pacifists, holding that war always causes more harm than good).

Judging politicians by their motives and intentions brings into the public sphere once more something that belongs to the private sphere (see also Sennet 1977) where, as we have just noted, principled stances like pacifism can exist—something the just war tradition wanted to be an alternative for. Adam Smith therefore held that our tendency to judge by actions (even though we do not have their consequences under our control) instead of solely by intentions, although it "has been in all ages the complaint, and is the great discouragement of virtue" (*Theory* II.iii.3.1), is in the end a "salutary and useful irregularity in human sentiments concerning merit or demerit, which at first sight appears so absurd and unaccountable" (*Theory* II.iii.3.2). To Rawls an ethical doctrine

that does not take the consequences into account "would simply be irrational, crazy" (*A Theory of Justice* §6).[19] Goodin writes that "those who
harbor a Ten Commandments view of the nature of morality see a moral
code as being essentially a list of 'thou shalts' and 'thou shalts nots'—a
list of things that are right or wrong in and of themselves, quite regardless of any consequences that might come from doing them" (1995, 10).
Especially deontologists tend to judge on that basis, also in the public
realm: "It is not enough, for them, that the right thing be done. They
also insist that it be done, and be seen to be done, for the right reasons"
(Goodin 1995, 47).

Utilitarianism, more about the consequences of an act than about
the actor and the act, has nonetheless a somewhat doubtful reputation,
sometimes on the mistaken assumption that it condones self-centered,
calculative behavior—utilitarianism would make expedience override all
other concerns. As one author puts it, "utilitarianism would lend itself to
abuse in precisely those kinds of situations in which ethical safeguards
are most needed" (Snow 2009, 560). This position—utilitarianism is not
bad per se, but prone to be misapplied in a self-serving way—is encountered quite often. Walzer sees the decision to drop atomic bombs on
Hiroshima and Nagasaki as an example of such a tilted utilitarian calculation that should have been "stopped short by the rules of war and
the rights they are designed to protect" (1992, 263–8). But that the calculation was biased means that the calculation was not really a utilitarian one. Utilitarianism does not prescribe that we should maximize our
own utility (or that of our group, organization, or people). The utilitarian credo of, in Hutcheson's famous phrase, "the greatest happiness for
the greatest number" (*Treatise* II.III.viii) is in fact agent-neutral, meaning that the consequences to everyone should weigh equally.[20] Although
utilitarianism is sometimes portrayed as a threat to individual rights
(Bentham gave some reason to do so when he called natural rights non-
sense upon stilts), the right to life would be better protected if everyone
would live by the utilitarian credo that the consequences to all persons
should weigh equally. Similar to Cicero's (consciously) erroneous denun-
ciation of Epicureanism on the basis that it would condone hedonistic
and self-seeking behavior, the negative verdict on utilitarianism may
therefore be a bit premature (see also Mill 1987b, 294–5).

The revolutionary moral idea behind the greatest happiness for the
greatest number is thus not that it puts happiness (or utility) to the fore
as the highest good, but its universalist outlook: each person's happiness
should count for the same.[21] Although this idea has some resemblances

with the "golden rule" in ethics that one should treat the other, and not just the members of one's own group, as one wants to be treated one-self (a dictum that goes as far back as Thales of Miletus and Confucius, and underlies to some extent Stoic cosmopolitism, Kant's categorical impera-tive, and the modern human rights doctrine) this thought was a relatively new one to most people when reformulated in the eighteenth century.[22] It was a plea for widening one's honor group, and at that time a much needed antidote to class justice and the like—that Godwin would res-cue Fénelon instead of his father or brother does not mean that utilitar-ians think that archbishops are inherently more worthy than their valets, but just that Godwin thought that the continued existence of Fénelon would contribute more to the general happiness. As far as we are dealing with fellow countrymen, this notion that the consequences for all should count for the same has become commonplace to the extent that we do not even see the revolutionary character of it any longer.

In our dealings with outsiders it is still rather novel, however, and perhaps the problem here is not so much that we are unwilling to ac-knowledge that our obligations to strangers go further than common sense morality holds, but that most of us would are disinclined to act upon those obligations. The difficulty with universalist moral theories seems to be that most people do not really *feel* they have obligations to outsiders (and, as said, loyalty lies more within the domain of senti-ment than reason). Although considered to be one of the precursors of utilitarianism, David Hume already wrote that "a man naturally loves his children better than his nephews, his nephews better than his cous-ins, his cousins better than strangers, where everything else is equal," and that he is not able to cure "that narrowness of soul" (*Treatise* III. ii.vii). We are more interested in preventing mishaps befalling those we love than in promoting the greatest happiness for the greatest numbers. In other words, agent-relative reasons are more important to us than agent-neutral reasons, meaning that the relationship in which the sub-ject (stranger or friend) stands to us, matters (Parfit 1987, 27).

It is therefore a bit too optimistic to think that explaining to people that they have obligations to those not so near and dear is enough to induce them to actually act upon those obligations. According to Brian Barry, there is "a gap between acknowledging that some rule, univer-sally adhered to, would advance one's conception of the good and having a motive (based on nothing but the pursuit of one's conception of the good) for adhering to the rule" (1995, 45). The conscientious utilitarian, for instance, "may well be required by utilitarianism to do more than psychologically he can bring himself to do," especially if he or she wants to compensate for the self-centered choices of others too (Goodin 1995, 67).[23] At first sight, it seems that the selflessness universalism requires makes it too demanding for most people—if true, that would be a rather disappointing conclusion. Yet, as we have seen in the first two chapters, honor can function as a motive to do the right thing, against one's immediate self-interest. Can honor also help us to rise above narrow group loyalties, to live by a more outward looking ethic, and to choose loyalty to principle—justice—over loyalty to our own group? If so, honor could form a solution to the problem it itself created. Honor is something exclusive, making that we care above all about the members of our honor group, but perhaps honor can also form an incentive to make that group a larger one.

Widening honor to facilitate utilitarian ethical calculations

Widening the Honor Group

Most authors who deemed honor an important motive, but had a fairly universalist outlook nonetheless, held such an enlargement of the honor group possible. Hume, although of the opinion that we tend to be partial in our own favor, and that our sympathy with the public interest is in general too weak to have much influence on our own conduct, at the same time observed that we often do act with an eye to the greatest happiness for the greatest number. Hume thought that we generally do so from a concern for our own reputation, however, and not so much from a love of virtue or a sincere concern for the public interest. Although we in general praise the intention to do well because circumstances decide what the consequences of act will be (*Treatise* III.iii.i), yet insofar as just conduct was concerned it was, for Hume himself at least, not so much the intention, but the consequences that counted.

Utilitarianism's main protagonist, Jeremy Bentham, who supposedly stated that Cicero's *De Officiis* was an "attempt to teach morals by declamation" (cited in MacKendrick 1989, 254), held a similar view.[24] In *An Introduction to the Principles of Morals and Legislation* he expanded upon Hume's ideas on the role of reputation; where for Hume utility was the standard we normally use for distributing praise and blame, and to good effect, it was for Bentham also the standard we all *should* use, precisely because, as also Hume had noted, the concern for reputation can keep the conduct "of each in the line which promotes the general happiness."[25] That latter phrasing is from John Stuart Mill (1987a, 251), who, defending Bentham against the allegation that he made "the approval of our fellow creatures" into the foundation of morality, wrote that public sanctions have their value "not as constituents or tests of virtue, but as *motives* to it; as means of making the self-interest of the individual *accord* with the greatest-happiness principle" (1987a, 249).[26] Bentham himself defined the love of reputation, a semi-social motive in his view, as

> neither more nor less than the desire of ingratiating one's self with, or, as in this case we should rather say, of recommending one's self to, the world at large. In a good sense, it is termed honour, or the sense of honour (. . .). In a bad sense, it is styled, in some cases, false honour; in others, pride; in others, vanity. In a sense not decidedly bad, but rather bad than otherwise, ambition. In an indifferent sense, in some cases, the love of fame: in others, the sense of shame. And, as the pleasures belonging to the moral sanction run indistinguishably into the pains derived from the same source, it may also be styled, in some cases, the fear of dishonour, the fear of disgrace, the fear of infamy, the fear of ignominy, or the fear of shame (*An Introduction to the Principles of Morals and Legislation* X.xxii).

After goodwill (which almost by definition coincides with the principle of utility), this love of reputation was the motive with the best chance of corresponding with the principle of utility (*Principles* X.xxxviii).

That the concern for reputation is a more selfish motive than benevolence was also for Bentham not an issue: in contrast to what one might think, utilitarianism, actually quite logically because it is rather indifferent regarding what motivates beneficial conduct, is not necessarily hostile to honor and the concern for reputation, even if they are not the purest of motives. Mill wrote in his defense of utilitarianism that it is therefore unjust to criticize utilitarianism for asking too much: the greatest happiness for the greatest number is a standard, and an act is right if it contributes something to that greatest happiness. But that does not mean that our acts should be motivated by that standard; in all likelihood they are not, writes Mill, and "utilitarian moralists have gone beyond almost all others in affirming that the motive has nothing to do with the morality of the action" (1987b, 289). This is somewhat similar to the observation, made in the section on intentions, that consequences, not intentions, determine the permissibility of an action. Not unlike Scanlon, Mill held "that a right action does not necessarily indicate a virtuous character, and that actions which are blamable, often proceed from qualities entitled to praise. When this is apparent in any particular case, it modifies their estimation, not certainly of the act, but of the agent" (1987b, 292).[27] According to Sen, Bentham and Mill belonged *Middling* to a tradition which deemed "the removal of manifest injustice" more *approach* important than searching for a perfectly just society (2009, 7). Although utilitarianism is often deemed utopian, in that sense the works of Bentham and Mill form a realistic political theory. But most modern consequentialists, not adhering to this "realization-focused" approach (Sen 2009, 7) of classical utilitarianism, do not see a role for honor to bridge the gap between our natural tendency to pursue our self-interest, and our moral obligation to further the general interest.

These modern consequentialists might be right, though: it has to be feared that in the real world honor will rarely motivate people to do what is in the interest of the greatest number; most people are still concerned about their reputation, but it is one of shortcomings of the honor ethic that this concern is generally limited to how they are viewed by the members of that same honor group that we now want to widen by the use of honor. The democratization of honor might have led to an enlarging of the honor group, but this has stopped at the national borders. Although Mill and Bentham thought that we seek the approval of our "fellow-creatures," and even the "world at large," it is, stuck as we are on what Kohlberg called the conventional level of moral development, mainly the opinions of our friends, colleagues, and fellow-countrymen that matter to us. It is no coincidence that the Stoics, who rejected honor, espoused a more cosmopolitan ethic than Cicero (see also Long 2008), who deemed honor important, and wrote that our most important moral obligations are those to our parents and our country (*De Officiis* I.58). Honor is by nature very much a group phenomenon (see also Welsh 2008, 4, 10), and different from what Mill hoped, it is in practice therefore not very well suited for aligning self-interest with the greatest happiness for the greatest number principle.

The "narrowness of soul" Hume mentioned probably plays a role here. Even if we know that it would save lives to donate some of our surplus money to, say, hunger or malaria fighting organizations, we are free to not donate, without any stain on our honor. Smith thought that if "a man of humanity in Europe"

> was to lose his little finger tomorrow, he would not sleep tonight; but, provided he never saw them, he will snore with the most profound security over the ruin of a hundred millions of

his brethren, and the destruction of that immense multitude seems plainly an object less interesting to him, than this paltry misfortune of his own (*Theory* III.iii.4).

Smith expected the impartial spectator to be a check on this partiality, and it is for that reason mainly that Amartya Sen prefers Smith's impartial spectator over Rawls' justice as fairness. As Sen sees it, Rawls' idea is a demand for impartiality in a closed form (Sen 2009, 54), seeing that outsiders, more specifically those who do not belong to our nation, are not involved and are not a party (Sen 2009, 123). Sen believes that Smith's impartial spectator does take into account the viewpoint of other parties, "from far as well as near" (Sen 2009, 131). So different from what is the case in Rawls' *A Theory of Justice*, nonmembers of society play a role in this, what Sen calls, open impartiality (2009, 134).

Sen might give Smith too much credit here, though: he overlooks that Smith's impartial spectator functions within a society, and tends to follow the conventions of that society rather closely. Smith "rejected the Stoic's 'absurd and unreasonable' cosmopolitan assertion that we should aspire to collapse the natural concentric structure of human relationships through the proper use of reason" (Forman-Barzilai 2005, 201). Although the impartial spectator might help to overcome physical distance, enlarging our perspective and enabling us to feel sympathy for those who suffer faraway, it is probably not very well suited to help understand, and feel sympathy for, those who are *culturally* distant (Forman-Barzilai 2005, 207). Smith's "man within, the great judge and arbiter of our conduct" is dependent on real spectators. In the end the opinions of those real spectators matter most to us, and perhaps it is only to be expected that our partiality to our own group does not impede our reputation in the eyes of its members. Tellingly, the fact that the population of Patusan held Jim in high esteem brought him only partial satisfaction; he longed for the esteem of his equals, and Jim clearly did not think the "dark-skinned" inhabitants of Patusan to be quite that (nor did Marlow or, for that matter, their creator Conrad). And probably Jim was also not too concerned about what the Muslim pilgrims he abandoned might think of him. As Locke wrote, it is the "dislike and condemnation of his own club" that man cannot bear (*Essay* I.iii.12). So, where loyalty as group loyalty generally asks too little or, maybe more accurately, the wrong thing, universalist moral systems like utilitarianism probably ask too much, at least in some contexts.

To end with a less pessimistic note: maybe such a cosmopolitan outlook is not really what is required from most of us. According to Mill,
"it is a misapprehension of the utilitarian mode of thought, to conceive it
as implying that people should fix their minds upon so wide a generality
as the world, or society at large" (1987b, 290). This is, Mill writes, not
only too demanding, but also unnecessary as the overwhelming majority of us are in no position to augment the general happiness anyway
(1987b, 290)—politicians are an obvious exception. But the conclusion
that it is all right for everyone else to only look after their own narrow
group of family and friends would be too easy—what we would like to
find is a middle ground between particularistic loyalty to the group and
the hard to attain universalism that loyalty to principle asks for. Taking
a look at the difference between a fairly exclusivist and a very universalist ethic, namely the military and medical the ethic respectively, might
help us here. Although we tend to give priority to the interests of those
whose opinion matters to us, that is, to our honor group, patients clearly
do not belong to the honor group of a doctor. But a doctor who fails to
treat these patients impartial might lose the esteem of his or her peers.
This is different for, for instance, members of the military (including
military medical personnel); they might lose the esteem of their peers
by acting too impartial. What we see in the medical profession is that a
concern for reputation does not help to widen the honor group (which
remains limited to colleagues), but that it can bring people—doctors and
nurses—to take the interests of outsiders seriously. To explore this further, we have to return for a final time to our example of war.

Dual Loyalties and Professional Loyalty

Considering the power group loyalties have over us it is not surprising,
nor necessarily a cause for condemnation, that soldiers primarily worry
about the safety of their colleagues, which they (similar to politicians
and the public) think more important than that of the local population.
At the same time, a strong loyalty to colleagues and the organization is
at odds with what a regular professional ethic entails.[28] That professionals are in general more loyal to their profession, their professional ethic,
and their clients, than to their organization and their colleagues sets
a profession apart from other occupations. Surgeons care more about
the judgments of their peers, for instance the verdicts of their professional association—in a sense their honor group (see for professions as

honor groups Sessions 2010, 140–53)—than about the opinions of their employer of that moment. Also, they place their own professional judgment above that of the management that supervises their work, based on the conviction that their training, education, and professional experience makes their judgment more informed than that of those at a higher level in the organization, usually having a different background and training. Because their profession is the focus of their loyalty professionals pay more attention to the interests of clients than to those of their colleagues and organization. A professional is typically someone who "works relatively independently of his colleagues, but closely with the clients he serves" (Mintzberg 1983, 190). This, incidentally, also explains why professionals can switch from one employer to another without too much pain in the heart.

Contrasting the ethic of the medical profession, probably the most professionalized profession, with that of the military profession shows that both point out quite clearly whose interests should be most important, but also that they point in opposite directions.[29] Medical ethics is not about how to behave towards colleagues, but about patients and medical care, and about providing patient care impartially, while the gist of the codes, oaths, and values in most militaries is mainly about the organization and colleagues; there is little in them that regulates the behavior of soldiers towards civilian populations. Not surprisingly, being subject to two dissimilar professional ethics leaves military medical personnel with a somewhat complex professional identity as they are neither purely soldiers nor simply doctors or nurses. And their belonging to two different honor groups results in tensions between the wish to give priority to the interests of colleagues, and the demands that an outward looking ethic poses. One could say that in the military medical profession the two examples of this chapter, war and utilitarianism, meet.

The term for this tension between different loyalties is dual loyalty or, somewhat less commonly, "mixed agency" (Howe 1986). In military medical ethics it consists of the "role conflict between the clinical professional duties to a patient and obligations, express or implied, real or perceived, to the interests of a third party such as an employer, an insurer, the state, or in this context, military command" (London et al. 2006).[30] Such conflicts can occur when military medical personnel must choose who to help first: a seriously wounded insurgent or civilian, or a somewhat less seriously wounded colleague, or when their presence during unlawful interrogation is presented as in the interest of the detainee.[31]

A few years ago an International Dual Loyalty Working Group drew up ten guidelines to resolve these dilemmas (Dual Loyalty Working Group 2002; see also London et al. 2006), yet the net result was a plea to give preference to the medical ethic over military considerations, that is, to be loyal to the patient under almost all circumstances. Drawing on the findings of that working group, some have appealed for a rights based framework "that privileges the protection of vulnerable people from state-sponsored harm, no matter the alleged justification" (London et al. 2006, 387).[32] Although the authors recognize that "in wartime, the exigencies of battle pose unique challenges incomparable to the civilian context because of the scale of the threats to life, unpredictability, and the levels of violence" (London et al. 2006, 385), and that military necessity sometimes justifies deviating from what is normal ethical medical practice, they agree with the Dual Loyalty Working Group's first guideline that "the military health professional's first and overruling identity and priority is that of a health professional" (London et al. 2006, 388). The underlying idea is that "medical ethics during wartime are not fundamentally different from those applicable in peace" (London et al. 2006, 389). This is in line with the opinion of the World Medical Association, laid down in the *WMA Regulations in Times of Armed Conflict*, that there is no difference between medical ethics in war and in peace.[33]

On first sight, these guidelines are more a denial of the tensions than anything else. They ask for a universalist ethic (see also Gross 2006) in which friend and foe count for the same, in a context of violent conflict where, as we have noted, such an all-encompassing ethic is difficult to live by. This way out also suggests that the moral dilemmas military medical personnel face are not really dilemmas but just tests of integrity: it is clear what is the right thing to do, yet there is considerable pressure (from peers, or the prospect of furthering one's own interest) to choose the wrong course of action (Coleman 2009, 105–6). One might think that loyalty to colleagues is nothing more than such a pressure. But if loyalty amounts to a value, and for most members of the military (including military medical personnel) it is in fact a rather important one, then there is a dilemma again (see also Coleman 2009, 112).[34]

Michael Gross rejects in *Bioethics and Armed Conflict* (2006) the WMA standpoint as an example of utilitarian thinking that is blind to the fact that in war returning as many soldiers to duty as quickly as possible is, and should be, the guiding principle of all medical efforts.

* Has Ok. sufficiently defended the universalist impulse?

That serves not only the military as a collective "fighting force" best, but, in the end, also the survival of the political community it serves. Gross believes that, different from what the WMA claims, war does transform medical ethics (2006, 324). From that viewpoint it is perhaps even defendable that military medical personnel sometimes let their sense of military duty override their obligations to their patients (see also Clark 2006, 577). It would also explain why the largest part of the military codes, military oaths, value systems, and culture is antagonistic to the idea that the plight of local civilians counts for the same as that of a Western soldier. But his ethic took shape when the main task of Western militaries was the defence of their own territory; with the shift from wars of self-defence to humanitarian interventions military necessity may play less of a role in the future (see also Gross 2006, 330).

Meanwhile, loyalty as defined and demanded by most organizations today, military or not, boils down to loyalty to the organization and colleagues—employees who want to do their work based on loyalty to principle do not always fare well. They sooner end up as martyrs for a good cause than as moral exemplars for their employing organization. Consider, for instance, the case of Captain Lawrence Rockwood who in September 1994 was deployed to Haiti to remove the dictator Cedras, but also to end gross human rights violations. Rockwood had joined the military to protect the weak and defenseless, but he soon found out that the safety of own personnel was the main concern of both the U.S. forces and the politicians that had sent him to Haiti. Cedras' men tortured and killed political opponents, yet Rockwood's superiors proved unwilling to do something about it. Frustrated, Rockwood followed his conscience against orders, and hitchhiked to a nearby prison to inspect it. Having gained access to the facility, a U.S. military attaché convinced him to give up his solitary attempt. Rockwood underwent psychiatric evaluation and was found normal although somewhat tensed. Refusing to resign because he was convinced that he had done the right thing, he was court-martialed for disobedience and conduct unbecoming an officer (Wrage 2002). As a witness for his defense appeared My Lai hero Hugh Thompson, Jr. (the helicopter pilot who tried to end the killing of Vietnamese villagers by U.S. soldiers in 1969)—another man who remained loyal to his principles and paid the price for it.[35] The military is of course not alone in its lack of enthusiasm for this kind of detachment. To state the obvious: most organizations will think that they cannot have too many employees taking an impartial, "objective" view on matters like Rockwood (and Darby and Princen) did.

Yet one could wonder whether group loyalty is really that helpful to an organization in the longer run, given that this form of loyalty at least partly consists of the suspension of independent judgment, while loyalty to principles, not asking for the suspension of independent judgment, can be expected to benefit one's organization and outsiders alike. The idea of professional loyalty suggests that there exist some shades of gray between loyalty to a limited honor group and the perhaps too demanding loyalty to principle. Rockwood later stated in an interview that he had moral obligations surpassing the ones he owed his immediate superiors. But these were not obligations to a universal principle, as his "cause was the professional and ethical integrity of the Armed Forces."[36] As an officer, Rockwood tried to emulate men like the just mentioned My Lai hero Thompson and Hitler's adversary and attempted assassinator Claus Schenk von Stauffenberg (Wrage 2002, 47). The latter was, although clearly denouncing blind group loyalty, not acting from universal principles either; his motive was loyalty, yet not to the Germany as it was, but to an idea of what Germany should be (see also Fletcher 1993, 154; Van Creveld 2008, 372). Whistleblowers, likewise, sometimes profess to act from values their organization believed in when things were still good (see also Hirschman 1970, 76–105).

So, although not as principled as loyalty to principle, professional loyalty can form a middle ground between group loyalty and loyalty to principle, and is thus perhaps an attainable ideal. Who is loyal to a profession generally identifies him or herself with an honor group that is not too large, that is, that does not include the whole of mankind, and is loyal to something that is sufficiently substantial and concrete, yet quite principled at same time—professional loyalty is clearly more akin to loyalty to principle than to group loyalty. As it stands, the demands of group loyalty and loyalty to principle will continue to conflict, and the fact that most organizations tend to stress group loyalty might be behind the many attempts to cover-up after incidents. Given that those who "tell" every now and then not just find themselves out of a job, more protection for whistleblowers, not disloyal of character yet just not willing to suspend independent judgment, is perhaps a good idea.

Conclusion

Freud wrote in *Civilization and Its Discontents* that it would be wrong to love a stranger, "for my love is valued by all my own people as a sign of my preferring them, and it is an injustice to them if I put a stranger on a par with them" (1961, 66).[37] That we give priority to the interests of friends, family, and colleagues testifies to the importance of thick moralities, and suggests that it is more than a matter of flawed common sense morality that nearness matters. To return once more to Godwin's example of the archbishop and the valet/father/brother in the burning house, and to the reality that being impartial is in some instances asked too much: one could argue, as Susan Mendus does, that there is a difference "between the requirements which govern our choice of principles" on the one hand, and "the requirements that govern our decisions about day-to-day actions" on the other (2002, 55). Whether we may make decisions on partial grounds depends on the context, Mendus writes, and in the context of Godwin's burning house partiality in decision-making is not only legitimate, but even required. In line with the argument in this chapter, one could say that there is in general more room for partiality and loyalty in the private than in the public sphere. As with most distinctions, there will remain some problems of demarcating the areas in which impartiality is required, but the real problem is that there are cases in which it is evident that one should be impartial, but in which people are tempted to act on partial grounds nonetheless (Mendus 2002, 59)—doctors working for the military might be an example.

One could argue that moral reasoning (and being moral) is about placing ourselves in the position of someone else for a moment, as for instance Thomas Nagel asks us to do in his *The View from Nowhere* (1986; see also Welsh 2008, 204); a title that suggests a view that resembles the view from where Hume's judicious spectator and Smith's impartial spectator were standing. Although Hume allowed that "sympathy with persons remote from us, [is] much fainter than that with persons near and contiguous," it is precisely for that reason that "it is necessary for us, in our calm judgments and discourse concerning the characters of men, to neglect all these differences, and render our sentiments more public and social" (*An Enquiry Concerning the Principles of Morals* V.ii).[38] Taking a completely objective, detached view might be hard to attain and often supererogatory, but moral progress in all likelihood does involve a shift towards a more impersonal, agent-neutral morality (Nagel 1986, 185–8).

Such a universalist morality is not something completely imposed from outside, writes Nagel, but "answer[s] to something very important in us," and reflects "our disposition to view ourselves, and our need to *accept* ourselves, from outside" (1986, 198). Nagel thinks that it is therefore quite possible to harmonize our own projects and actions with universal requirements that are just as well part of us (1986, 198). If true, this means that weighing the consequences to all concerned more equally is not the psychological impossibility it appeared to be; as we have seen in the previous section on the military and the medical ethic, group loyalties (and the same probably goes for national identities) are often not as natural as some think, but are in fact constructed, and imposed from the outside (see also Galston 2010, 402). Education and socialization might make a difference here, and contribute something to enlarging the limits of the honor group beyond its normal, narrow boundaries.

So although acting impartial is asked too much (and supererogatory) in many cases, on other occasions we probably should be able to do so, at least to some extent. In *What We Owe To Each Other* Thomas Scanlon described thinking about right and wrong as "thinking about what could be justified to others on grounds that they, if appropriately motivated, could not reasonably reject" (1998, 5). Mere distance (psychological, cultural, or physical) and the absence of ill intent are not such grounds. Contra the somewhat too relativistic particularism of thick moralities one could argue that, especially in today's globalizing world, we should be able to come a bit closer to the solidarity utilitarianism asks for (see also P. Singer 1997). In fact, as we have seen, the conversion of the aristocratic notion of honor into a more democratic form of honor already brought a widening of the honor group although, as said, not yet transcending national frontiers.

Unclear is whether this process has to stop there. Emphasizing group loyalty might seem somewhat outdated to those who, in the words of one author, have moved on to a new "ethical demand of the hour," and now adhere to a "transcendental humanism" (Coker 2008, 124). Such a transcendental humanism lies behind the doctrine of the *Responsibility to Protect*, coined in 2001 and not much later embraced by the UN, which basically sets a limit to the sovereignty of states that seriously fail to protect their subjects. Although somewhat utopian according to some, the question is what the ratio should be like if we for whatever reason do not agree to the belief that every individual counts as much as another in our dealings with strangers too.

We have seen that such a universalist outlook is something to be valued in the public sphere. Not so clear is to what extent loyalty might be a praiseworthy or even necessary quality for those who are not politicians, or policymakers, but want to be, say, loving parents, or good friends and colleagues. Loyalty seems to be a quality that is, in fact, meant to be more beneficial to those who are near and dear to us than to outsiders. A world without loyalty, with for instance parents taking an objective view to their children, or friends looking in a similar vein towards their friends, would be rather inhospitable. Viewed in that light, loyalty might qualify as a value (see also S. Keller 2007).

The same can be said of Royce's conception of loyalty to a cause, which is somewhat similar to loyalty to principle. As Royce put it when he explained his idea of loyalty to loyalty, it is good for a person to be loyal, from which he concluded that we should choose our causes, and then serve them, in such a way that, as a result, there "shall be more loyalty in the world rather than less" (1995, 57). According to Royce, I am not able to find a plan of life by looking within, since there is no "inborn ideal naturally present within myself" (1995, 16). The alternative route consists of looking outside oneself—society suggests plans of life to us by way of models that we can imitate—but that might lead us to just mimicking what others do (1995, 16–17). In being loyal to a cause, or plan of life, suggested by our social order yet at the same time deemed worthy of our commitment if we look within, the conflict between subjective will and conformity is resolved, writes Royce (1995, 20). Loyalty "is a devotion to a cause, outside the private self, and yet chosen by this individual self as his cause" (1995, 94). Loyalty can, in this rather specific interpretation of Royce that is, lie between the at times too conformist ethic of honor, the subject of the previous chapters, and the perhaps too subjective notion of integrity, not coincidentally the topic of the next chapter.

4

Internalizing Honor: Integrity

The question what someone would do if he or she were invisible has been a recurring theme since Plato's tale of Gyges' ring, and touches upon a fundamental flaw of the ethic of honor: it can be reduced to a matter of not being found out. That dependency of honor on the presence of a public is the main reason why we turn to integrity in this chapter. <u>Integrity, in the sense of upholding one's personal principles</u>, is the virtue that can make someone, <u>provided his principles are morally sound, do the right thing, even when there are no witnesses present, and in spite of being tempted otherwise.</u>

Integrity internalizes honor

Integrity as Loyalty to Oneself

In the previous chapter, dealing with another drawback of honor (its exclusiveness) we have seen that loyalty comes in two basic varieties: loyalty to a group (which can range from one's primary group to one's country) and loyalty to a principle (such as justice, or respect for human life). Although in real life most people probably have a propensity to the first form, group loyalty, most philosophers and ethicists have a preference for loyalty to principle, and they seem to have good reasons for that; where group loyalty requires the suspension of independent judgment, loyalty to principle, on the whole, does not. But where should these principles stem from? It would seem obvious to look for these principles outside oneself, be it in a moral tradition, religion, or the values society dear, yet some believe that the highest form of loyalty is loyalty to the principles and values you find within yourself.

This loyalty to one's own principles and values is what we often have in mind when we use the term integrity, but other meanings abound; today integrity has so many meanings that the term has come to signify everything and nothing. Integrity is a "much-used term but very much in need of analysis" (Wakin 2000, 115). Notwithstanding this profusion of meanings, the term has a rather restricted connotation in most of today's organizations, where it is mainly negatively formulated, and as such concerned with the things an employee should not do: for example, taking gifts of a value above a certain threshold, being careless with sensitive information, or taking office supplies home for private use. Although this narrow definition of integrity is very much alive in most organizations, this is clearly not what integrity as a virtue is about.

In general, integrity as a virtue has a wider meaning outside that organizational context, although it is somewhat hard to pin down. It can, for instance, stand for "wholeness," which is actually closest to its original meaning (the Latin *integer* stands for "whole" or "complete"). This meaning of the term goes back to the ancient idea, present in the works of Plato, Aristotle, and Cicero, that one cannot have one virtue without the others, and that all the virtues are interrelated (see for instance Cicero *Tusc. Disp.* II.32 and *De Officiis* II.35). Being just is of little value if one lacks the courage to defend it, while courage is of not much use without practical wisdom to guide it. This unity of the virtues also suggests that one cannot be a moral person in one sphere of life, and wanting in morals in another. Somewhat resembling this definition of integrity is the view of integrity as being consistent over time, and it is integrity in this sense that asks us to be steadfast, and not to give up our once dearly held beliefs under pressure. Admiration for this kind of integrity might explain the dislike some feel for politicians, who many see as the embodiment of inconsistency, changing positions whenever there are votes to be gained, and compromising when they should show some persistence. What complicates matters somewhat is that some hold that integrity can also demand the balancing and reassessing of our own principles and values in the light of new circumstances (Cox, La Caze, and Levine 2003, 2–5, 17, 41).

To circumvent these definitional subtleties, "possessing integrity" is sometimes simply used as a synonym for "being ethical" (see also Cox, La Caze, and Levine 2003, 56); someone is thought to possess the virtue of integrity to the extent that he or she upholds moral principles. Yet, although upholding moral principles is of course a good thing, this definition is so general that it does not help us understand what this virtue is really about. In all likelihood, we should locate integrity somewhere between the narrow definition of integrity as simply conforming to the rules of one's organization, and the all-too-wide definition that equates it with ethical behavior. If we seek the meaning of the term in its use, and want to stay close to the everyday understanding of integrity already hinted at in the above, we can take integrity to mean something as living by, and being loyal to, one's own values and principles (see also Appiah 2010, 209). That suggests that we not only have moral obligations to others, near and far, but also to ourselves, and especially an obligation to live in accordance with our own moral principles. To return to Conrad's *Lord Jim* once more: although honor is its main topic, the novel can also be read as a tale about integrity; Jim's acts are not those of the man he in his own eyes is, or wants to be. That failure to live up to his own high principles, and not his lack of courage per se, seems to be his essential flaw. In a quintessentially modern, yet somewhat puzzling phrase, we could say he fails to be "loyal to himself."

Defined as loyalty to personal principles and values, integrity, not requiring the suspension of independent judgment, obviously resembles loyalty to principle to quite an extent (one could say it is a subspecies), but with the important qualification that integrity requires us to be loyal to our *own* principles and, in that way, to who we really are. Who does not do so, like Jim, is therefore disloyal to him- or herself; he or she is self-deceiving. Although this loyalty to oneself might seem to amount to loyalty to a very small group indeed (just like justice can be seen as loyalty to a very large group, as we have seen in the preceding chapter), some see it as very principled, and even the basis for all other virtues (Wakin 2000). Yet, can a virtue that is devoid of any fixed content really perform that function?

Before we can answer that question, and the question to what extent people should (and can) be loyal to their personal principles, we first have to come to a better understanding of what integrity as loyalty to personal principles means—which in this case can best be done by taking a brief look at its genealogy. As said, "being loyal to yourself" is a very modern phrase that would have been unintelligible for most authors from before, say, the eighteenth century because they probably would not have subscribed to the first, and certainly not to the second, of the two assumptions underlying the notion of integrity: 1) that an individual has innate moral principles and 2) that those are unique to him or her. So, where does this relatively new notion spring from? In the philosophy of Cicero and the Stoics we encounter views that, on the surface at least, seem to resemble integrity as we understand it today, so we should (re)turn to them first.

Integrity and Conscience

Cicero held that the heaviest sanction for unethical conduct does not consist of legal penalties (that can often be avoided), but lies in the corruption of one's own morals (*De Officiis* III.38). Yet, in Cicero's view someone's "own" morals largely originate from his or her relations with others. He could therefore hold that ignoring public opinion testifies to a lack of principle (*De Officiis* I.99). That goes rather against modern intuitions about what integrity is—sticking with one's principles *against* public opinion, among other things. On first sight, the Stoics came closer to the contemporary idea of integrity with their idea that someone's social roles, descent, and the like were masks behind which an individual's true self was hidden. But a closer look learns that the divine spark the Stoics thought all people carry within themselves stands for a universal cosmic wisdom, that is, for knowledge of a principle outside one's self, and not for the kind of personal values integrity asks us to stand up for. It seems therefore that, different from loyalty, integrity in the sense of loyalty to your own principles really is a recent virtue—we have already seen that in the seventeenth-century John Locke did not believe that man had innate moral principles, and the modern idea of integrity would have been incomprehensible to him.

It was the Romantic era that brought us the notion of an inner moral compass that is truly individual and unique, and it is in the work of Jean-Jacques Rousseau, who in the opening statement of his autobiographical *Confessions* claimed to be "unlike no one in the whole world" (1953, 17), that this notion of conscience as an inner voice is most influentially expressed.[1] Like Hume and Smith, Rousseau was an intellectual heir to the ancients, with the important difference that he was above all indebted to the Stoics (and especially to Seneca), as shows from his rejection of honor as a bona fide motive.[2] But he differed from the Stoics by his embracing of feeling as something both worthwhile in itself and a guide in matter of morality. In the *Profession of Faith of the Savoyard Vicar*, part of his pedagogical work *Emile*, he wrote that "everything I sense to be good is good; everything I sense to be bad is bad" (1991, 267). According to Rousseau, "too often reason deceives us. (. . .) But conscience never deceives; it is man's true guide" (1991, 286). A few pages further:

> Conscience, <u>conscience! Divine instinct, immortal and Celes-</u><u>tial voice, certain guide of a being that is ignorant and limited</u> <u>but intelligent and free; infallible judge of good and bad which</u> <u>makes man like unto God; it</u> is you who make the excellence of his nature and the morality of his actions (1991, 290).

Conscience, Rousseau wrote in the fifth book of *Emile*, is the most enlightened philosopher, and we do not need to read Cicero's *De Officiis* to be an honest man (1991, 408). <u>That so many people do not listen to</u> <u>their inner voice is, in Rousseau's view, because its sound is lost in the</u> <u>murmuring around us</u>—and because most people put far too much value on how others see them.[3] This was also the Stoic view.

In this view, and different from what the proponents of the honor ethic think, the presence of spectators does not always keep someone on the path virtue. In fact, Rousseau thought that the opposite is true in modern bourgeois society, where it is easy to hide one's conduct from the public eye, where a position is sought by altering one's public appearance, and where the pursuit of fame replaced the pursuit of virtue (*Lettre à M. d'Alembert*; see also Sennet 1977, 119). Rousseau was therefore also rather skeptical about of the arts and the sciences, as they "owe their birth to our vices," more specifically to our vanity (*A Discourse on the Arts and Sciences*). Different from Erasmus, Mandeville, and Hume, Rousseau drew the conclusion that this should make us suspicious about their supposed benefits. Not that the wise man is indifferent to glory, to the contrary, but if he sees how it is distributed in modern society, where "rewards are lavished on wit and ingenuity, while virtue is left unhonored," his virtue, that might have turned to the advantage of society with a little emulation, "droops and dies away in obscurity and indigence" (*A Discourse on the Arts and Sciences*).

Rousseau thought that this could be different in a small republic where the conduct of every citizen is seen by his or her fellow citizens, and in his proposals regarding the Polish constitution he therefore advised that Poland should contract its boundaries, and if that was not possible, to divide the country and opt for a federal system.[4] Rousseau thought (not unlike Montesquieu in *De l'Esprit des Lois*) that small countries "prosper simply because all the citizens know and watch one another" (*Considerations on the Government of Poland*; see also Gay 1979, 532-3). According to Rousseau, human nature was not better in earlier, simpler times, "but men found their security in the ease with which they could see through another," something which "prevented their having many vices" (*A Discourse on the Arts and Sciences*).[5] But that is not the case in the society Emile is going to live in, and to make sure he will lead a moral life nonetheless Rousseau is going to educate Emile to become the opposite of Gyges, that is, as someone who does not need the gaze of others as a check on his behavior. Or, as Peter Gay put it, "Rousseau has intended Emile to grow up as no one before him had grown up: into an autonomous man. Kant's affection for Emile was no accident" (1979, 545).

As we have seen in the second chapter, thinkers such as Adam Smith tried to demonstrate the impossibility of such an individualistic morality by pointing out that the praise and blame of our fellow citizens form a looking glass by which we can examine the appropriateness of our conduct (see for instance Smith *Theory* III.1.5). Smith was "sympathetic to Rousseau's insistence that commercial society is fundamentally driven by a vanity that threatens to corrupt its participants" (Hanley 2008, 137–8), but his impartial spectator certainly does not represent some inborn rule that goes against the norms of society. It is a "socialized conscience," or social censor (Forman-Barzilai 2005, 208), and in that sense it bears some distant resemblance to George Herbert Mead's generalized other and Freud's super-ego. Although it might seem flawed to us, for thinkers from Cicero to Smith the terms good and virtuous were close to synonymous with what was considered honorable in a society (both meanings are present in the Latin *honestum*). According to Locke, for instance,

> everywhere *virtue* and praise, *vice* and blame, go together. *Virtue* is everywhere that which is thought praiseworthy and nothing else but that which has the allowance of public esteem is called virtue. *Virtue* and praise are so united that they are often called by the same name (*An Essay Concerning Human Understanding* II.xxviii.11).

Hume wrote in *Of the Standard of Taste* that

> we must allow some part of the seeming harmony in morals may be accounted for from the very nature of language. The word

virtue, with its equivalent in every tongue, implies praise; as that of *vice* does blame: And no one, without the most obvious and grossest impropriety, could affix reproach to a term, which in general acceptation is understood in a good sense; or bestow applause, where the idiom requires disapprobation.

Hume wrote elsewhere that "the intercourse of sentiments, therefore, in society and conversation, makes us form some general unalterable standard, by which we may approve or disapprove of characters and manners" (*An Enquiry Concerning the Principles of Morals* V.ii). Locke, Hume, and Smith therefore held that observing what people praise and blame, instead of looking within oneself, is indispensable as a heuristic tool to discover what is the moral thing to do. As one author wrote about Hume's moral philosophy: "It is not that virtue is approved because it is virtue, but that virtue is virtue because it is approved" (Hill 1987, 543).

Still, the idea that what is good and true for one person is not necessarily so for another proved so powerful that in the late eighteenth century the idea grew

> that each individual is different and original, and that this originality determines how he or she ought to live. Just the notion of individual difference is, of course, not new. (. . .) What is new is the idea that his really makes a difference to how we're called on to live. The differences (. . .) entail that each one of us has an original path which we ought to tread; they lay the obligation to live up to our originality (Taylor 1992a, 375).[6]

Jim, for instance, considered himself unique too. As far as his colleagues on board were concerned, they "did not belong to the world of heroic adventure," and Jim felt that "the quality of these men did not matter; he rubbed shoulders with them, but they could not touch him; he shared the air they breathed, but he was different" (Chapter 3). Later, Jim does not want to be confounded with his partners in crime because "he was not one of them; he was altogether of another sort" (Chapter 7). That Jim, who before his life on the sea had fantasized about "saving people from sinking ships, cutting away masts in a hurricane, swimming through a surf with a line" (Chapter 1), had jumped ship too did not change his heroic self-image a bit. Although he could no longer claim to be a man of honor as that at least partly depends on how others see you, he could persist in seeing himself as hero, also after his failure to act in accordance with that self-image when it was tested, by separating his doings from his being. Marlow, describing a meeting with Jim at the time of the hearings:

> There he sat telling me that just as I saw him before my eyes he wouldn't be afraid to face anything—and believing in it too. (. . .) He must have led a most exalted existence. Can you fancy it? A succession of adventures, so much glory, such a victorious progress! and the deep sense of his sagacity crowning every day of his inner life (Chapter 8).

Richard Sennet writes in *The Fall of Public Man* that this distinction between being and doing is a quintessential feature of "intimate society," which reversed the "dictum that praise or censure should apply to actions and not to actors; now what matters is not what you have done, but how you feel about it" (1977, 263).[7] While "a man in heroic society is what he does" (MacIntyre 1985, 122), a Romantic like Rousseau believes that "his sins will be overlooked, because he believes implicitly in everything he does and is: that he is good is everything, what he does matters little" (Roche 1974, 574).

Later, this idea that we all possess unique personalities, and that our concern for how others see us is what bars us from being our true selves, would echo in the humanistic psychology of Abraham Maslow and Erich Fromm.[8] As Fromm writes, in language that he seems to have borrowed from Rousseau:

> Here also we find the irrational distortion of a normal attitude: man naturally wants to be accepted by his fellows; but modern man wants to be accepted by everybody and therefore is afraid to deviate, in thinking, feeling, and acting, from the cultural pattern (1949, 164).

It is as a result of such ideas that the norm today is that we should choose our own way through life, not needing the help judgments of others may offer or the check that the sense of shame can be.[9] Independence is then the ideal to strive for, the way one wants to be, other-directedness is seen as the regrettable reality, and the way too many people are.

The term other-directedness is from sociologist David Riesman, who wrote that "the characterological struggle that holds the center of the stage today is that between other-direction and inner-direction, as against a background in which tradition-direction gradually disappears from the planet" (1950). And there is a clear winner:

> all power, not merely some power, is in the hands of the actual or imaginary approving group, and the child learns from his parents' reactions to him that nothing in his character, no possession he owns, no inheritance of name or talent, no work he has done is valued for itself but only for its effects on others (Riesman 1950, 49).

At present these ideas resonate in popular psychology, self-help literature, and our notion of integrity. But it is clear that it was only as a result of inner-directedness having become the new ideal that Riesman could arrive at the conclusion that people were getting more other-directed. As Sennett explains:

> Riesman believed American society, and in its wake Western Europe, was moving from an inner- to an other-directed condition. The sequence should be reversed. Western societies are moving from something like an other-directed condition to an inner-directed condition—except that in the midst of self-absorption no one can say what is inside (1977, 5).

According to Stephen Holmes, the current emphasis on individuality "is a product of a peculiarly modern style of social conditioning" (1993, 191).

Also in matters of morality, independence from what others might think has come to be considered the highest good (which of course resembles the ideas of the Stoics). Following examples and adjusting one's behavior so that it coincides with what is praised and condemned in one's society, as authors from Cicero to Smith advised us to do, is seen as falling short of that ideal. According to Kant, for instance, nothing could be more detrimental to morality than wishing to derive it from examples (*The Groundwork of the Metaphysics of Morals* BA 30).[10] To know what is the moral thing to do, we have to look within: "a public-spirited citizen must do a bit of soul-searching—must decide what he or she most truly and deeply believes to be right and good—before it is possible to live with integrity" (Carter 1996, 10). Today, we consider conscience, as an inner voice, not only important because it should tell us what is right; it has become something with "independent and crucial moral significance," and most of us hold that listening to our moral feelings is "something we have to attain if we are to be true and full human beings" (Taylor 1994, 28). The idea that it is important to be able to "look at yourself in the mirror"—a telling phrase as it suggests that it is reckoned to be of less importance what others think of one's conduct—replaced Smith's idea that the praise and blame of others form a necessary looking glass.

One could even say, as James Bowman does in *Honor: A History*, that doing what your "inner self" tells you, against external pressure, is now considered the honorable and courageous thing to do (2006, 206). That seems to have been the kind of glory Rousseau was after when he wrote his *Confessions*. According to Edmund Burke, it was his vanity that caused Rousseau "to publish a mad confession of his mad faults, and to attempt a new sort of glory from bringing hardily to light the obscure and vulgar vices, which we know may sometimes be blended with eminent talents" (cited in Mansfield 1987, 689).[11] Rousseau himself was rather candid about his not always being able to live up to his own ideals. After a misstep:

> I did not fear punishment, but I dreaded shame: I dreaded it more than death, more than the crime, more than all the world. I would have buried, hid myself in the centre of the earth (. . .). I felt no dread but that of being detected, of being publicly and to my face declared a thief, liar, and calumniator (1953, 88).

It appears, as regards this "new sort of glory," that "a guilty or shameful secret when spoken of publicly becomes at the same time something else—a matter of pride" (Schneider 1977, 44; see also R. Williams 1983, 138), and that shamelessness is sometimes seen as a "form of freedom and courageousness" (Tarnopolsky 2010, 8). "I may be no better, but at least I am different" wrote Rousseau, a founding father of the genre of intimate autobiography, in the opening sentences of the *Confessions*.

G. Thomas Couser writes in his book on autobiographies that "autobiography is the literary form, and democracy the political form, most congruent with this idea of a unique and autonomous self" (1989, 13). According to John Sturrock, in his book on the autobiographical genre,

> The tension in autobiography derives from the conflict in it between the will to apartness and the will to association; and if the

evidence of the will to apartness pervades all autobiographical narrative, then the evidence of the will to association lies in the existence of autobiography itself, as the most sociable of literary acts (1993, 18–19).

Sturrock thinks that in Rousseau's case "the urge for an autobiographical vindication" is absolute (1993, 146), and that his *Confessions* are a monument of *amour propre* (1993, 156). Sturrock also suspects that "for an autobiographer there can be no disgrace in having been disgraced, since to admit it is a creditable act" (1993, 55), and that "there may be more vanity in broadcasting our failures than our triumphs, since to broadcast failure is to demand recognition from others that the world has done us an injustice in underestimating our true worth" (1993, 119). That last remark refers, incidentally, to Hume's short autobiography *My Own Life* (in which, as we have seen, Hume calls the love of literary fame his ruling passion). Hume's account of his life (meant as a prefix to his collected works) is rather unlike most modern autobiographies, though; Hume modestly opens with the remark that "it is difficult for a man to speak long of himself without vanity; therefore I shall be short."

The unique self that Rousseau claimed to possess and that the notion of integrity presupposes is, just as integrity itself, a comparatively new construct, and something also Conrad's Jim prided himself on. When narrator Marlow talks about Jim's case with a friend, the German trader and butterfly collector Stein, the latter is quick with his diagnosis: "I understand very well. He is romantic." Only death—"One thing alone can us from being ourselves cure"—can cure us from that. When Marlow says that "strictly speaking, the question is not how to get cured, but how to live," Stein answers: "How to be! *Ach*! How to be!" A difficult question because man is fickle. As Stein puts it: "he wants to be a saint, and he wants to be a devil—and every time he shuts his eyes he sees himself as a very fine fellow." But "because you not always can keep your eyes shut there comes the real trouble—the heart pain—the world pain," caused by not being able to live up to one's own self-image (Chapter 20). Earlier in the story Marlow already remarked that "no man ever understands quite his own artful dodges to escape from the grim shadow of self-knowledge" (Chapter 7). A man or woman of integrity is the rare person who, in spite of everything, has found an answer to the question of how to be, and, more important, succeeds in living by it.

> For himself

✳ Matured definition of integrity

Can We be Loyal to Our Personal Principles?

There are some problems with this notion of integrity, however, especially in its most common meaning of being true to oneself and one's deeply felt principles, in other words: of "being loyal to oneself." First of all, although many see integrity as an important virtue, whether or not it is in fact a virtue depends on the values and principles someone actually wants to live by (see also Wakin 2000, 115)—to use Stein's words: does he or she aspire to be a devil or a saint? Rawls notes in *A Theory of Justice* that "of course the virtues of integrity are virtues, and among the excellences of free persons. Yet while necessary, they are not sufficient; for their definition allows for most any content" (§78). There is nothing in integrity that precludes a malevolent dictator, a mobster, a terrorist, or, for that matter, Conrad's most illustrious character: the ivory collector Kurtz from the *Heart of Darkness* (a novel about our inner depths by most accounts), of rightfully claiming to be a person of integrity (see also Margalit 1996, 49). According to Margalit, "our hesitation about calling Eichmann a man of integrity stems not from any conceptual considerations" (1996, 49). Although Rousseau thought that integrity presupposes goodness, holding that a whole and integrated person cannot be immoral (Grant 1997, 86), one could say that the immoral pirate Brown actually did a better job living according to his principles than "moral" Jim (even the rusty Patna was, according to Marlow, true to herself when she began to take in water). In their *Integrity and the Fragile Self*, Cox, La Caze, and Levine take a position similar to that of Rousseau—one cannot be a person of integrity and evil at the same time (2003, 8–9)—yet they are rather alone in holding this view, as they themselves admit, and do not offer much to substantiate their view on top of that.

Non-conformist evildoers who act against the norms of wider society, out of deeply felt principles or not, are sometimes even admired for their unashamed disregard for social conventions and the consequences of their actions for themselves and others. Some members of the terrorist Baader-Meinhof Group met with quite some sympathy in Europe and the United States, the above-mentioned Kurtz had an admirer in the narrator of the story (the same Charles Marlow we already know from *Lord Jim*), and thief and writer (and sympathizer of the Baader-Meinhof Group) Jean Genet was declared a saint by Jean-Paul Sartre. In that light, it is perhaps not a good idea to see integrity as the equivalent of being ethical. Rawls deems integrity a secondary virtue; more about form rather than matter, and definitely not the basis for the other virtues (*A Theory of Justice* §78).

Nonetheless, there are times when virtues of form are in demand. Especially when it is not clear what is just or good, we want our beliefs at least to be our own, originating from within. As Rawls writes, "in times of social doubt and loss of faith in long established values, there is a tendency to fall back on the virtues of integrity: truthfulness and sincerity, lucidity and commitment, or, as some say, authenticity" (*A Theory of Justice* §78). It is not a one to one relationship, but evidently sticking to your own, personal values and principles is more likely to be admired when the general feeling is that there are no shared societal values and principles. One can, for instance, be in total disagreement with someone else yet still deem him or her a person of integrity (as was possibly the case with some admirers of the Baader-Meinhof Group, and Marlow's admiration for Kurtz in *Heart of Darkness*). This relativistic side of integrity presupposes that different persons have values and principles that are not only different from each other, but also unique in a way that makes these values and principles central to who they are. That might be a common view today, but we have already seen that historically this notion of unique selves has arrived on the scene relatively recently. This aspect of integrity is closely related to two attendant virtues of integrity: sincerity and, especially, authenticity.

Lionel Trilling explains in his classic *Sincerity and Authenticity* (1971) that there are important differences between these two latter virtues, even if they appear roughly similar. Sincerity serves a social purpose; in order to be reliable for others one says what one truly thinks, without distorting information, holding it back, or deceiving. In brief, do what you say, and say what you think. This is less straightforward than it might seem: there is something ambiguous about being oneself for other-directed reasons. Taking pride in speaking your mind, and possibly even being rather blunt in an effort to pass for sincere, is for instance not always authentic. Now and then we "play the role of being ourselves, we sincerely act the part of the sincere person, with the result that a judgment may be passed on our sincerity that is not authentic" (Trilling 1972, 11). This is not the case with authenticity itself, however: in the case of authenticity, being ourselves is an end in itself.[12] How others might feel about that is considered irrelevant. Evidently, as a moral ideal, this is bound to have its catches too. For understandable reasons, some definitions of integrity emphasize sincerity more than authenticity.

Partly building upon Trilling's work, Charles Taylor observes in *The Ethics of Authenticity* (1992b) that we tend to confuse two aspects of authenticity: that of matter and that of manner. The first is all about the content of our strivings, while manner is about the way we do things. Now, it is probably possible to look within ourselves to find our own way to do things, and this own way is in that case self-referential in the sense that we use it as a means of expressing ourselves.[13] This does not apply to matter, though. It is a mistake to think that our goals should come from within, should be an expression of ourselves, and can in that way be self-referential too. Taylor argues that this is impossible because human life is fundamentally dialogical (1992b, 33), that is, we define our identity through engaging in an exchange with significant others. Although we choose our own goals, we necessarily choose them within a tradition and a framework. We only find fulfillment in what has significance outside ourselves, and confusing these two kinds of self-referentiality "lends legitimacy to the worst kinds of subjectivism" (1992b, 82). This is, by the way, not a point of view only communitarians hold: not unlike Taylor, although possibly leaving somewhat more room for choice, Rawls holds that the many associations of society

> simplify decision by offering definite ideals and forms of life that have been developed and tested by innumerable individuals, sometimes for generations. Thus, in drawing up our plan of life we do not start de novo; we are not required to choose from countless possibilities without given structure or fixed contours (*A Theory of Justice* §85).

To return to Taylor: he illustrates his point by elaborating on the way artists see their own role. Since Romanticism, Taylor writes, artists are looking for, and finding, individual ways of expression. Yet good artists, although often having found a form that is unique to them, in general aspire to articulate something beyond themselves, and their own sentiment. Art that is mainly about the artist's personal feelings, and Taylor thinks that in modern art this is too often the case, is generally not very interesting (1992b, 82–91).

Some characters of fiction, created by writers who did aspire to articulate something beyond their selves, also point to the problematic side of having to find your own way, and raise questions about the feasibility of the Rousseauian ideals. Conrad's Jim is an obvious case in point, but a better example is Tolstoy's character Konstantin Levin, from *Anna*

Karenina, who looked inside for what to do with his life, and was consequently, as Tolstoy portrays him, always at a loss about what to do (until finding the answer in Christianity). In the life of his opposite, the young officer Andrej Wronski, there was, although somewhat superficial, also something to be envied: as an officer he had access to a code that told him what he was expected to do in almost every situation. To a large extent this code still consisted of the "very exotic notions" Tocqueville saw as characteristic of honor in ancient times. For instance, in his day Wronski's code

> laid down as invariable rules: that one must pay a cardsharper, but need not pay a tailor; that one must never tell a lie to a man, but one may to a woman; that one must never cheat anyone, but one may a husband; that one must never pardon an insult, but one may give one and so on (Part III, Chapter 20).

This reminds of Mandeville, who wrote that a

> man of honour must not cheat or tell a lie; he must punctually repay what he borrows at play, though the creditor has nothing to show for it; but he may drink, and swear, and owe money to all the tradesmen in town, without taking notice of their dunning. He must make no attempts upon his friend's wife, daughter, sister, or anybody that is trusted to his care, but he may lie with all the world besides (*Fable* vol I 245).

As to that last point: Wronski's code stipulated that you could have a playful affair with a married woman, but that you cannot run away with her (probably running away with your mistress would bring things too much in the open—as we have seen, in most honor cultures that what is not spoken of publicly does not exist). His affair with the married Anna Karenina was not a "brilliant, graceful, worldly liaison," which the world would have accepted, and even applauded, "but a sort of Wertherish, desperate passion" that both lovers took much too seriously, and got her pregnant; something that his code did not cover. After Wronski broke the code completely by leaving the military for Karenina, he had no idea what to do next. Mrs. Karenina fared considerably worse, though.[14]

Tolstoy was a great admirer of Rousseau (and wore a medallion with his picture around his neck as an adolescent), and although *Anna*

Karenina can be read as a—sympathetic—critique on Rousseauian ideals of independence and naturalness, that was most likely not what Tolstoy, who is thought to have modeled Levin after himself, meant it to be. That is different with Stendhal's *The Red and the Black*, which can be read as a much more explicit critique on the ideas of Rousseau (see Boyd 2005 for a different reading), pointing out the impossibility of unmediated desires, and stressing our need for models to follow. The novel, published in 1830 (the year the restoration government of Charles X, background of Stendhal's novel, ended), tells the story of Julien Sorel, the son of a carpenter (and carpeting was the trade Rousseau had in mind for his pupil Emile, because it was "clean and useful") who, wanting to advance in life, opted for the clergy (the black) because a career in the army (the red), the days of Napoleon being over, seemed no longer feasible.[15] The shift (described by Tocqueville) from an aristocratic conception of honor to a more democratic one made Julien's struggle (and longing) for honor possible, writes Walzer: "the struggle for honor that raged among aristocrats, and that played such a large part in early modern literature, is now entered by everyman" (1983, 252; see also Boyd 2005, 376–7). And, writes Walzer on the next page,

> Since he has no fixed rank, since no one knows where he belongs, he must establish his own worth, and he can do that only by winning the recognition of his fellows. Each of his fellows is trying to do the same thing. Hence the competition has no social boundaries short of the national frontier, nor does it have any temporal limit (1983, 253).[16]

When the major of the small town of Verrières offers him a job as a tutor in his household, Julien is afraid that he will have to eat with the servants. His unwillingness to do so

> was not natural to Julien; he would, in seeking his fortune, have done other things far more disagreeable. He derived this repugnance from Rousseau's *Confessions*. It was the one book that helped his imagination to form any idea of the world (*The Red and the Black* Book I, Chapter 5).

An affair with the major's wife, Mme. de Rênal, never really materializes—mainly because of a lack of novels that could offer guidance.

> The young tutor and his timid mistress would have found in three or four novels, and even in the lyrics of the Gymnase, a clear statement of their situation. The novels would have outlined for them the part to be played, shown them the model to copy; and this model, sooner or later, albeit without the slightest pleasure, and perhaps with reluctance, vanity would have compelled Julien to follow (Book I, Chapter 7).

Later, in Paris, he has a new love affair above his station, but this time Rousseau's novel *La nouvelle Heloise* serves as a model of what to feel—and although it ended in disaster, this affair at least did take off. That did not bring Julien the recognition he sought, as birth still mattered to those above him; they made him feel that he was of common descent, and their inferior in wit and manners. Interestingly, social distinctions do not seem to play much of a role in Conrad's *Lord Jim*, published just seventy years later. In another aspect, Jim does resemble Julien; he too needed models, and opted for a life on the sea only after a course of "light holiday literature." In fact, Jim had imagined himself as a Crusoe-like

> castaway, barefooted and half naked, walking on uncovered reefs in search of shellfish to stave off starvation. He confronted savages on tropical shores, quelled mutinies on the high seas, and in a small boat upon the ocean kept up the hearts of despairing men—always an example of devotion to duty, and as unflinching as a hero in a book (Chapter 1).

Jim, Levin, Wronski, and Julien Sorel demonstrate that unmediated feeling is almost impossible, and that we need something outside ourselves—a standard, tradition, or model—to show us which way to go. Rousseau himself describes in his autobiography how he, in his youth, came to prefer the *Parallel Lives* of Plutarch to novels, and, as he put it, even "became the character whose life I was reading" (1953, 20–1).

Lastly, and following up on Taylor's remark about man's dialogical nature, it is the question whether we can know if those who claim that they are following their own moral compass are actually doing so. To begin with, they could of course be willingly deceiving their public, yet that would imply that their claim to integrity is a deliberate lie, as they themselves would know. Much more relevant (and interesting) is the question if they could not be deceiving themselves: how can they, although sincerely believing that they are following an innate moral rule, possibly know whether they are in fact doing so? This is especially hard to answer when someone is acting against the opinions of others, and that is what the virtue of integrity calls for when one's principles are at odds with the general opinion. Chances are that we are then dealing with, as Bernard Williams phrased it,

> a man who thinks that he is just, but is treated by everyone else as though he were not. If he were given merely that description of himself, it is less clear how steady his motivations would prove. Moreover, it is less clear how steady we think they should prove. For given simply that description, there is nothing to show whether he is a solitary bearer of true justice or a deluded crank (1993, 99; see also Miller 1993, p. ix; Robinson 2009, 262).

Williams seems to refer to Wittgenstein here, whose argument against the idea of a private language suggests that there are three possibilities if someone claims to follow an innate moral rule: 1) he or she is indeed following a rule and does so consistently; 2) he or she follows a rule, but is not entirely consistent. That what is considered morally right on one occasion is not what is deemed morally sound on another instance; 3) he or she claims to follow a rule but his or her judgments are in reality totally random. The problem here is that neither the rule follower nor the audience can determine which of the three alternatives we are dealing with.[17]

The followers of an innate rule find themselves in the same position as Daniel Defoe's Robinson Crusoe who, alone on his island, tried to keep track of what day it was by means of a calendar (enabling him to keep Sundays, although he soon gave that up), and named the native he befriended Friday, because Crusoe thought it was on a Friday that they had met. But until his rescue there was for him no way of knowing whether Thursday or Monday would have been a more appropriate name, and in fact Crusoe learned that he had missed a day or two after his isolation was lifted. *The Adventures of Robinson Crusoe*, glorifying Tocqueville's quiet virtues (which the industrious and orderly Crusoe certainly possessed), was the first book Rousseau's pupil Emile had to read. His future wife Sophie, incidentally, lends Emile *Les Aventures de Télémaque*, written by Fénelon, the Archbishop of Cambray, who, as might be remembered from the previous chapter, in case of a fire had more chance of being rescued by the utilitarian Godwin than the latter's own father. But it was the account of Crusoe's adventures that was to help Emile to live his life unaffected by a corrupted society—a society that Crusoe, who spent years teaching his parrot to call him by name, dearly missed (Alexander Selkirk, the castaway Crusoe was modeled after, allegedly danced with his cat during the four years he spent alone on his island). And although we have just seen that light literature made Jim fantasizing about a Crusoe-like adventure at the beginning of his career, he missed society dearly when he was in Patusan where he, surrounded by many, was as isolated as Crusoe had been.

What we can learn from the impossibility of a private language (and Crusoe's calendar) is that we can only consistently follow a rule, or act on a principle, moral or otherwise, if there is a public that can tell us whether we are in the right or in the wrong. As we have seen, it is one of the functions of honor to make us see what the right course of action is. But a problem that John Stuart Mill hinted at might well be hampering this function in democratic times. Although Mill (like Tocqueville) considered social tyranny and conformity to be greater dangers to individual freedom than the state, he nonetheless held that we have a right to warn someone if we think him at fault, or even a fool, and it seemed to him that

> it would be well, indeed, if this good office were much more freely rendered than the common notions of politeness at present permit, and if one person could honestly point out to another that he thinks him in fault, without being considered unmannerly or presuming. We have a right, also, in various ways, to act upon our unfavourable opinion of any one, not to the oppression of his individuality, but in the exercise of ours. We are not bound, for example, to seek his society; we have a right to avoid it (though not to parade the avoidance) (. . .). We have a right, and it may be our duty, to caution others against him (1993, 145).[18]

No doubt Mill saw no contradiction between his advice to render this good office more often, and his fear for too much conformism; pointing out to someone that we think him in fault was in his view probably in agreement with Cicero's conception of honor as the "agreed approval of good men," while the conformism Mill feared resembled the applause of the masses that also Cicero rejected. But Mill would not have used the term honor in relation to the rendering of this "good office." Interestingly, he was very modern in his use of the term honor as more or less synonymous with integrity, and spoke of honor and personal dignity as "that feeling of personal exaltation and degradation which acts independently of other people's opinion, or even in defiance of it" (1987, 153). Nonetheless, one could say that this element in Mill's work (i.e., that it is important to point out to someone that we think him in fault) stems from what Gertrude Himmelfarb describes as Mill's easily overlooked indebtedness to an "older liberal tradition, the tradition of Montesquieu, Burke, the Founding Fathers, and Tocqueville. It is a tradition that is eminently modern and yet resonant of classical thought" (1974, p. xxi). According to Richard Boyd, "Tocqueville, Mill, and other 'aristocratic liberals' of the 19th century worried about what happens when aristocratic honor gives way to the sway of 'public opinion'" (2005, 374), and Boyd sees Stendhal's *The Red and the Black* "as an immediate precursor to Tocqueville's criticisms of tyrannical public opinion" (2005, 367).

Rendering the "good office" Mill speaks of is in our day even more contrary to custom than it was in Victorian England, and it seems that it can only perform its function as a check, for instance on our tendency (noted by Mandeville, Hume, and Smith) to overvalue ourselves, when criticism does not amount to a narcistic injury in its own right (for the virtue of rudeness see Westacott 2006, especially 13). One should give (and get) some honest critique every now and then, because, as Amitai Etzioni writes in words that somewhat remind us of those used by Mill, "it is unrealistic to rely on individuals' inner voices and to expect that people will invariably do what is right completely on their own" (1995, 36), something that follows from Etzioni's assumption that "individuals' consciences are neither inborn nor—for most people—self-enforcing" (1995, 30).[19] Interestingly, and notwithstanding the fact that Fromm and Riesman were likeminded as far as the bigger picture is concerned, Riesman, who, as we have seen, was rather negative about other-directedness, nonetheless thought that

> the "humanistic conscience" which Erich Fromm describes as "man's recall to himself," is, to be sure, an inner voice. It can be silenced by external authority. But it can also be muted when other people refuse to remind the individual how his conduct looks to them (1950, 304).

Such a refusal, now, could be seen as testifying to a lack of moral courage; a virtue that at first glance has a lot in common with the virtue of integrity.

Integrity, Moral Courage, and Honor

Moral courage is an important subspecies of courage, not only because we need people who blow the whistle if necessary (like Sergeant Darby did on his colleagues in the Abu Ghraib case), but also because we want people to correct a friend or colleague when they think him in the wrong—this is especially important if we assume that innate moral rules are either weak or non-existent. The idea that you should be able to withstand the unfavorable "opinion of the many" (the phrase goes back to Plato's *Crito*) is in fact a very old one. It was already a recurring theme in Plutarch's biographies—Gaius Pompey's decision-making, for instance, was fatally hampered by his wish to be liked and esteemed by his friends (*Pompey* 67). In the portrayal of Cato Minor we read, conversely, how this great-grandson of the censor Cato Major (and contemporary of Gaius Pompey) went out without tunic and shoes to habituate himself to be ashamed only of what was really shameful (Plutarch *Cato Minor* 6). At that time, the final years of the Roman republic, Cato Minor's incorruptibility was already seen as somewhat of an anachronism that reminded of older, better times, and paradoxically Cato gained fame by not seeking it (see also Sallust *Catilinae Coniuratio* 54). This ability to withstand unfavorable opinion is of course not the same as an insensitivity to honor, as honor depends on the "agreed approval of good men," and is thus a completely different matter, at least from Plutarch's perspective.

The term moral courage itself makes one of its first appearances in *The Philosophy of Courage* by Horace Porter, a U.S. General of the Civil War, who thought it more important than physical courage (1888). He did not define it, though. Miller does, and according to him "moral courage has come to mean the capacity to overcome the fear of shame and humiliation in order to admit one's mistakes, to confess a wrong, to reject evil conformity, to denounce injustice, and to defy immoral or imprudent orders" (2000, 254). Its beneficiaries are probably more often outsiders than those who belong to one's honor group. Paradigmatic examples are for instance those few in Lt. Calley's platoon who refused to participate in the My Lai massacre in Vietnam, and Hugh C. Thompson, Jr., the already mentioned helicopter pilot who tried to stop it. Miller's definition of moral courage as consisting of, among other things, the ability to overcome shame also suggests that the person who does not care at all about how others think of him or her is not, in fact, morally courageous. This similar to the way a person without fear of bodily injury is not really physically courageous (because he or she has no fear to conquer)—it was on that ground that Plato had Socrates for a moment maintaining that in battle the better trained soldier is less courageous than the one who lacks training, since a well-trained soldier has less reason to be afraid and thus less fear to overcome (*Laches* 193).

Clearly, the differences between the two forms of courage are more important: whereas the word "physical" in the term physical courage refers to what is at stake, life and limbs, the word "moral" in the term moral courage refers to the higher end that this form of courage aims at (and not to what is at stake in the case of moral courage: reputation, esteem, popularity, etc.).[20] It is therefore by definition motivated by a moral cause, at least in the eyes of the agent and those who label his act morally courageous. By definition, but not as a logical necessity it: is of course possible to put one's reputation to risk for an immoral end, and the main distinction between physical and moral courage therefore lies in what is put in harm's way, respectively one's life and one's reputation (seen in that light, reputation courage would perhaps be a more appropriate term than moral courage).[21] Interesting here is that if there are outsiders who see someone as morally courageous, this can be said to exclude him or her from actually being so, at least to some extent: although losing the esteem of peers, for compensation he or she (a whistleblower or conscientious objector, for instance) will get support from at least some others in wider society, heralding him or her as an example of moral courage.

Physical and moral courage were pretty hard to tell apart in the centuries that standing up for your beliefs, if they were not in line with those held by the state or the church, would not only impede your reputation but also your physical existence (see also Miller 2000). It is only from the nineteenth century onwards that we treat physical and moral courage as separate entities (Miller 2000, 263). Yet one could argue that these two forms of courage are still interrelated, and Miller holds this position: who lacks physical courage will probably not have much moral courage.[22] But seeing it as an derivative of physical courage, as Miller clearly does, suggests that moral courage ranks somewhat lower than physical courage, and that it is easier attainable for an average person since it is not one's life and limbs that are at stake, but only one's reputation or popularity (see for instance Castro 2006, 69).

But it is not clear at all to what extent we can with reason blame someone who fails to speak out because he or she cannot bear the contempt of others; as Locke pointed out, we fear the opinions of others more than we fear hell or jail (*Essay* I.iii.12). Although most of us would probably judge a lack of moral courage harsher than a lack of physical courage for the reason that practicing the former is considered less demanding, this might underestimate the extent to which people dread being held in contempt by those whose judgment matters to them. Sometimes death is chosen to avoid shame, as for instance Jim did after his failure in Patusan. Other famous examples are the chaste Roman noblewoman Lucretia, who killed herself after being raped, and the Japanese sailors who in the Second World War stepped cheerfully in their Kaitens, manned torpedoes offering no chances of survival (Miller 2000, 273–6). It looks as if these Kaiten pilots, somewhat resembling Japan's kamikaze pilots from the same era, did not have much of a choice, given the all-pervasiveness of the Japanese shame culture at that time.[23] One could even argue that the Japanese soldiers who surrendered surpassed in courage (although in moral courage rather than physical courage) their many colleagues who did fight to the death to avoid disgrace (also the motive behind the Samurai practice of hara-kiri). According to Godwin, somewhat similar, it was probably "more courageous to resist the social pressure to duel than to give in to it" (Appiah 2010, 169, see also 35). At present video testaments maneuver potential suicide bombers into a position that is somewhat similar to that of the Kaiten pilot. Such testaments function not only as propaganda; they also make it impossible to not execute the planned attack without massive loss of face.

We can find examples closer at home as well: the courageous soldier is sometimes neither fearless nor someone who has overcome his or her fears, but, as Mandeville and quite a number of military sociologists have pointed out, someone fearful of what colleagues think of him or her. Armed forces have adapted their organizations on the assumption that the existence of strong bonds between soldiers is the most important factor in combat motivation (Keegan 1976, 53, 72–3), and every military promotes loyalty to the honor group.[24] The motivation behind many acts of physical courage thus partly boils down to being more afraid of being considered a coward than of dying (see also Bourke 2005, 214; Dollard 1944, 46; Miller 2000, 178; Rachman 1990, 45). Seeing that expecting anything else would simply raise the bar too high, most people, in spite of Aristotle's view that courage should be motivated by a noble cause to deserve that predicate, will deem these acts courageous nonetheless.[25] For instance, we consider the U.S. and RAF airmen who in World War II continued to fly their missions while knowing that their chances of surviving a tour of duty were slim (about 10 percent during some periods) courageous, even if peer pressure played a large role in their valor (Rachman 1990, 36–7).[26]

There is another side to this, however. Especially in the military, honor, in its modern guise of social cohesion, can lead to the kind of group loyalty that is potentially dangerous to those who fall outside the honor group.[27] This loyalty to the honor group can stop someone from showing moral courage, as this type of courage in general brings moral disapprobation from one's peers. So, our moderate standpoint concerning the motivation behind a virtuous act—not that important—backfires here. If physical courage is motivated by the wish to gain esteem or save face, and thus does not meet the Aristotelian requirement regarding noble intention, it is not very likely to be accompanied with the equally important virtue of moral courage. The things that foster physical courage most, strong group loyalty and the wish to avoid shame, inhibit moral courage. Although especially visible in the armed forces, this mechanism is, of course, in a less extreme form present in many groups and organizations: the stronger the loyalty to the group, the less likely moral courage is to occur. As we have briefly noted in a previous chapter, most employees probably work more for recognition than for money, and for many people colleagues form their most important honor group.

On first sight, then, there is some similarity between the virtue of moral courage and integrity; like integrity, moral courage asks us to uphold our principles when others disagree, and perhaps even hold us in contempt for sticking to them. But there is an important difference: moral courage aims at a moral principle outside oneself, whereas integrity clearly does not—in view of the fact that a devout Nazi could also claim to possess this good quality (see also Margalit 1996, 49). Some famous examples of integrity were in fact motivated by principles and values that were not very personal at all, and were therefore actually instances of moral courage. For instance, we already noted in the chapter on loyalty that people like Von Stauffenberg, in the eyes of many a paradigmatic case of integrity, often do not act on strictly personal values that are at odds with national values (or organizational values in the case of whistleblowers), but on ideas about what their country (organization, for whistleblowers) should stand for (and perhaps once stood for). The same holds for My Lai hero Hugh Thompson and Captain Lawrence Rockwood (from the previous chapter). Their behavior can also be seen as an example of professional loyalty; as we have seen, professional loyalty is loyalty to an ethos originating outside oneself, and is thus free from the subjectivity integrity suffers from. What's more, persons loyal to their profession have that characteristic that we were looking for in integrity: they will not unquestioningly follow their peers, as ultimately the object of their loyalty is their professional ethic, and not their honor group, which will mainly consist of colleagues.

Conclusion

A paramount quality of many definitions of integrity is their imprecision; possessing integrity is often simply seen as tantamount to being ethical. This very broad view on integrity is widespread and has possibly contributed to integrity being one of the most used moral terms—perhaps from time to time because of lack of a more comprehensive moral vocabulary (Cook 2002, 337). In a more specific meaning, integrity requires of us that we live according to our own personal values and principles, and it even seems to imply that we have a moral obligation to do so. The relationship between integrity, in this meaning, and some other virtues central to this book is in general an uneasy one. For instance, integrity defined as loyalty to personal principles can collide with loyalty to one's nation or organization.

But most of all integrity is at odds with honor as a reward for virtue; integrity resembles the Stoic and Platonic ideal that virtue should be its own reward. It is especially this hostility towards honor, public opinion, and the like that sets integrity apart from virtues such as honor and loyalty, and it is also this non-conformist side of integrity that makes it closely related to modern virtues such as autonomy, authenticity, and sincerity. One could even argue that it is either honor tied to public codes, or integrity based on private codes (assuming such a thing is possible), but that one cannot have both (Challans 2007, 88–9).[28] Stressing internal honor—the gaze of imaginary others will be sufficient enough for honor to function, so that the actual presence of others is no longer needed—offers no middle ground. Although on first sight internal honor resembles integrity to quite an extent, with honor and integrity from time to time being used as synonyms, internal honor presupposes an internalized other, say Smith's impartial spectator, and is therefore still based on adherence to a public code.

Thus far this chapter—in many aspects the reverse of the chapters on honor—has cast doubt on the idea that integrity is a virtue. But there is another side to this too: that the notion of integrity does not always give due attention to the inescapable frameworks we live in and by does not change the fact that it has itself become a part of that framework. Today we cannot but see ourselves, and judge others, in the light of integrity and its attendant virtues (Taylor 1992a/b), at least to some extent. In the final pages of his voluminous *Sources of the Self* Taylor writes: "what I hope emerges from this lengthy account of the growth of modern identity is how all-pervasive it is, how much it envelops us, and how deeply we are implicated in it" (1992a, 503). As we have seen in the introduction, even Conrad admitted that the theme of *Lord Jim*, lost honor, "may be condemned as artificial" (*Author's note to 1917 edition*). That many people nowadays say that they consider it important to be able to look at themselves in the mirror illustrates the extent to which integrity itself has become a part of our moral space, and a criterion by which we evaluate others and ourselves. Most people today hold their inner personal principles and values very dear, and make an effort to live by them.

Also, it is evident that in some instances being principled is what is called for. Although a problematic virtue, integrity is also a virtue that aims high. As we already noted in the previous chapter, one could say that someone's integrity is tested when it is plain what is the right thing to do, yet with considerable pressure to choose the wrong course of action (see Coleman 2009), as for instance Jim did. In *Lord Jim* the pirate Brown refers to the role of invisibility in Jim's jump from the Patna with his remark, quoted in the introduction, about "saving one's life in the dark," and it is an important limitation of honor that it is powerless in such situations. In a way this was also the situation Ellison's invisible man and Smith's man of low condition found themselves in (the position of Gyges and Well's invisible man was different; they deliberately sought invisibility in order to have the freedom to act immorally).[29] To put it somewhat dramatically: especially when no one is around, when those around are letting their moral standards go, or when the norms of a group or organization are the wrong ones in the first place, sticking to one's principles seems a laudable thing to do. In line with the distinction between group loyalty and loyalty to principle from the previous chapter, one could argue that without expecting people to be men or women of principle to at least some extent, they could hide behind the fact that they were just doing as others did.

The question is whether these principles should be truly personal principles, or internalized societal principles. As we have seen in the above, the latter seems to be the more promising option. Integrity is overwhelmingly vague, and in its most common meaning much too subjective. One could even wonder whether integrity is really that outward looking and inclusive—the motivation behind sticking to one's own principles can be rather self-serving, more about maintaining one's own morals, the ability to look oneself in the mirror, and a certain self-image, than about its possible beneficiaries. If loyalty is about giving priority to the interests of a particular individual or a group, integrity as a special kind of loyalty can be seen as giving priority to the interests of oneself. In that aspect, it resembles pacifism (and perhaps also the doctrine of double effect) as outlined in the previous chapter. Integrity is a virtue that has everything to do with good intentions and what Weber called *Gesinnungsethik*—it does not ask us to take the consequences of our standpoint into account. Similar to what is the case with loyalty, there is probably more room for it in the private than in the public sphere, where consequences count for more. That we now and then confuse those spheres might, incidentally, explain the harsh judgments passed on politicians now and then: according to Ruth Grant, in her book *Hypocrisy and Integrity*, integrity lies within someone's reach insofar as he or she is dealing with either friends or foes, since one can be candid with both categories. That is why integrity is often listed as a military virtue: integrity lies within the reach of the soldier because he or she is almost always dealing with either friends (in the form of colleagues) or foes. But politicians have often to do with intermediate categories, compelling them to build coalitions and compromise, which requires being less than truthful now and then. Hypocrisy is therefore "is a regular feature of political life, and the general ethical problem of hypocrisy and integrity is quintessentially a political problem" (Grant 1997, 3).

When asking for integrity one should always specify that this is on the precondition that one's personal principles are good—a quite odd and unsatisfying construction. It appears that integrity as a particular form of loyalty—namely to one's own principles—is as gray a virtue as group loyalty. But on second thought the difference between integrity and honor is, in this aspect at least, not that big because with honor all depends on whether the norms of the honor group are the right ones. We have already seen that there is no contradiction in referring to the "honor of thieves." Likewise, loyalty to principle is a laudable thing insofar as that principle is a morally sound one, and that is not always the case; Wronski's loyalty to a rather eccentric honor code made him think that it was acceptable to not pay his tailor. In this aspect, honor, loyalty, and integrity differ from, for instance, wisdom, courage, justice, and respect; always good things to strive after. That brings us to what might be the main drawback of integrity: it is not clear what integrity, a second order virtue, has to offer that is not covered by more substantive, first order virtues that are desirable for what they are, such as, for instance, (moral) courage, justice, or, indeed, respect. So, yes, there is a need for something that is less dependent on the presence of a public than honor, and also more inclusive and outward looking, but integrity is not the ideal candidate to perform that role.

5

Denying Honor:
Respect and Humiliation

In the previous chapter we concluded that we need something more comprehensive than honor or loyalty, and less subjective than integrity. Justice and moral courage were mentioned, but it lies at hand to think that the third option suggested, respect, might be a more suitable candidate, not in the least because it is more in line with the topic of this book as it is clearly related to, and by most accounts a descendant of, the old notion of honor. What further speaks for respect is that, contrary to what is the case with honor, it is not a constant-sum game: to have respect for outsiders does not diminish the amount of respect left to show one's near and dear.[1] What's more, where honor, loyalty, and integrity are often seen (correctly or incorrectly) as virtues, respect lies more in the domain of duty-based ethics, which is on the whole a somewhat less self-regarding strand of thought than virtue-ethics. We already saw in the chapter on loyalty that virtue ethics is mainly about the agent and his character, and in that aspect, although we in general reserve the epithet virtuous for behavior that is socially beneficent (as, among others, Mandeville and Hume have pointed out), the main alternative to duty-based ethics is somewhat self-regarding. Aristotle's idea of virtue as excellence of character, for instance, is on the whole a lot less considerate of others than Immanuel Kant's categorical imperative, or Bentham's notion of the greatest happiness for the greatest number.[2] For Aristotle, the good life took precedence over the moral life (Nagel 1986, 195, 197). Finally, respect has a much more modern ring to it than honor and loyalty.

Kant described respect (*Achtung*) in his *The Groundwork of the Metaphysics of Morals*—partly a response to Cicero's *De Officiis* according to Sensen (2010)—as something we owe to all rational beings in their capacity of being free and autonomous, that is, of being able to follow the moral law they set to themselves. This is of course the literal meaning of the word autonomous. Such rational beings (Kant avoided the term *human* beings for them because he did not think that was the same thing) have intrinsic dignity, regardless of their social status and achievements, and they exact respect on the basis of this dignity (*The Groundwork* BA 79). In that aspect there is evidently an important difference between honor ethics and Kantian ethics: honor is a hierarchical concept (for a different view, see Welsh 2008; F. H. Stewart 1994, 132–3), while respect is a much more egalitarian one. This is only true, however, for "recognition respect," due to all persons, and not for "appraisal respect," based on conduct or character and often called esteem (see Darwall 2006, 122; see also Appiah 2010, 13, 130). Because we have dignity we are, as Kant put it, never to be treated as means only, but always, at least partly, as ends too (*The Groundwork* BA 66–7). Where loyalty, although it always has an object, is in fact depending on the preferences and likings of a subject (the one who is loyal), respect is object-generated; a person can claim respect from us regardless of our own inclinations, attachments, and tastes (Dillon 2008).

This still leaves somewhat elusive what respect actually *is*, probably also to those who insist most on getting it. Yet, to make the argument that respect is what we are looking for, and that a lack of respect for others, something that can amount to humiliation, is to be avoided, it is necessary to know what concepts such as respect, self-respect, dignity, and, especially, humiliation stand for. Not surprisingly, establishing this will to a certain extent turn out to be a reengagement with some of the terms encountered in earlier chapters.

Respect, Dignity, and Humiliation

If we say that someone possesses the virtue of honor, or is a man or woman of honor, we usually mean that he or she behaves honorably, and claims his or her due share of honor for it (this latter aspect is what Aristotle described under magnanimity and ambition). Although Appiah argues that the heart of the psychology of honor consists of the receiving *and* giving of respect (2010, p. xix), we normally do not mean that such a person is particularly good in honoring others. Honor is about getting recognition from one's peers (and is in that sense intertwined with group loyalty) and by definition exclusive—the honor group can be large, and perhaps even include a whole nation, but it cannot include mankind since it then would lose its meaning. Respect is different: although those who demand respect the loudest might see it differently, respect is not about claiming respect for oneself, but about having respect for others who do not necessarily belong to one's own group. Having an attitude of respect is consequently much more inclusive than having a sense of honor: it is about having respect for insiders and outsiders alike. Respect, first of all, sets important limits on what we can and, much more so, cannot do to others; respect is often negatively formulated, and as a rule implies that a person should not be discriminated, abused, harassed, and so on—the things that many organizational codes of conduct forbid, although too often solely with regard to colleagues. Secondly, more positively phrased, respect signifies giving proper attention to someone, and seeing him or her for what he or she is, as opposed to a disrespectful attitude of indifference or even neglect (Dillon 2008). The sequence here is not coincidental: although certainly not more laudable, one could say that the first meaning of respect is the most important as it sets a minimum standard.

The respect we owe to ourselves is self-respect, and today many seem to agree with Rawls that this is "perhaps the most important primary good" (*A Theory of Justice* §67; see also Margalit 1996, 124; Dillon 2008). In the introduction we noted that honor concerns both the value that someone allocates to himself and the value others place on him (Cooley 1922, 238), and we see this duality reappear in Rawls' definition of self-respect as something that "first of all includes a person's sense of his own value," but is also based on "finding our own person and deeds appreciated and confirmed by others who are likewise esteemed and their association enjoyed" (*A Theory of Justice* §67; see also Margalit 1996, 124). Stressing the latter element, Joseph Raz writes, somewhat similar to the way in which Rawls tried to secure self-respect for everyone by (among other things) limiting the role of shame (see Chapter 2), that "self-respect requires the absence of shame (. . .). The self-respect of those who are ashamed of their nationality, gender, sexual preference, or race, for example, is damaged" (1995, 24). Self-respect is in that aspect somewhat similar to honor, as both our self-respect and our honor partly depend on how others value us. But self-respect is not the same as self-esteem, a ranking concept based on how people see their own achievements (Margalit 1996, 44–8).

Dignity, an etymological descendant of the Latin *dignitas* and according to Kant the basis for our claim to respect, replaced honor in its role of status in a hierarchically ordered society (Taylor 1994, 27; Berger 1984, 151). It is telling that when Cicero wrote about *dignitas*, or social honor, the emphasis was on someone's own dignity, and one's duty to realize it fully, while recent views on dignity underline the dignity of others, and see it as a basis for rights (Sensen 2010). This is in line with the difference between honor as something one claims from others, and respect as something one has for others. As we have already noted in a previous chapter, dignity, akin to the difference between self-respect and self-esteem, is also different from *dignitas* (something not everyone shares in and meaningless when evenly distributed) in the important aspect that it is inclusive and lacks degrees. According to Rawls, for instance, "men have equal dignity," and although this does not imply that "their activities and accomplishments are of equal excellence" (*Theory* §50), there is no contradiction here because "criteria of excellence" lose their validity outside the narrow traditions they stem from (*Theory* §50). Margalit writes that from a present-day perspective *dignitas* is morally less relevant than dignity because of its hierarchical character (1996, 42, 43, 51). Remember that it was out of a concern for their *dignitas* that Coriolanus, Catiline, and Caesar jeopardized the Roman republic. Although dignity, just like honor, can be a ground for action (Welsh 2008, 200), for instance as a driver of "the global movement for human rights" (Appiah 2010, 195), it as a rule will not lead to the kind of exploits of which the sole aim is personal aggrandizement. Emphasizing its egalitarian character, Peter Berger writes that dignity, contrary to *dignitas*, "relates to the intrinsic humanity divested of all socially imposed roles or norms. It pertains to the self as such, to the individual regardless of his position in society" (1984, 153).

Berger points also to another aspect of dignity here, one which does not so much refer to our intrinsic value, but has everything to do with dignity being the descendant of *dignitas*: like honor, dignity bridges self and society, and honor and dignity equally "require a deliberate effort of the will for their maintenance—one must strive for them, often against the malevolent opposition of others—thus honour and dignity become goals of moral enterprise" (Berger 1984, 153). This aspect of dignity is somewhat less egalitarian, and seems to be the thing we refer to when we say that someone behaves with "great dignity." Dignity is in that case the external aspect of the self-respect we feel for ourselves as human beings (Margalit 1996, 51–2). Even though it is something external, people value this side of dignity too, and consider a breach of it humiliating. With reason, because dignity, as the external aspect of self-respect, "is not a show: it is not pretending to have self-respect, but the demonstration of it" (Margalit 1996, 53).

Given that both self-respect and dignity are partly (though not exclusively) externally determined, one could say that honor is an element of self-respect as a form of personal honor, and of dignity as the classless descendant of social honor. Especially this external aspect is important in here, as it is the dependence of self-respect and dignity on the opinions of others that makes people prone to humiliation. Some characters of fiction spring to mind, from Achilles to the protagonist of Stendhal's *The Red and the Black*, Julien Sorel. And, not to forget, Jim from Conrad's *Lord Jim*. Narrator Marlow describes Jim after a—perceived—insult:

> His ears became intensely crimson, and even the clear blue of his eyes was darkened many shades by the rush of blood to his head. His lips pouted a little, trembling as though he had been on the point of bursting into tears. I perceived he was incapable of pronouncing a word from the excess of his humiliation (Chapter 6).

Jim's reaction to feeling humiliated—blushing—points to the close relationship between humiliation and shame. You cannot humiliate someone who is immune to feelings of honor and shame—a state of mind some Cynics and Christian hermits strived for.

Humiliation can then be defined as the injury of someone's self-respect or dignity (either as "intrinsic humanity" or the external aspect of self-respect). This definition comes, as much more in this section, from Avishai Margalit's *The Decent Society* (1996, 9, 51), written with the idea that honor and humiliation should be central in political thought because they are so in people's lives (1996, p. ix). Although clearly more related to hierarchical notions such as honor and shame than to more egalitarian notions such as conscience and guilt, humiliation itself is as a rule (though not always) about the social goods we are all equally entitled to in our quality of human beings, such as self-respect and dignity, and thus not so much about the hierarchical notions of self-esteem or *dignitas*. It is, for instance, on the basis of the distinction between *dignitas* and dignity that Margalit distinguishes mere insult from humiliation: the former "denotes injury to one's social honor," whereas the latter "injures one's sense of intrinsic value" (1996, 119–20). Humiliation often consists of rejecting a person from the human common wealth, for instance by ignoring him or her, or treating him or her as subhuman (1996, 100–12).

Margalit also makes a distinction between humiliation in a normative and a psychological sense that is, although problematic, relevant for

Feeling humiliated
vs.
Being
humiliated

the remainder of this chapter: who is humiliated in a psychological sense feels humiliated, who is humiliated in a normative sense has a sound reason to feel humiliated, and although not all authors differentiate between these two meanings, they do not always apply to the same case (1996, 9)—we have just seen that Jim felt humiliated when he mistakenly thought that he had overheard Marlow speaking ill about him. Although Margalit writes about humiliation within a society, there is, as we will see, reason to think that this distinction is also valid on an international level. In addition, Margalit stresses that not only persons but also conditions can humiliate, and he mentions colonialism and Arabs working in the Israeli-occupied territories as examples (1996, 101–2, 150). But even if conditions can humiliate, humiliation is in the end always a result of human actions or inactions. Humiliation can occur without someone having intent to humiliate, though—humiliating someone by not seeing him or her is an example of that (Margalit 1996, 9). The socially invisible central character of Ellison's *Invisible Man*, for instance, was "defined" by such "past humiliations" of being overlooked; they *were* him (Chapter 23).

The type of humiliation Margalit writes about—treating others as subhuman—is humiliation "with a big **H**," to be distinguished from humiliation "with a small **h**." It is William Ian Miller who makes this distinction, and he defines humiliation with a small **h** as the deflation of pretension, and "the consequence of trying to live up to what we have no right to" (1993, 145; see also 133, 137)—Conrad's Jim and Stendhal's Julien Sorel might be examples of that. Humiliation with a big **H** is also the deflation of pretension, but in that case "the claim of the torturer, the concentration camp guard, the ideologies of ethnic, racial and religious genocide, is that the humanity of their victims is a pretense" (Miller 1993, 165). Clearly, those humiliated with a big **H** have more reason to complain than those humiliated with a small **h**, if only because a lack of respect for the life of the humiliated typically accompanies the former—a point we will briefly take up later. This distinction between two forms of humiliation nuances the aforementioned idea that humiliation in generally relates to dignity, and not to *dignitas*. Humiliation with a small **h** has in fact everything to do with breeches of someone's status, or social honor (which resembles the Roman notion of *dignitas*), while humiliation with a big **H** involves the morally more important notion of human dignity.[3]

Shades of humiliation

In line with his own distinction between normative and psychological humiliation, Margalit writes about humiliation in pluralistic societies that a "vulnerable group with a history of humiliations and suspicion of its surroundings, especially suspicion of the dominant culture, is liable to interpret any criticism as humiliation" (1996, 181), while Miller points out that people with a low status in society tend to feel humiliated more often than that they actually have reason to (1993, 144). This also holds true on a global scale: today some citizens of non-Western societies might feel they are the lower-status people Miller refers to. An example can illustrate how this economy of respect works out in practice.

Honor, Respect, and Humiliation as Motivational Factors

Some authors who claim that we tend to overlook that honor can be a motive for political violence think that Western cultural and economic hegemony, foreign policies in general and the way the West deals with the Israeli-Palestinian conflict in particular, but also insensitivity to migrants at home and military presence abroad, have produced a sense of humiliation that was a root cause of the terrorist attacks of the previous decade in New York, Bali, London, Casablanca, and Madrid. These observers think that honor and shame, supposedly waning in the West, are still important in many non-Western societies. The reverse image of the consensus that guilt replaced shame in Western societies is the equally widely held view that, for instance, the Arab world is still a shame culture—that, too, appears to be beyond dispute these days (see for instance Bowman 2006, 15–39; F. H. Stewart 1994, 103).[4] Interestingly, some Islamists underwrite such somewhat general observations about the difference between the West and the rest, especially the one that "the most basic sense of honor" has disappeared in the West, its permissiveness in their view being a clear sign of this (Buruma and Margalit 2004, 134). Different from some Western authors, they do not see this demise of honor as a moral improvement.

The idea of a feminine West is widespread. Ian Buruma and Avishai Margalit point out in their book on stereotype views of the Western world (titled *Occidentalism*) that the suggestion that the West lacks a sense of honor and community is part of a strand of thought that goes back a long way and has many different manifestations (2004). Some past examples of occidentalism are the Japanese views of the West during World War II, and Romantic criticisms (such as that of Rousseau) of modern society in eighteenth-century Europe.[5] The common denominator is the view that calculative, scientific thinking, mercantilism, and an absence of honor and community, characterize the West. The *Gemeinschaft* gave way to the *Gesellschaft*, in the words of the nineteenth-century sociologist Ferdinand Tönnies (1955). Western culture is so individualistic that it has lost its willingness to make sacrifices (Lewis 2003, 17), and references to earlier "shameful" retreats by Western militaries from Vietnam, the Lebanon, and Somalia have to substantiate the image of a weakened West (Lewis 2003, 125). Such views perhaps explain why many suicide attacks are aimed at democracies: terrorists see them as soft (Pape 2005, 39, 44-5). There might even be a shaming element in a suicide attack that presents "a challenge to a spectator's own lack of faith or inaction" (Burke 2004a, 35).[6] This is in line with the Western fear that the willingness to accept and inflict casualties for political or religious goals is today relatively high in non-Western societies with young populations and dim prospects for the ambitious (see for instance Huntington 1996, 116–21; Kaplan 2002), and some see this as just as problematic for the West as its own reluctance to bring sacrifices (and inflict casualties) in defense of its interests (see for instance Bowman 2006; Nafziger and Walton 2003, 260; Pape 2005, 44).

But this negative view of the West does not explain the terrorist attacks we have witnessed in the previous decade. For an explanation, we should look at the other side of honor: sensitivity to honor and shame makes people vulnerable to humiliation. This is about what Bowman calls "reflexive honor": the need to get back, if only because not doing so is humiliating in itself (2006, 6; see also F. H. Stewart 1994, 64–71). Although Locke felt that a gentleman should be willing to let a small insult go unpunished (Tarcov 1984, 140–1), it might be remembered that Mandeville, although he deemed honor a chimera, did not think he would react very philosophically if someone would spit in his face. Reflexive honor can be distinguished from cultural honor, to be found in "the traditions, stories and habits of thought of a particular society" about, for instance, the proper use of violence (Bowman 2006, 6), or sex. Also testifying to the close tie between honor and humiliation (and for that reason quoted here instead of in an earlier chapter) is that Miller defines honor, in his book on humiliation, as

> the keen sensitivity to the experience of humiliation and shame, sensitivity manifested by the desire to be envied by others and the propensity to envy the successes of others. To simplify greatly, honor is that disposition which makes one act to shame others who have shamed oneself, to humiliate others who have humiliated oneself. The honorable person is one whose self-esteem and

social standing is intimately dependent on the esteem or envy he
or she actually elicits in others (1993, 84).

Miller's definition points again to the worrying fact that a strong sense
of honor often comes with a tendency to do whatever is necessary to even
the score, in the hope that revenge will lift some of the dishonor felt. If
such views are at least partly accurate, we should take honor and humiliation serious as motivational factors.

As said, many already do see honor and humiliation as the key to
understanding the psychological mechanisms behind terrorism. But although one might think that "learning what motivates enemies does not
mean sympathising with them," and ask potential critics "to stop confusing justification with explanation" (Burke 2005a; see also Saurette
2006, 518–19), attempts to understand terrorism form a source of confusion. Understanding is an ambiguous term that can mean a lot of things,
ranging from looking for explanations for an act, or excusing that act,
to even justifying it, and these different meanings are not always easy
to tell apart. While it is clear what explaining means, that is, looking
for causes, the difference between excusing and justifying can be more
elusive. An excusable act is wrong, killing an innocent civilian for instance, but is in view of the circumstances only considered blameworthy
to a limited extent, for example because the death of that innocent civilian was necessary to rescue many others.[7] Justified deeds form a more
uncomplicated category: an act is justified if it is not wrong in the first
place, implying that there is no blame to be attributed to begin with.
This is for example the case when someone kills his or her attacker (or
when a state wages war) in self-defense. Interestingly, these distinctions
surface in discussions on terrorism and torture (of planners of terrorist
attacks, for instance) alike.

The idea that there is a link between humiliation and terrorism, a
thought which Western observers hold as an explanation and the perpetrators of terrorism as a justification, is fraught with problems—the
justifying variety of course much more so than the explaining variety.
That these problems are less obvious in the case of the explaining variety
means that this variety asks for some more "systematic critique" than the
justifying one (Walzer 2004, 52). As Walzer sees it, "the real cause of
terrorism is the decision to launch a terrorist campaign" (2004, 62; see
for a similar view Elshtain 2007). Yet, although some authors do blame
U.S. foreign policies (see for instance Stern 2004a; Challans 2007, 182),
we will see below that in reality most authors clearly try to stay aloof

from excusing terrorism, looking only for causes in an attempt to explain it.[8] But explaining violence can by itself look rather similar to implicitly excusing violence (see also Pinker 2011, 689). In the case of terrorism looking for causes might seem to imply that terrorists have no free will, absolving them somewhat from their responsibility; it suggests that part of the responsibility for the recent terrorist attacks aimed at the West lies with the West itself (see also Bowman 2006, 232).

That brings us on some rather slippery ground, as it is not at all clear whether most terrorists actually act out of feelings of humiliation. Apart from the fact that much of the evidence is anecdotal, it is also somewhat naive to believe terrorists on their word when they say that they are motivated by humiliation. Perhaps some terrorists claim to feel humiliated because that is what they have heard and read in the media, providing them with a ground that sounds remotely legitimate. In reality, more profane (though sometimes related) reasons, such as envy, personal failure, or the wish for self-glorification, might well play a role, of course (see also Borowitz 2005; Goldhagen 2007). Poverty and lack of opportunity, on the other hand, do not seem to be important factors; somewhat disturbingly, most perpetrators of the attacks of recent years were of well-educated, middle class backgrounds, and some had lived in Western societies for quite some time.

Humiliation on the Global Level

At a time that many people see honor as something obsolete, one might expect that injured honor is easily overlooked as a potential cause of terrorism; we already noted that some authors claim that humiliation is an underrated factor in international relations. Thomas Friedman, for instance, writes that if he has "learned one thing covering world affairs, it's this: The single most underappreciated force in international relations is humiliation" (2003; see for somewhat similar remarks Bowman 2006, 22; Saurette 2006, 496).

In reality, quite a number of authors who have been looking for "a root cause" behind the terrorist attacks of recent years have put forward the view that humiliation plays an important role here. In fact, Islam historian Bernard Lewis wrote already in 1990 that the rejection of the West by many Muslims is partly "due to a feeling of humiliation—a growing awareness, among the heirs of an old, proud, and long dominant civilization, of having been overtaken, overborne, and overwhelmed by those whom they regarded as their inferiors" (1990). Since then, many

authors have espoused similar views. The line of thought that some terrorists feel that their culture is superior to Western individualism, yet at
the same time fear that in today's world their way of life is threatened
and that their honor is at stake, has by now developed into a broadly
shared point of view. In addition to Friedman himself and Bernard
Lewis, many others have dwelled with different amounts of empathy
(although always staying clear of excusing, let alone justifying) on this
relationship between humiliation and violence. Among them are Samuel
Huntington (in *The Clash of Civilizations*), Dominique Moïsi (*The Clash
of Emotions*), Ian Buruma and Avishai Margalit (in their *Occidentalism*),
Jason Burke (best known for his book *Al Qaeda*), and, probably most
famously, Jessica Stern, and together they have turned the idea that such
a relationship exists into something close to accepted knowledge.

Huntington, for instance, thinks that Islam is a civilization whose
people "are convinced of the superiority of their culture and are obsessed
with the inferiority of their power" (1996, 217). They have this sense of
superiority, together with a conviction of universality and a desire to
expand, in common with the West (1996, 217–18). But where the West,
despite its diminishing role in the world, can still maintain this feeling of
superiority (Huntington 1996, 218), in Muslim countries, according to
some authors lagging behind in more than one respect (see for instance
Lewis 2003, 87–92; Hanson 2002, 270; see also Moïsi 2007, 10), "the
modern successes of Christian empires were felt as an intolerable humiliation" (Buruma and Margalit 2004, 40). As a result, writes Huntington,
many in the Islamic world think that Western culture—seen as inferior,
morally degenerate and, consequently, weak, but at the same time also as
seductive—threatens their way of life (1996, 213).

Jason Burke, writing with somewhat more nuance (and empathy)
than Huntington and focusing more explicitly on the relationship between humiliation and the rise of radicalism, holds that the motives
that lie beneath the rise of Muslim radicalism and Islamist terrorism
are more political than religious (2004a, 24–6; see also Bowman 2006,
22; Pape 2005, 16–17; Stern 2004b, 6). And although "individuals and
groups turn to terrorism for a variety of reasons, some of which, though
not all, may be shared by others" (2004a, 24), Burke thinks that humiliation is among the most important causes. In his view, "the mother lode
of resentment underlying the appeal of radical Islam" is

the profound sense of humiliation, disenfranchisement and
emasculation felt by hundreds of millions of young Muslim men

faced with the apparent military, political and, increasingly, cultural dominance of the West. This is increased by a collective memory of the past glories of Islamic civilization (2004b).

Elsewhere, Burke states that the

perception that a belligerent West is set on the humiliation, division and eventual conquest of the Islamic world is at the root of Muslim violence. The militants believe they are fighting a last-ditch battle for the survival of their society, culture, religion and way of life (2004c).

Like Burke, terrorism specialist Jessica Stern thinks that "the reasons that people become terrorists are as varied as the reasons that others choose their professions: market conditions, social networks, education, individual preferences" (2010). Yet, also like Burke, Stern holds that humiliation is a reason many terrorists share. Looking back on the interviews she conducted for her book *Terror in the Name of God: Why Religious Militants Kill*, Stern writes that, although she "came to despair of identifying a single root cause of terrorism" as those "interviewed cite many reasons for choosing a life of holy war," in the end "the variable that came up most frequently was not poverty or human-rights abuses, but perceived humiliation. Humiliation emerged at every level of the terrorist groups I studied—leaders and followers" (2003). Stern's research was not limited to Islamic terrorism, and that suggests that humiliation can be a motive behind non-Islamic terrorism as well.

Stern further found that the "purpose of terrorist violence, according to its advocates, is to restore dignity. Its target audience is not necessarily the victims and their sympathizers but the perpetrators and their sympathizers" (2004a). Elsewhere, Stern warns that "prominent Islamists such as Sayyid Qutb and Ayman Zawahiri, the intellectual leaders of the Muslim Brotherhood and of Al Qaeda, respectively, argue that violence is a way to cure Muslim youth of the pernicious effects of centuries of humiliation at the hands of the West" (2004b, 285). The intellectual backers of terrorism she refers to here are not so much referring to humiliation as a cause to explain or excuse terrorism, but try to justify terrorism, and present humiliation as a valid reason.[9] It is at this juncture that the explainers and the justifiers part company. Although the justifiers, underwriting the popular thesis that humiliation causes terrorism, follow roughly the same line of reasoning as the explainers,

they go considerably further than the latter when they claim that violence "restores the dignity of humiliated youth" (Stern 2003). Al Qaeda's
second man Ayman al-Zawahiri, for instance, claimed that the New
World Order is humiliating to Muslims (Stern 2004b, p. xviii; see also
Stern 2004c). Stern thinks that al-Zawahiri believes that fighting the
new world order "frees the oppressed youth from his inferiority complex,
despair and inaction, making him fearless and restoring his self-respect"
(Stern 2004d). As Stern sums up this view:

> The "New World Order" is a source of humiliation for Muslims.
> And for the youth of Islam, it is better to carry arms and de-
> fend their religion with pride and dignity than to submit to this
> humiliation. Part of the mission of jihad is to restore Muslims'
> pride in the face of humiliation (2003).

Stern states in the final chapter of her book on terrorism that she considers humiliation an "important risk factor" for the future (2004b).

But even if injured honor plays a role in the motivation of some terrorists, this of course does not justify terrorism, just like injured family
honor is not a legitimate reason for honor killings, no matter how important the family honor is to the murderer. According to Walzer, insults
"are not occasions for war, any more than they are (these days) occasions
for duels" (1992, 81). Walzer refers to states here, but there is no compelling reason why terrorists should have more leeway in this. Margalit,
although writing on humiliation, depicts physical cruelty as the greater
evil (1996, 148), and it is this evil terrorists have opted for. There are,
writes Walzer, some "obvious and crippling questions" (1992, 205) for
who nonetheless thinks that violence is a justified means of restoring
dignity. The therapeutic violence al-Zawahiri proposed somewhat reminds of Sartre's acceptance of violence as a last resort for young Alge-
rians (2001). Addressing Sartre's remark, made in 1961 in defense of the
Algerian revolt against French rule, that "to shoot down a European is
to kill two birds with one stone, to destroy an oppressor and the man he
oppresses at the same time: there remain a dead man, and a free man"
(Sartre 2001, 148), Walzer wondered if a one-to-one relationship—one
European for one Algerian—is necessary. In that case, there might not
be enough Europeans (1992, 205).

Also, the fact that some terrorists feel humiliated does not mean that
they also have much of a *reason* to feel that way. Not all humiliation they
might feel amounts to normative humiliation (in Margalit's terms), or

humiliation with a big **H** (Miller's terms), for instance. Although some of today's terrorists might think that they are treated as sub-human, not being able to live up to the pretension of being a superior civilization perhaps explains a part of the frustration underlying Islamist terrorism. The founder of the Kashmiri militant group Muslim Janbaz Force had started the movement because "Muslims have been overpowered by the West. Our ego hurts. We are not able to live up to our own standards for ourselves" (Stern 2004a).[10] This deflation of pretension is evidently humiliation with a small **h**, and resembles a breach of someone's *dignitas* in older times. It touches more on someone's self-esteem than on his or her self-respect. Notwithstanding these arguments there will always be a few who feel they are deeply humiliated, and, although humiliation does not legitimatize terrorism, are not willing to react in a non-violent way. Revenge—reflexive honor in Bowman's terms (2006, 6)—is often the motivation (Moïsi 2007, 10).[11]

The above is therefore of more than just theoretical interest. Of course, an easy conclusion would be that the disrespect that potential terrorists feel is not really the problem of the West, especially since it is more perceived than actual (i.e., psychological rather than normative, to use Margalit's terms again), and if actual more often unintentional than intentional, and does not justify terrorism nor excuse it in any case. Yet cases such as the Danish cartoon crisis that sparked off after the newspaper *Jyllands-Posten* published twelve cartoons critical of Mohammed in September 2005 illustrate how a perceived lack of respect can have real consequences for, for instance, one's interests abroad.[12] A more recent example is the Quran burning in 2011 in Florida, leading to the killing of UN staff in Afghanistan, and the anti-Islam film *Innocence of Muslims*, which resulted in the killing of the U.S. ambassador to Libya, Christopher Stevens. Although seldom admitting to it, it stands to reason that governments now and then base their foreign and domestic policies on the assumption that (perceived) humiliation can cause violence. The question is whether that would be a wise policy.

The distinction between humiliation with a small **h** and with a big **H** cannot always clarify things in cases like these, as the character, extent, and genuineness of the humiliation felt as a result of, for instance, cartoons or films is difficult to assess from where a third-person is standing. For similar reasons, Margalit's distinction between normative and psychological humiliation is probably not of much more use here, although it is clear that those who take offence at a film or cartoon are not personally insulted. It is also quite possible to avoid being confronted with a film or cartoon while, on the other hand, the authors of these works often do aim at contributing to an ongoing societal debate. Yielding to everyone who feels offended by a drawing seems a bad idea, since there is probably no end to that.[13]

But sometimes it is not possible for the person who feels humiliated to just look away, for instance because this feeling is the result of foreign policies or, more specifically, Western military presence in Arabic countries, which bin Laden and his likes time and again labeled as part of a crusade. Regarding the question whether the West should intervene in the affairs of other nations, one could argue that politicians should at least take into consideration that some will see such an intervention as humiliating. Especially if the aim of the intervention is actually to fight terrorism; Burke writes that

> we need to recognise that doing things that enrage millions, even if we feel that anger is wrong-headed and misdirected, will make us more of a target. Before the invasion of Iraq the UK was fairly low down the target list for the militants (2005a).

Many seem to share that view. The claim that Western militaries fought terrorism in Iraq and Afghanistan so that they did not have to fight it at home lacked credibility in the eyes of many people, who probably did not think that plotters of terrorist attacks need Afghan desert for their scheming. Terrorists did not plan the September 11 attacks "in training camps in Afghanistan but, rather, in apartments in Germany, hotel rooms in Spain and flight schools in the United States" (Pillar 2009).

On the other hand, giving in to the demands of political Islamists seems a dead end street because "no conceivable concessions, short of acquiescence to their scheme of expunging Western influence from the Islamic world and bringing Taliban-like regimes to power throughout it, can appease bin Laden, his followers, and his allies" (Bergen and Lind 2007). Also, our double standards (already noted in the chapter on loyalty) in tolerating regimes with bad human rights records, such as the regimes of Saudi Arabia, Syria, Sudan, Algeria, and, until recently, Afghanistan, Iraq, and Libya, might suggest that we consider the peoples those regimes repress to have "neither concern nor capacity for human decency" (Lewis 2003, 80), and that is perhaps just as humiliating as invading a country. This perception of being seen as subhuman might amount to humiliation with a big **H**, and also clearly meets Margalit's definition of humiliation as rejecting people "as beings capable of freedom, since it is freedom that makes them humans rather than things" (1996, 119).

Humiliation on the Local Level

Most of those who bring up humiliation to justify the therapeutic violence that should restore their dignity are at worst humiliated in an indirect way, being treated, or considering themselves being treated, *as a group* as second-class, by something as abstract as the West. This is the humiliation at the level of civilizations that in recent years was central in much of the argumentation of the explainers of terrorism. To many this humiliation on an international level will seem somewhat abstract, and rather hard to relate to.

But there are also very direct forms of humiliation that are consequently harder to ignore than the humiliation at the global level that both the backers (such as bin Laden and al-Zawahiri) and explainers of terrorism mention, and that would bring anyone to despair, regardless of whether one belongs to a shame culture or not. A case in point is the young Palestinian who has to undergo some indignities at an Israeli checkpoint before being allowed through. John Elster has noted that "most writers on the Palestinian suicide bombers emphasize the intense resentment caused by the daily humiliations that occur in interaction with the Israeli forces" (2005, 245). One of these writers is Stern, who wrote that "one need not spend many days in Gaza before understanding that fear and humiliation, constants of daily life there, play at least some role in certain Palestinians' decisions to become martyr-murderers" (2010; see also Moghadam 2003, 73; Held 2008, 26; Buruma and Margalit 2004, 138). Writing about the "real or perceived national humiliation by Israeli policies," Stern points out that even "repeated, small humiliations" can "add up to a feeling of nearly unbearable despair and frustration, and a willingness on the part of some to do anything—even commit atrocities—in the belief that attacking the oppressor will restore their sense of dignity" (2004b, 62).[14] As Western military personnel have in recent years been manning checkpoints and searching houses in faraway countries, it has to be feared that for instance some Iraqis and Afghanis are now also familiar to with such small humiliations.

Perhaps, such offensive behavior is often unintended (see also Fontan 2006). For example, in Iraq some felt humiliated because allied troops had to do what the Iraqis themselves could not: doing away with the Saddam Hussein regime (see also T. L. Friedman 2003). As one Iraqi

Shiite put it: "The greatest humiliation of all was to see foreigners topple Saddam, not because we loved him, but because we could not do it ourselves" (Fontan 2010, 2), while an Iraqi insurgent told *The Observer* that "there is no greater shame than to see your country occupied" (Burke 2004d). As Sennett explains his book *Respect* (2003), dependency erodes self-respect.[15]

Some instances of unintended humiliation by occupying forces in their dealings with the local population are perhaps a result of having insufficient knowledge of local sensitivities, and of "a lack of cultural relativity in their occupation 'technique'" (Fontan 2006, 219).[16] These are, what Thomas Friedman calls, "the daily slights and miscommunications that come with any occupation" (2003). Respect is to some extent a matter of manners and etiquette, though, and these can be learned (see also Darwall 2006, 143), at least to some degree—although many will remain at a loss about what to say to Iraqis who take offense at a female police officer directing traffic (Fontan 2006, 219).

[margin handwritten note: Calls for cultural training]

In other instances, for example when interrogating prisoners in Iraq, it has been a deliberate tactic, based on the handbook assumption (also held by those who explain terrorism by referring to humiliation) that Arab culture is a shame culture, making use of supposed taboos on dogs, nudity, and homosexuality (see also Saurette 2006, 509). That handbook used might very well have been Raphael Patai's infamous *The Arab Mind*, writes Seymour Hersh:

> The notion that Arabs are particularly vulnerable to sexual humiliation became a talking point among pro-war Washington conservatives in the months before the March 2003 invasion of Iraq. One book that was frequently cited was 'The Arab Mind,' a study of Arab culture and psychology, first published in 1973, by Raphael Patai, a cultural anthropologist (. . .). The Patai book, an academic told me, was 'the bible of the neocons on Arab behavior.' In their discussions, he said, two themes emerged— 'one, that Arabs only understand force and, two, that the biggest weakness of Arabs is shame and humiliation' (2004).

In Abu Ghraib Prison, Guantanamo Bay Detention Camp, and other facilities, detainees have been humiliated as part of a policy to "soften up" prisoners before investigation. As it is widely known (and certainly within the military) that information extracted from prisoners by using harsh interview techniques is often unreliable (see also Shue 2006; Miles

2006, 7–13),[17] one wonders whether the ill treatment of prisoners is intended to serve any real purpose to begin with. The ticking time bomb that is often called upon in this context probably only exists in the minds of those who hold that inhumane treatment is on occasion excusable, or even justified (see also Shue 2006). Since "history does not present us with a government that used torture selectively and judiciously" (Shue 2006, 234), it is a good thing that international law forbids torture categorically (see also Fiala 2005). Under certain circumstances the sheer possession of power is by itself enough to induce people to misuse it.

Stern wrote in an essay published seven months after the invasion of Iraq that "the word humiliation, alas, is now coming up in Iraq as well" (2003). Three years later she described how incidents such as in Abu Ghraib had made terrorist groups even stronger (2006a), while "interrogation techniques intended to extract information by humiliating the enemy help our enemies 'prove' that humiliating Muslims is our goal" (2006b). Stern holds that "events in Iraq have shown that a war cannot be prosecuted against terrorists without giving some thought to what motivates new recruits to the terror cause" (2004d), and in her opinion humiliation is the biggest factor in it. Posing the question "why a growing majority of Iraqis has chosen to resort to violence in order to bring an end to the occupation of Iraq," political scientist Victoria Fontan points to humiliation by occupying troops as an important catalyst for the growth of the insurgency (2006, 218–20).

A report of the bipartisan U.S. Senate Armed Services Committee that states that the harsh treatment of prisoners "increases resistance to cooperation, and creates new enemies" underlines that view (U.S. Senate Committee on Armed Services 2008, p. xii). Navy General Counsel Alberto Mora told the committee that "there are serving U.S. flag-rank officers who maintain that the first and second identifiable causes of U.S. combat deaths in Iraq—as judged by their effectiveness in recruiting insurgent fighters into combat—are, respectively the symbols of Abu Ghraib and Guantanamo" (U.S. Senate Committee on Armed Services 2008, p. xii). Aside from human rights violated, the gains of degrading prisoners clearly do not outweigh the losses.

The committee points out that incidents such as in Abu Ghraib are not necessarily the result of moral flaws at the individual level; the larger organization and the political leadership can contribute to an ethical climate that makes disrespectful behavior more likely to occur. Many in Abu Ghraib believed that humiliating prisoners was permitted, among other things because Secretary of Defense Rumsfeld's decision in

December 2002 to allow the use of aggressive interrogation techniques at Guantanamo Bay (such as the removal of clothing and the use of fear of dogs) and President Bush's statement that the Third Geneva Convention did not apply to Al Qaeda and Taliban detainees. The detainee abuse that harmed the cause of the West in Iraq so much was therefore not, as some have maintained, a matter of "a few bad apples" acting on their own (U.S. Senate Committee on Armed Services 2008, p. xii and xxiv). In the case of Abu Ghraib, "the military and civilian chain of command had built a 'bad barrel' in which a bunch of good soldiers became transformed into 'bad apples'" (Zimbardo 2007, p. x).

If true, this would mean that the influence of a virtuous disposition is often fairly limited, possibly in particular when needed most.[18] This is basically the view Marlow, and the French third lieutenant with whom he discussed the case of Jim, take regarding the latter: although Jim might have had the best disposition, every possible inducement to courage, and the lieutenant mentions "the eye of others" here, had been lacking (Chapter 13). We have seen throughout this book that honor can motivate to do the right thing, and that is also true in war (see also Demetriou 2013).[19] But insofar as honor plays a role in cases like Abu Ghraib, it is mainly a negative one. According to Paul Robinson, "in so far as honour is a relative good, the easiest way to go up is to push others down. Honour can thus encourage people to humiliate those over whom they acquire power" (2009, 264). Elsewhere, Robinson writes that "nonsoldiers lie outside the military honour group; as such they are felt to deserve no respect" (2007b). Although that might be put somewhat polemically, a survey conducted by the U.S. military found that only 47 percent of the American soldiers and 38 percent of the marines in Iraq were of the opinion that non-combatants should be treated with dignity and respect (Mental Health Advisory Team 2006).[20]

Social psychologists point out that people with high ethical standards often find ways to justify their unethical behavior, thus sparing themselves the guilt and shame that normally follows not living up to one's own standards (Bandura 1999, 194).[21] Especially dehumanization, a notion that is fairly similar to humiliation and consists of purposely disrespecting people, can open the door to more serious forms of unethical conduct (see for instance Bandura 1999, 200; Moller and Deci 2010, 43–4; see also Slim 2007, 218). For instance, an unpublished U.S. Army general's report on Haditha found that statements of their chain of command "had the potential to desensitize the Marines to concern for the Iraqi populace and portray them all as the enemy even if they are noncombatants" (Bargewell 2007).[22] According to the same social psychologists the remedy lies in humanization, a not so clearly defined concept that, not surprisingly, seems to be the opposite of humiliation, and includes the affirmation of common humanity, instead of distancing oneself "from others or divesting them from human qualities" (Bandura 1999, 202–3).[23] The famous Milgram experiments on obedience showed that it is more difficult to be cruel, or indifferent, when the other has a face (Smith and Mackie 2000, 402).

Today that face is probably not always there, as drone operators take out insurgents from a control room thousands of miles away. Some fear, and this would be in line with what we have noted in the chapter on loyalty, that killing might get a bit easier with such a distance (physical, but also psychological) between a soldier and the horrors of war (see for instance P.W. Singer 2009, 395–6; see for a different view P. Lee 2012).[24] That latter remark brings us, very briefly, from respect per se to respect for human life. Evidently, the latter, respect for something, is different from respect per se, which normally signifies the respect we show to our fellow humans, and which was central to most of the above. Nonetheless, respect for human life, although not the same thing as respect as such, does border on respect in its negative formulation (i.e., insofar as it is about what we cannot do to others), if only because one cannot plausibly claim to respect someone without respecting his right to life.[25]

Conclusion

To show someone respect is to humble oneself at least somewhat (see also Hume *Treatise* II.ii.x). As Mandeville already noted, this is not always easy. Although respect costs nothing, it is nonetheless in short supply, and this scarcity is, writes Sennett, man-made (2003, 3). Honor is a group phenomenon, something that limits respect to members of that group (see also Welsh 2008, 4, 10), and which can have a possible downside in a lack of respect for the honor and dignity of outsiders (see also Wyatt-Brown 2005, 449–50; Elias 1965). The limited way most people define their honor group, and also their loyalty to that group, which makes that they give priority to the interests of group members, sometimes reduces nonmembers to outsiders who are not entitled to equal respect.

That can have serious consequences. Norbert Elias writes in *The Established and the Outsiders* (1965) that it depends on the situation whether outsiders who are (made to feel) ashamed of who they are, resort to violence or become apathetic. But there is a real danger, thinks Elias, that groups with a reputation for trouble want to live up to that image, for instance by behaving aggressively. Although real or perceived (i.e., normative or psychological in Margalit's terms) humiliation does not even come close to being a justification for the unlawful use of violence (something insurgencies often, and terrorism always, amount to), is not an excuse, and is probably too easily invoked as an explanation, the somewhat unsatisfying conclusion to the above must be that especially blatant cases of direct humiliation do make violence more likely to occur. The question whether that is something explainable, excusable, or even justifiable, is, although interesting, also fairly academic, since it will not alter the results very much.

Two remarks to finish with. First, Huntington and others, arguing that frustration over Western dominance has contributed to the rise of the radical Islam, suggest that people in the Arabic world are for the most part still motivated by old notions such as reflexive honor and group loyalty.[26] But although many authors have referred to that old motive when trying to explain the terrorist attacks of first years of the new millennium (and the intensity of the resistance to Western military presence in Iraq and Afghanistan), it is at the same time also clear that the majority of Muslims have no sympathy for the Islamist cause, do not sympathize with the terrorists' methods, and reject their extremism (Burke 2004a, 35). It is according to Burke especially attacks like the one in Madrid in 2004, making innocent victims but with the attackers making sure not to be killed in the process, that have alienated moderate Muslims from the radical ones (2005b; see also Pinker 2011, 504). On a still more optimistic note, one could even argue that the recent uprisings in the Middle East form an indication that more modern notions such as respect and dignity inspire most people in that region. The British foreign secretary William Hague said in an interview with BBC radio that "the real nature of the Arab world is expressed in Tahrir Square, not at Ground Zero." Then again, that might be a bit *too* optimistic, and many observers fear that tribal loyalties and religious strive will prove difficult to overcome.

Second, it seems likely that if individuals sometimes act from injured honor, states will do so too, although perhaps less often than in older times (Pinker 2011, 370). Although Walzer holds that "the moral significance of [notions about the honor of states] is dubious at best" (1992, 81), Thucydides thought that honor was nonetheless one of the main reasons for states to go to war. But according to Rawls we do not have much to fear from the liberal, democratic nations as "these peoples (. . .) are not swayed by the passion for power or glory, or the intoxicating pride of ruling. These passions may move a nobility and lesser aristocracy to earn their social standing and place in the sun; yet this class, or caste rather, does not have power in a constitutional regime" (1999, 47). This is probably a too rosy view of democratic politics; in Thucydides time democratic Athens was as concerned about its reputation as oligarchic Sparta was.[27] Although politicians often profess to promote modern notions as dignity and respect, there is a growing agreement that honor and reputation are still important in the relations between states, democratic or not (see for instance O'Neill 1999; Kaplan 2002, 131–2; Wyatt-Brown 2005, 445–9; Saurette 2006, 495–522; Bowman 2006)—although here too the term itself has become slightly out-of-date.

Conclusion

Not many people today will agree with Cicero's statement that a career in politics is preferable to a career in philosophy because the former brings more fame. Our choice for a plan of life should not depend on that. In the same way, we tend to think that people are to do the right thing for its own sake, and not for the sake of keeping face. Yet, the virtues discussed in this book are all in one way or another about face and reputation. Honor itself is of course by definition about how others see us, but so is loyalty, as we mainly care about how those belonging to our own honor group see us; to be disloyal to that group is often perceived as being dishonorable. Integrity, as we have seen, is also about how we view each other, yet only in an indirect way, as it asks us *not* to be led by how others see us. Respect, last of all, is not so much about how others see us, but about how we see them. But honor has clearly been the main theme, and the aim of this book was to make the case that the old arguments for honor are still convincing. A not-so-easy undertaking, as the notion is thought to have become seriously out of date, at least outside the military and some other pockets of resistance, while the term itself has just about disappeared from our moral language. It is easy to forget how relatively novel this situation is. Honor was deemed very important in the West all through the nineteenth century, and the honor driven practice of dueling—getting a shot at revenge after being disrespected—even persisted well into the twentieth century. But especially insofar as it is seen as something that depends on the good opinion of others, honor has lost much of its appeal since then.

Yet, even if honor has lost some of its legitimacy from the seventeenth century on, from Plato to the days of Mill philosophers always

155

had at least something to say on the subject. Most of today's authors are, with some notable exceptions, silent on the topic, or limit themselves to explaining how and why it has disappeared from the scene (see also Welsh 2008, 1). In that latter case, the explanation given is often based on a one-sided interpretation of Tocqueville that holds that the notion of honor was exclusively linked to the feudal, hierarchical societies of the past. Honor, it is consequently thought, disappeared with the disappearance of social stratification; because honor rests on distinctions, the gradual departure of class distinction brought the disappearance of honor. In reality, as we have seen, Tocqueville saw a role for honor in fairly egalitarian societies too. It was only an exotic (and outmoded) conception of honor that had disappeared. But in spite of the fact that honor is still an important motivator, the moral language in which honor still had a role has given place to two somewhat contradictory idioms that describe man primarily as an economic agent and an autonomous being respectively.

Both the modern notion of moral autonomy, harking back to the Stoics, and the economic view of man, slightly resembling the Epicurean view of man as purposely misrepresented in Cicero's work, are in their undiluted form not very well suited to motivate people to do what is good, as most of us at least occasionally do. One sets its aims too high, the other too low. Our present-day understanding of ourselves follows the ideals behind that first account rather closely, and in that sense we "are all Kantians now" (Adkins 1960, 2). That probably will remain the case until we see that, to put it somewhat pompously, we not only have a Judeo-Christian heritage, but a Greco-Roman one too. In our self-understanding and our ideals of autonomy resonate notions that stem from that first legacy, such as guilt and conscience, but one could argue that to understand our actual motives we should also take notions such as honor and shame, belonging to the second, older heritage, into account (see also Kinneging 1994, Kaplan 2002, 108–9; Bowman 2006). Although we use the word honor less frequently than our forebears did, the notion itself is in all likelihood still important in the form of the need for dignity, status, recognition, and, not to forget, respect.

While some of these notions have drawn considerable attention over the last few decades, the many publications on recognition, multiculturalism, and identity that resulted from this attention have in general not so much to say on honor, face, and reputation as motivators, both for the good and the bad. But if only the phrases have changed but the thing itself still exists, this is very likely at the cost of having somewhat lost sight on what makes human beings tick. Clearly, this is a loss; although many political and moral philosophers have strong ideas about how people ought to behave, a moral or political theory that does not take our actual motives into account seems a bit too academic. Expecting people to do what is right without a reward in the form of some reputational gain is for instance too demanding. John Dunn's remark that modern liberal political philosophy "belongs firmly to the Utopian genre" (1985, 9) is probably still true, and in order to be relevant some "motivational realism" (Galston 2010, 398) is in place.[1]

Besides motivating to actually do what is right, honor can also help *Real* to find out what is the proper thing to do, and it was mainly for these two *"heroes"* reasons that Cicero, Smith, and Hume deemed honor important. They did not expect people to be autonomous to an extent that was beyond their reach, but also avoided the extreme of viewing people as entirely controlled by their environment. Their idea that we all are (and should be) concerned about the opinions of those who matter to us, and now and then adjust our behavior accordingly, not only occupies the middle ground between self-serving and altruistic motives (see also Krause 2002, 11), but also between is and ought. Although it was Hume who provided for the most cited formulation of that distinction, he himself did not adhere to such a division between is and ought in his own work (see also Hanley 2011, 225), and freely based his prescriptions on his insights in man's most important motives and shortcomings. The famous passage that contains the is/ought distinction is more about the fact that the move from is to ought often goes without explanation than about the move itself (*Treatise* III.i.i).[2]

Perhaps we should follow Hume on this point and be somewhat less stringent too, and accept that it might be unrealistic to expect people to do what is moral from moral motives only. Often we follow moral rules, not because they are moral, but because not following them brings disesteem, and practice virtues, not out of a love of virtue per se, but because it brings praise, esteem and approbation. Where Smith wrote that man not only wants praise, but also wants to be praiseworthy, today it might be more enlightening to point out that the reverse is equally true: we want to be praiseworthy, but most of us also would like to receive some real praise in return. There might even be a more general lesson here, going beyond the subject of honor: political and moral philosophers should (if they are not already doing so), insofar as the motivation is concerned, look for a middle way between is and ought, or at least try to avoid a too exclusive focus on the latter.

Real audience

The objection that a good action undertaken for considerations of honor and reputation might not in every respect deserve the predicate moral is, meanwhile, a problem without many practical consequences. But if we do not pay due attention to the continued role of honor as an important motivator, we may also fail to address those downsides that are of practical consequence. Even in a more democratic form honor still comes with some serious shortcomings, mainly lying in it being something external (potentially reducing morality to not being caught), and in its exclusiveness (which limits the number of people who matter to us). In the world of today, that latter shortcoming is probably the most visible one, and it has everything to do with the role loyalty and distance play in this world.

Loyalty usually takes the shape of group loyalty—a form of loyalty that gives priority to the interests of an individual or a group—and not that of loyalty to principle or, somewhat in-between, a profession. The latter two types of loyalty are morally sounder than group loyalty: they have a wider scope and include more than just the interests of friends, colleagues, and fellow-countrymen. Pointing that out does not change anything by itself, though, and most people tend to give priority to the interests of those who belong to their own honor group. Although thinkers from Cicero to Mill thought that honor could motivate us to do what is right, and act in the general interest, honor probably cannot motivate to rise above group loyalty, seeing that, in general, the people whose interest we give priority to are also the people whose opinions matter most to us. The transformation of aristocratic honor into democratic honor enlarged the honor group, but it is not very likely that this widening of the honor group will transcend national borders any time soon. That might seem a somewhat bleak conclusion, but the coming of a more democratic conception of honor, as described by for instance Tocqueville, already meant a huge improvement compared to the older, aristocratic conception of honor that reduced most people to obscurity, covering them, in Smith's words, "from the daylight of honour and approbation" (*Theory* I.iii.2.1). What's more, the example of the medical ethic showed that it is perhaps not strictly necessary that the honor group includes the whole of mankind; a concern for reputation can motivate to take the interests of all into account when not treating outsiders correctly brings the loss of the esteem of insiders, that is, of the members of the honor group.

More dismal was the conclusion on integrity. Although integrity on first sight somewhat resembles the idea of internalized honor, it is in reality in many aspects the opposite of honor, and more aligned with current ideals such as authenticity and independence. Seemingly a virtue that has the advantage over honor that it is not dependent on (real or imagined) spectators, integrity, in its meaning of loyalty to personal principles, is in fact fraught with problems, with its overall vagueness and being much too subjective among the more important ones. What's more, this ideal of integrity, in this particular meaning that is, probably contributed a lot to the diminished position of honor (see also F. H. Stewart 1994, 51). This having lost sight of honor comes at a cost; the study of integrity showed, besides its own failings, above all our need for a public, and for models and codes to follow—more or less the things that honor offers. And although there are no clear-cut solutions to the shortcomings of honor, its limitations are not so serious that they form a sufficient ground to actually reject it altogether.

Even so, the final chapter before this conclusion elaborated on a modern descendant of honor, respect, which has the benefit over honor that it is more inclusive and outward looking. By looking into humiliation, basically the denial of honor and respect, that chapter also pointed to a potential drawback of overlooking the role honor plays at present: a reward for virtue in the political and moral philosophy from Cicero to Smith, honor is still a ground for action in our day—but regrettably sometimes in the form of therapeutic violence, political or otherwise. In that same chapter we noted that where honor is more about claiming honor than about honoring others, respect is in general about giving respect and being respectful. But if respect is a descendant of honor, it seems somewhat peculiar that honor and respect are so different in that important aspect. What to make of that?

In a short book on honor, titled *Honor* and referred to a few times in the above, anthropologist Frank Henderson Stewart defines honor as, "roughly speaking, the right to be treated as having a certain worth," and more specifically as the right to respect (1994, 21). Although on first sight Stewart's book is more about the internal aspect of honor (one's worth in one's own eyes), at least compared to this book that paid more attention to the external aspect of honor (one's worth in the eyes of others), Stewart suggests that seeing honor as a right to respect in fact resolves the contrast between the internal and the external aspect of honor; the first aspect "is honor viewed from the point of view of the bearer of the right," the second aspect is honor seen from the perspective "of those who have the corresponding duty" to treat that bearer respectful (1994, 147; see also 21). Although Stewart's definition of honor as a right to respect is not an answer to everything, it might also resolve (or at least reduce to a matter of emphasis) the just mentioned disparity between honor as claiming something, and respect as giving something. That we are concerned about honor means that we want respect from the world when we do right and act in the general interest, and that we see a corresponding duty to respect others, near or far, when they act well. Clearly, respect in this sense does not stand for a Kantian respect that we owe to all persons regardless of their achievements and doings, but for a right that can be won or lost. It is that right to respect that Jim forfeited when he jumped from the Patna.

So, we don't owe respect to everyone after all?

Notes

Introduction

1. Up till this point the story seems to be based on a true story. In 1880 the crew of the SS Jeddah abandoned its almost 1000 Muslim passengers when the pilgrim vessel appeared to be sinking. A French steamer rescued the Jeddah, and the story about a passenger mutiny that the crew had told was now discovered to be false. The report of the ensuing hearing can be read at http://www.plimsoll. org/images/14642_tcm4-165526.pdf.

2. Peter Berger's article *On the Obsolescence of the Concept of Honour* (1984), Peter Spierenburg's edited collection of essays *Men and Violence: Gender, Honor, and Rituals in Modern Europe and America* (1998), and Frank Henderson Stewart's book *Honor* (1994), are three examples of less recent publications on honor. Carlin Barton's *Roman Honor* (2001), and Laurie Johnson's *Thomas Hobbes: Turning Point for Honor* (2009) and *Locke and Rousseau: Two Enlightenment Responses to Honor* (2012), all deal with the role of honor in a specific period of intellectual history.

3. To complicate this straightforward picture a bit: although honor gained comes in gradations (some gain more of it than others), according to most theorists lost honor signifies something absolute; in general, one does not lose his or her honor to a degree. Conrad's Jim is an example of that. But then again, "whatever the theory [i.e., that honor is "a matter of all or none"], in practice there are likely to be people who exist in a gray region" (F. H. Stewart 1994, 123–4).

4. In a later work, Pitt-Rivers too distinguishes three facets: honor is "a sentiment, a manifestation of this sentiment in conduct, and the evaluation of this conduct by others" (cited in F. H. Stewart 1994, 13).

5. "In the history of peoples, shame has always been associated with honor and pride" (Kaufman 1989, 5; see also Appiah 2010, 16–18, 177; Barton 2001, 199–269).

6. Fossum en Mason, describing a couple in therapy: "Cal hung his head and averted his eyes. Judy became fearful and talked about herself as a hopeless person. 'I would like to drop through a trapdoor right now and disappear'" (1966, 5). Darwin suggested in *The Expression of Emotion in Man and Animals* (and referring

to the *Dictionary of English Etymology*) that the word *shame* might have its origin in *shade* (1965, 263).

7. The remark can be found at http://www.nydailynews.com/news/world/skip pers-embarrassed-costa-concordia-captain-failure-article-1.1008626.

8. According to F. H. Stewart, people in the seventeenth century began to consider having a "sense of honor," something internal, as more important than honor based upon public codes (1994, 44–5).

Chapter 1. Honor as a Social Motive

1. The Greek infantry soldier was part of an organized whole: with a shield on his left arm and a spear in his right hand he depended for protection on his neighbor on his right side (this, incidentally, caused the phalanx to tend to the right as every soldier sought cover behind the shield of his neighbor, and Thucydides explained that experienced commanders for that reason never put their armies exactly opposite of each other; *The History of the Peloponnesian War* 5.71.1). When the battle started the two armies ran at each other at full speed. After the first line had fallen, the second line stepped in. Aristotle's idea of courage as a mean between cowardice and recklessness (*Nicomachean Ethics* 1115) fitted the Greek phalanx therefore very well, as an excess or a deficiency of courage would likewise destroy the organized whole it was. To avoid the breakup of the phalanx— and thus losing the battle—holding your ground was deemed more important than individual heroic acts, but also more important than staying unharmed. So the Greek soldier had to overcome his natural instinct for self-preservation, and notwithstanding Du Picq's observation that the Greeks were mainly interested in the ideal depth of the phalanx (in general eight lines), this feat was accomplished by a combination of discipline and, like in the later Roman cohorts, honor (see also Hanson 1989 and 2002).

2. Although Cicero had written about the craftsmanship of Lucretius' *De Rerum Natura* in a letter to his brother years earlier, in *Tusculanae Disputationes* he denied having read it (Gay 1973, 99). According to Peter Gay, Cicero was a courageous man, and the reason for his denial must therefore "reflect a political position. Lucretius was to the dying Roman Republic much what Hobbes was to the seventeenth century, a disturber of the peace whose work was too great to be ignored but whose name was too disreputable to be praised" (1973, 99).

3. And Cicero might have been right to worry: "So far as direct influence on current affairs is concerned, the influence of the political philosopher may be negligible. But when his ideas have become common property, through the work of historians and publicists, teachers and writers, and intellectuals generally, they effectively guide developments" (Hayek 1990, 113).

4. That the Stoic Seneca quoted in his *Epistles* Epicurus more than any other author suggests that the differences between the moral philosophy of the Stoics and that of the Epicureans are in reality not that significant. The similarity

between Epicureanism and Stoicism was also noted by Michel de Montaigne, who wrote in *On Cruelty* that "in steadfastness and strictness of opinions and precepts, the Epicurean sect yields nothing to the Stoic."

5. More stoically minded philosophers opt for a different solution: according to Montaigne, for instance, we can overcome the fear of death by means of virtue. Going back to a dictum of Socrates, he wrote that "one of virtue's main gifts is a contempt for death, which is the means of furnishing our life with easy tranquility, of giving us a pure and friendly taste for it; without it every other pleasure is snuffed out" (*To Philosophize is to Learn How to Die*; see for a similar remark Cicero *Tusculanae Disputationes* I.74–5). But Montaigne did not convince everyone: although like Montaigne sympathetic to the Stoic position, Adam Smith nonetheless spoke of "the dread of death" as "the great poison to the happiness" (*The Theory of Moral Sentiments* I.I.i.13).

6. Illustrative of the modern view is Herbert Spencer's remark, in *The Social Organism* from 1860, that "those who regard the histories of societies as the histories of their great men, and think that these great men shape the fates of their societies, overlook the truth that such great men are the products of their societies" (1982, 387).

7. And Hobbes agreed with Aristotle that shame is not a virtue for a mature man: "Grief for the discovery of some defect of ability is shame, or the passion that discovers itself in blushing, and consists in the apprehension of something dishonourable; and in young men is a sign of the love of good reputation, and commendable: in old men it is a sign of the same; but because it comes too late, not commendable" (*Leviathan* I.6). But looking down on "good reputation is called impudence" (*Leviathan* I.6).

Chapter 2. Democratic Honor and the Quiet Virtues

1. In that letter Hume wrote: "Upon the whole I desire to take my catalogue of virtues from *Cicero's Offices*, not from *The Whole Duty of Man*. I had, indeed, the former book in my eye in all my reasonings." Hume wrote elsewhere that, as a philosopher, Cicero "enlarges very much his ideas of virtue, and comprehends every laudable quality or endowment of the mind, under that honourable appellation" (*An Enquiry Concerning the Principles of Morals* appendix IV), and added in a footnote that

> if Cicero were now alive, it would be found difficult to fetter his moral sentiments by narrow systems; or persuade him, that no qualities were to be admitted as *virtues*, or acknowledged to be a part of *personal merit*, but that were recommended by *The Whole Duty of Man* (*Enquiry* appendix IV, note).

2. According to Condren this idea of a tradition is an invention of the nineteenth century, and "a mythical projection of the academic *status quo*" (1985, 68; see also Gunnel 1986, 99).

3. On the other hand, it seems that "one may possess a concept without having a word to express it" (Ball 1998, 81). According to Bloom, "men of high intelligence, good will and learning reject an obvious point, clearly stated in the text, with the remark, 'No man in the sixteenth century could have thought such a thing!'" (1980, 130). So although the idea that we all have unique personalities is a novel one by most accounts, as we will also see in the chapter on integrity in this book, we should not exaggerate this; the same Alcibiades to whom Pocock referred, describes in Plato's *Symposium* Socrates as completely unlike all others (217–22). Then again, Arendt's description of the public realm of the Greek polis as "the only place where men could show who they really and inexchangeably were" (1958, 41) does sound somewhat anachronistic.

4. As political theorist Peter Euben put it:

> understanding is necessarily a matter of self-understanding. That means that changes in how we understand ourselves (including ourselves as interpreters of texts) alter how we understand a text or culture even as our interpretation of that culture alters our sense of self and the prejudices that animated our initial inquiry. This (always incomplete) historical consciousness requires both an awareness of the strangeness or otherness of what which we are trying to understand and an assumption of commonality sufficient to engender mutual interrogation (1990, 16).

Skinner and Pocock take a more positivist stance, although Skinner writes that his precepts "are only claims about how best to proceed; they are not claims about how to guarantee success" (1988, 281).

5. Confusing is that Mandeville also suggests that politicians and moralists equated virtue with self-denial because that doctrine was advantageous to society. Were they just mistaken in what is truly good for society?

6. In their wars under the Ancien Régime the French did not use their muskets to engage the enemy from a safe distance, but to fire from very close, and to subsequently press the attached bayonet into the opponent. This tactic required that one held one's fire while marching forwards (reloading took too long), meanwhile receiving fire from the enemy. This all was, so they thought, in accordance with their culture of braveness, and of course very different from the English ways. During the First World War, the French paid the price for their boldness (Lynn 2003, 111–44).

7. That "greater circumspection" is not always necessary. Peters and Waterman describe in their famous management book *In Search of Excellence* how

> the manager of a 100-person sales branch rented the Meadowlands Stadium (New Jersey) for the evening. After work, his salesmen ran onto the stadium's field through the players' tunnel. As each emerged, the electronic scoreboard beamed his name to the assembled crowd. Executives from corporate headquarters, employees from other offices, and family and friends were present, cheering loudly (1982, p. xxiv).

According to the authors this was a tactic borrowed from Napoleon, "who was a master ribbon-granter" (1982, 268). Although most companies use this tactic, it is "top performers almost alone who use it extensively. The volume of contrived opportunities for showering pins, buttons, badges, and medals on people is staggering at McDonalds, Tupperware, IBM, or many of the other top performers. They actively seek out and pursue endless excuses to give out rewards" (1982, 269). For the rest, it is important to create a situation in which "virtually everybody wins regularly" (1982, 57), since "all of us are self-centered suckers for a bit of praise" (1982, 55)—"Label a man a loser and he'll start acting like one" (1982, 57). To sum it up, "the message that comes through so poignantly in the studies we reviewed is that we like to see ourselves as winners. The lesson that the excellent companies have to teach is that there is no reason why we can't design systems that continually reinforce this notion; most of their people are made to feel that they are winners" (1982, 57).

8. According to Hume, "the author of the *The Fable of the Bees* betrayed himself when he maintained that private vice was public benefit: for as virtue consists in public utility or good, how can that what is a public good be a vice?" (cited in Kerkhof 1992, 218n11).

9. And these were especially Roman models: "Throughout the eighteenth century the intellectual and moral outlook of the educated remained predominantly Roman" (Kinneging 1994, 101).

10. Hume thought

> that the sentiments of those, who are inclined to think favourably of mankind, are more advantageous to virtue, than the contrary principles, which give us a mean opinion of our nature. When a man is prepossessed with a high notion of his rank and character in the creation, he will naturally endeavour to act up to it, and will scorn to do a base or vicious action, which might sink him below that figure which he makes in his own imagination (*Dignity or Meanness of Human Nature*).

11. J. B. Stewart writes in his book on Hume's political and moral philosophy that, according to Hume,

> our feelings about ourselves and others, based on comparisons with the standard of worthiness prevailing within our society, are outstanding as causes of behaviour, and, therefore, are of great importance to the moral, economic, and governmental institutions of every group and nation (1963, 60).

And Peter Jones writes in his book on Hume that

> in Hume, as in Cicero, we find that man's natural resistance to unbridled scepticism is strengthened by his social nature, and the public judgments it generates; and that those very same judgments ensure that discussions of value, in art as in morals, satisfy all man's needs for objectivity

and rationality, without *a priori* thought on the one hand, and without having to concede a place to religious claims and practices on the other (1982, 187).

12. Hume continues:

> For as parents easily observe, that a man is the more useful, both to himself and others, the greater degree of probity and honour he is endowed with; and that those principles have greater force, when custom and education assist interest and reflection: For these reasons they are induced to inculcate on their children, from their earliest infancy, the principles of probity, and teach them to regard the observance of those rules, by which society is maintained, as worthy and honourable, and their violation as base and infamous. By this means the sentiments of honour may take root in their tender minds, and acquire such firmness and solidity, that they may fall little short of those principles, which are the most essential to our natures, and the most deeply radicated in our internal constitution.

13. Burke wrote about British prejudices that "instead of casting away all our old prejudices, we cherish them to considerable degree, and, to take more shame to ourselves, we cherish them because they are prejudices; and the longer they have lasted, and the more generally they have prevailed, the more we cherish them" (1967, 84).

14. As Hume phrased it elsewhere:

> it is certain that, while we aspire to the magnanimous firmness of the philosophic sage, and endeavour to confine our pleasures altogether within our minds, we may, at last, render our philosophy like that of Epictetus, and other *Stoics*, only a more refined system of selfishness, and reason ourselves out of all virtue as well as social enjoyment. While we study with attention the vanity of human life, and turn all our thoughts toward the empty and transitory nature of richness and honours, we are, perhaps, all the while flattering our natural indolence, which, hating the bustle of the world, and drudgery of business, seeks a pretence of reason to give itself a full and uncontrolled indulgence (*An Enquiry concerning Human Understanding* V.i; compare Mandeville *Fable* vol. I 161).

15. Adam Smith wrote that Epicureanism "is, no doubt, altogether inconsistent with that which I have been endeavouring to establish" (*The Theory of Moral Sentiments* VII.ii.2.13).

16. Hayek, a self-declared heir to Hume and Smith, wrote that "we all know that, in the pursuit of our individual aims, we are not likely to be successful unless we lay down for ourselves some general rules to which we will adhere without re-examining their justification in every particular instance" (1990, 66).

17. Smith's description of the difference between a gentleman and a "man of low condition" reminds somewhat of Robert Louis Stevenson's *Strange Case of Dr Jekyll and Mr Hyde*; Dr. Jekyll was a distinguished member of London society, who, being somewhat envious of the liberty the anonymous members of lower strata enjoyed, invented an alter ego, Mr. Hyde, to be able to, in Smith's words, abandon himself to profligacy and vice—just like Gyges, Griffin, and Sebastian Caine had done.

18. Illusory superiority, also called the above average effect, is now among the more robust findings of today's social psychology. According to Hume, that tendency to overvalue ourselves is not necessarily a bad thing. In a section called *Of Greatness of mind* he wrote that a talent we have is useless if we don't know that we have it, and that it is therefore "more advantageous to overrate our merit, than to form ideas of it, below its just standard" (*A Treatise of Human Nature* III.iii.ii).

19. According to Williams, "it is accepted that the world of Homer embodied a shame culture, and that shame was later replaced, in its crucial role, by guilt." But, he continues, "these stories are deeply misleading, both historically and ethically" (1993, 5).

20. But according to apologists of the duel the practice of dueling had a civilizing effect, as "they teach a man the forms to observe in his interactions with others and increase his stock of urbanity and wit" (Nye 1998, 9; see also Appiah 2010, 32). According to Mandeville, for instance,

> those that rail at dueling don't consider the benefit the society receives from that fashion: if every ill-bred fellow might use what language he pleased, without being called to an account for it, all conversation would be spoiled. Some grave people tell us, that the *Greeks* and *Romans* were such valiant men, and yet knew nothing of dueling but in their country's quarrel: this is very true, but for that reason the kings and princes in *Homer* gave one another worse language than our porters and hackney coachmen would be able to bear without resentment (*Fable* vol. I 242–3).

In other words, "the prospect of having to face an opponent in arms restrained men in social intercourse; they thought twice before they said a wrong word" (Spierenburg 1998, 9). Different from Mandeville, both Hume and Smith did not see much of value in the practice of dueling (Appiah 2010, 33–4).

21. This position, also the position of Friedman and Becker, has been criticized. Gunnel writes that in

> the work of John Stuart Mill, who apparently knew very little about the actual substance and practice of natural science, we have (. . .) one of the first clear examples of the suggestion that, because natural science is a paradigm of rationality, this mythical method could be extended to the field of social studies in order to emulate the success of the natural sciences (1986, 149).

According to Peter Winch, "Mill states naively a position which underlies the pro-
nouncements of a large proportion of contemporary social scientists" (1958, 66).

22. Gunnel writes that "Dahl argued that empirical and normative inquiry,
political science and political philosophy, reflected the 'logically' distinct character of 'decisions about what *is* and decisions about what *ought* to be,'" while Dahl's
colleague David Easton "argued that 'facts and values are logically heteroge-
neous' and that ethical evaluation and empirical explanation involve two different kind of propositions that constitute the difference between 'causal and value
(moral) theory.'" According to Easton, writes Gunnel, "the latter 'can ultimately
be reduced to emotional responses'" (Gunnel 1986, 160–1; see also Easton 1965,
7 and Dahl 1991, 5, 123).

23. Fukuyama writes: "Not only is the neo-classical economic perspective insufficient to explain political life, with its dominant emotions of indignation,
pride, and shame, but it's not sufficient to explain many aspects of economic life
either" (1995, 18).

24. French economist Serge-Christophe Kolm, however, struggles. About
"moral social feedback" he writes that

> The classical opposition between "self-interested" and moral motivation
> misses this [i.e., social feedback] very important cause of moral behavior.
> For this reason, among others, this opposition appears overly naive, super-
> ficial, and ill-defined. (. . .) Indeed a taste for fame or for other people's
> approval, or a dislike for their reprobation or contempt, can constitute
> sufficient motives of moral behavior, yet they are not moral motivations.
> However, the individual is moulded by culture, and culture is shared val-
> ues. Hence is being judged good or not-bad by others that different from
> the same judgment applied to oneself? Can really one be moral motivation
> the other not be? On the other hand, individuals who are concerned by
> other people's view of them in itself (that is, not as a means for further
> purposes) are "interested" in this opinion (1996, 392–3).

25. But according to one author there is a reevaluation of shame going on "that
casts shame as at least potentially a positive, not a destructive emotion" (Leys
2009, 124), and is it even so that "shame (and shamelessness) has replaced guilt
as a dominant emotional reference in the West" (Leys 2009, 4). Dodds wrote
already in 1951 that our "ancient and powerful" guilt-culture is in decline (1951,
26n106).

26. Although some might think that being capable of changing your behavior because of how others judge it, or how an impartial spectator might judge
it, presupposes a free will, and that, conversely, rejecting the idea of a free will
implies believing that praise and censure do not have much influence, this is not
necessarily the case. Writes Hayek, again another economist and Nobel laureate (and this one saw himself standing in the British tradition of, among others,
Hume and Smith),

all those factors whose influence is sometimes inconsistently denied by those who deny the "freedom of the will," such as reasoning or argument, persuasion or censure, or the expectation of blame, are really among the most important factors determining the personality and through it the particular action of the individual (1990, 74).

"We assign responsibility to a man, not in order to say that as he was he might have acted differently, but in order to make him different," we read one page further. Something which "requires that the individual be praised or blamed, whether or not the expectation of this would in fact have made any difference to the action" (1990, 75). At the same time, Hayek, but Hume and Smith too, stopped well short of B.F. Skinner's determinism; clearly, altering your behavior to bring it into conformity with what is considered right and proper presupposes some degree of freedom, although Hume did write that it "is only upon the principles of necessity, that a person acquires any merit or demerit from his actions, however the common opinion may incline to the contrary" (*Treatise* II.III.ii). What they adhered to is the compatibilist/consequentialist view on moral responsibility, that is, the view "that determinism poses no threat to moral responsibility since praising and blaming could still be an effective means of influencing another's behavior, even in a deterministic world" (Eshleman 2009). The competing view is the so-called merit based view of moral responsibility: praise and blame are in place if an actor "deserves" such praise or blame (Eshleman 2009).

27. "Success in Goffman's social universe is nothing but what passes for success. There is nothing else for it to be. For Goffman's world is empty of objective standards of achievement," writes MacIntyre (1985, 115).

28. "One cannot, for Aristotle, do ethics without doing moral psychology; one cannot understand what a virtue is without understanding it as something a man could possess and as something related to human happiness. Morality, to be intelligible, must be understood as something grounded in human nature" (MacIntyre 1969, 49; see also Aristoteles *Nicomachean Ethics* 1102a). Responding to MacIntyre, Ronald F. Atkinson finds "a thought extravagant the suggestion that Hume was the last representative of the Aristotelian tradition" (1969, 58).

29. "Dipping at will into the psychological level" is a bad idea according to Mary Douglas too (1987, 34), because "such psychic satisfactions do not work reliably enough to carry the weight of explaining. If they work sometimes and sometimes do not, the question is just pushed back into the form of asking what switches on the public-spirited emotional attitudes" (1987, 31).

30. Communitarians claim to do better: "In short, the communitarian self—part member, part creative and critical—is a rather well empirically grounded concept and one on which a communitarian philosophy can build constructively" (Etzioni 1995, 34).

31. To name three canonical examples: Cooley (1922) and Goffman (1958) both saw humans as essentially led by pride, shame, and the fear of losing face, and Riesman (1950) portrayed the modern employee as other-directed.

32. Elsewhere, Fukuyama states that "the satisfaction we derive from being connected to others in the workplace grows out of a fundamental desire for recognition" (1995, 6). Like Smith, Fukuyama thinks that

> beyond subsistence levels, economic activity is frequently for the sake of recognition rather than merely as a means of satisfying natural material needs. The latter are, as Adam Smith pointed out, few in number and relatively easily satisfied. Work and money are much more important as sources of identity, status, and dignity, whether one has created a multinational media empire or has been promoted to foreman. This kind of recognition cannot be achieved by individuals; it can come about only in a social context (1995, 7).

33. According to Allan Bloom, Rawls is

> writing hundreds of pages to persuade men, and proposing a scheme of government that would force them, not to despise anyone. In *A Theory of Justice*, he writes that the physicist or the poet should not look down on the man who spends his life counting blades of grass or performing any other frivolous or corrupt activity (1987, 30; compare Rawls *Theory* § 65).

Elsewhere, Bloom wrote that "Rawls's man cannot withstand unfavorable public opinion. Rawls tries to provide him with esteem no matter what his life plan may be; Rawls's man is in every way dependent, 'other-directed'" (1990, 328).

34. According to Finley, in *The World of Odysseus*, "when everyone attains equal honour, then there is no honour for anyone" (1993, 118). Something disagreed with by the Dodo from Lewis Carroll's *Alice's Adventures in Wonderland*, who said after a race: "*Everybody* has won, and all must have prizes."

35. Scottish theorists such as Hume and Smith were, writes Hayek, "very far from holding such naïve views, later unjustly laid at the door of their liberalism, as the 'natural goodness of man,' the existence of a 'natural harmony of interests,' or the beneficent effects of 'natural liberty'" (1990, 60).

36. The arguments in this chapter might throw a different light on the debate in the 1990s between communitarians and liberals. The discussion was mainly about the Rawlsian notion of autonomy, and its (im)possibilities. The fact that communitarianism was to a large extent a reaction on Rawls' work suggests that it was not liberalism itself that was at stake, but a specific sort of liberalism that came into existence only fairly recently.

Chapter 3. Defining the Honor Group: Loyalty and Distance

1. "Throughout Europe, honor had become less of a personal attribute by 1900. In earlier days, one person's actions had repercussions for the honor of his family at the most; now they had repercussions for a much larger group, the nation in particular" (Spierenburg 1998, 12).

2. This change started when in 1969 psychologist and former conscript dr. J. E. Hueting told in a television interview that some Dutch military personnel—including Hueting himself—had committed serious war crimes, in Hueting's view comparable with those of the French in Algeria and the Americans in Vietnam (1969 was also the year the My Lai massacre reached the media). He was called a traitor and worse. The Netherland's biggest newspaper called his performance on television "sickening." Hueting had to go into hiding.

3. The moral, according to Conrad: "Yes, material may fail, and men, too, may fail sometimes; but more often men, when they are given the chance, will prove themselves truer than steel, that wonderful thin steel from-which the sides and the bulkheads of our modern sea-leviathans are made" (2007, 645–6).

4. The Kosovo War of 1999 numbered 78 days of bombardments and killed about 500 civilians, but ended with a zero NATO death toll (Shaw 2005, 10, 22). Although 35 percent of the bombs and missiles used were "smart," "one cannot help but note that the precision would have been higher still had the aircraft operated at lower altitudes (and greater risk)" (Cook 2004, 127).

5. Although "we consider it a worse moral error if the police were to injure or kill innocent bystanders than for them to fail to apprehend suspected criminals at large," in military missions in far-away countries it is not considered a worse moral error to kill or injure innocents "than to fail to apprehend suspected terrorists, or even belligerents" (Challans 2007, 17–18).

6. In earlier days soldiers considered bows, catapults, and firearms to be the weapon of choice of cowards, yet it seems that today's use of unmanned weapon systems push things even further by excluding risk altogether. But the difference between running no risks and running a limited risk is not merely gradual, and that raises the question to what extent risk is fundamental to the military profession, and whether the elimination of risk will change it. According to Welsh,

> For men to join in battle is generally thought to be honorable, but not if they are so situated as to be able to kill others without exposing themselves to danger whatever. On the contrary, the willingness to risk one's life—it could be in an act of passive resistance—comes as the test of honor we most often hear invoked (2008, 4).

Time journalists Ghosh and Thompson observed that people in Waziristan, the region in Pakistan where drones killed many Taliban leaders, see the use of unmanned aircraft as dishonorable and cowardly (2009). That latter fact is, perhaps understandably, not a big concern to everyone. It is nonetheless ironic that robot manufacturer iRobot named its latest creation for the military "Warrior" (incidentally also the temporary name of an upgraded Predator version—the name Reaper for the bigger brother of the Predator, a drone especially designed as a "hunter-killer," seems more adequate). Even so, after initial reluctance possibly due to the perceived dishonorableness of their use, militaries have now embraced the use of drones (P. W. Singer 2009, 216–7)—just like they eventually accepted bows and catapults in those earlier days.

7. Baitullah Mehsud, the Pashtun commander of the Pakistani Taliban, claimed that each drone attack brought "him three or four suicide bombers" (Thompson and Ghosh 2009), mainly from the families of the victims of the drones. Using drones is an effective method, though: an UAV killed Mehsud in August 2009.

8. It was in fact for these reasons, maintaining the support of the local population and increasing the safety of own troops, that NATO changed its tactics in Afghanistan, something that reduced the amount of civilian casualties significantly. That the extra caution stemmed more from self-serving motives than from moral considerations suggests that the consequences for the local population would count for less if the expediency argument would no longer hold. That is a rather unsatisfactory conclusion. Probably, taking civilian deaths seriously as such, that is, as something to be avoided independently of what is in it for the military, would result in the postponement or cancellation of particular missions in even more cases than the aforementioned reasons of expedience in recent years already led to (see for instance Dadkhah 2008).

9. But in modern warfare there are always innocent casualties, hence the contingent pacifist's conclusion that under present conditions wars should not be fought (Fiala 2010). As it basically rules out war completely, this position is in effect similar to absolute pacifism (Coady 2008, 136), opposing war altogether. According to most authors contingent pacifism is therefore still too strict, since it has the undesirable outcome that it forbids wars of self-defense and, more generally, does not allow war even in cases where *not* fighting a war seems the immoral thing to do. So although not differentiating much between intended and unintended civilian casualties, many (contingent) pacifists seem quite concerned about retaining their own purity of intention.

10. Fundamental to the principle of double effect is "the claim that there is a stronger presumption against action that has harm to the innocent as an intended effect than there is against otherwise comparable action that causes the same amount of harm to the innocent as a foreseen but unintended effect" (McMahan 1994). Acts that have evil consequences, such as innocent casualties, are permitted if four conditions are met: 1) the act is not bad in itself (such as for instance bombing residential areas in war would be), but good or morally indifferent; 2) the direct effect is good (for instance the bombing of military infrastructure in war), and the bad side effect is not a means to the one's end (the opponent is not brought to capitulation by civilian deaths resulting from bombing military infrastructure); 3) the intention is good (it is the destruction of the military infrastructure that is intended, not the deaths of civilians living nearby); and 4) the (intended) good effects (the destruction of the military infrastructure) outweigh the unintended bad effects (civilian deaths), i.e., the chosen means, with its evil effects, should be proportional in light of the intended outcome (see

for instance Anscombe 1961; Walzer 1992, 153). Similar to the just war tradition as a whole, the principle of double effect consists of a mixture of consequentialist (the proportionality condition) and non-consequentialist elements (the emphasis on right intention). But the third proviso, about intention, is clearly central to the principle, and in theory not differentiating between intended and unintended civilian casualties might bring us back to pacifism, "since almost all contemporary warfare involves the killing of innocent bystanders in large numbers" (McMahan 2009). In practice, doing without this distinction is in fact likely to lead to *less* restrained warfare because, given that noncombatant casualties are in almost every situation a foreseeable consequence, it would turn the immunity of civilians into a dead letter fairly rapidly (see also Coady 2008, 142).

11. The authority whose permission is needed should therefore ask the bomber pilot (or the planner of the mission?) about his intentions, and permission should depend on the answer. Holding intentions relevant in such a way is prone to lead to "double-think." Elizabeth Anscombe pointed out that if intention is "an interior act of the mind" that can be "produced at will," then you only have to "'direct your intention' in a suitable way. In practice, this means making a little speech to yourself: 'what I mean to be doing is...'" (1961, 58). The principle of double effect is hence likely to be misapplied in a self-serving way; with some double think even the terror bomber can hide behind the principle, since all he "requires for his purpose, and therefore all he needs to intend, is that the civilians should *appear* to be dead long enough for the government to be intimidated into surrendering" (McMahan, 1994; see also Quinn, 1989). The terror bomber could argue that the civilian deaths he caused are an unintended side effect, since making civilians appear dead long enough requires actually killing them (Quinn, 1989).

12. This adds up to what Walzer calls the idea of double intention. The first intention should be to hit the target and not something else. The second intention consists of two rather separate aspects: 1) efforts should be made to reduce the number of civilian casualties; 2) when needed, at increased risk to oneself. There are some complexities here, though. For instance, although the use Unmanned Aerial Vehicles (UAV's) might be safer for the local population than other ways of delivering firepower by air (see for instance Lin, Bekey, and Abney 2008, 52–3), it falls short in the risk acceptance aspect. The use of ground troops or low flying manned aircraft would amount to a sufficient indication of the acceptance of risk to oneself, and thus of a good intention, but if that would also increase the risk to the local population one might ask what the point is, as it would boil down to accepting higher risks to oneself *and* the local population just to prove your good intention. Walzer's emphasis on "accepting cost to oneself," stemming from his wish to see proof of a good intention, does not seem to allow for the possibility that sometimes risks to the local population can be reduced *without* increasing the risk to Western military personnel.

13. Combatants, on the other hand, are legitimate targets, and when they get killed it is therefore not the presence or absence of intent per se that matters, but

the *correctness* of the intention. For example, the wish to secure peace and pun-
ish evildoers are legitimate motives, revenge and hatred are not (see for instance
Aquinas *Summa Theologiae* II-II, Q. 40, art. 1).

14. Virtue ethics calls for the development of good inclinations—we are virtuous when doing the right thing gives us pleasure (Kohlberg famously denounced
virtue ethics as "a bag of virtues approach"). Testifying to a fairly Calvinistic
view on human nature, duty-based ethics asks us to follow moral rules against
our natural (selfish) inclinations.

15. Walzer's pessimism about the "endlessly permissive" logic in war seems
at odds with his own "accepting cost to oneself" stipulation that (although for
Walzer primarily needed as a proof of good intention) suggests he thinks that
soldiers should be able to rise above their own concerns. Yet, the two examples
from World War II that Walzer uses to illustrate his idea of double intention
both involve military personnel reducing the risks to their own occupied populations (1992, 157).

16. If we look at the arguments rendered pro and against the ban on torture
we see, likewise, that not only the arguments for lifting this ban are always based
on expediency, but that the defense of the ban on torture is also often based on
a fairly pragmatic argumentation. In support of the prohibition of torture it has
been argued that torture yields information of questionable quality; would alien-
ate the public at home and one's allies alike; and has the effect of strengthening
the resistance to one's cause. These rationales for the ban on torture are of course
just as well about "what is in it for us" as the rationales that the defenders of
torture put forward, and thus do not really amount to a moral argument. In *De
Officiis* Cicero claimed that there is no contradiction between what is virtuous
and what is expedient, but without offering convincing substantiation, and for
that reason possibly more based on hope than on anything else.

17. It is not only the distance to the (intended or unintended) victims that
matters here, but also the distance to those who (willingly or unwillingly) caused
these casualties. Although insurgent forces are responsible for most of the civilian casualties in Afghanistan (around 77 percent in 2011; United Nations Assistance Mission in Afghanistan 2012, 1), these draw considerably less media
attention, and cause much less moral outrage, than those caused by Western
soldiers. Although partly natural since Western militaries profess to bring good,
the blind eye turned to the atrocities the other side commits seems somewhat
unfair. This unevenness is perhaps an indication of the fact that distance (in this
case the cultural and psychological distance to the perpetrators of the atrocities)
is more important than intention and proportionality.

18. The media could play an important role here by paying more attention
to these victims, but can only do so if journalists work independent from the
military. Recent years have shown that embedded journalists mainly write about
their own countrymen in the military, and pay much less attention to the suffering of the local population than journalists working independently from the

military (The Hague Centre for Strategic Studies 2008; see also Carruthers 2011, 8, 229–34). Media researcher Eric Louw wrote about the U.S. military that "a key requirement of the Pentagon's PR-ized warfare model is the need to keep media corralled in order to black out news of 'blood' (especially of dead civilians)" (2003, 223; see also Carruthers 2011, 8, 222). This is the more to be regretted since the media can also function as a check on the behavior of military personnel. The media coverage of modern conflicts poses considerable limitations on Western troops, and in that way it helps troops to make true their expressed ambition (that is, by some members of militaries) to be "a force for good."

19. Rawls rejects the "doctrine of the purely conscientious act," which

> holds, first, that the highest moral motive is the desire to do what is right and just simply because it is right and just, no other description being appropriate; and second, that while other motives certainly have moral value, for example the desire to do what is right because doing this increases human happiness, or because it tends to promote equality, these desires are less morally worthy then that to do what is right solely in virtue of its being right (*A Theory of Justice* §72).

Although such undiluted adherence to one school of ethics might be common in academia, most people will consider both the intentions and the consequences of an act (Nagel 1986, 166). In Lewis Carroll's *Through the Looking Glass*, Alice listens to Tweedledee's poem about the walrus and the carpenter feeding on oysters:

> "I like the Walrus best," said Alice: "because you see he was a LITTLE sorry for the poor oysters." "He ate more than the Carpenter, though," said Tweedledee. "You see he held his handkerchief in front, so that the Carpenter couldn't count how many he took: contrariwise." "That was mean!" Alice said indignantly. "Then I like the Carpenter best—if he didn't eat so many as the Walrus." "But he ate as many as he could get," said Tweedledum. This was a puzzler. After a pause, Alice began, "Well! They were BOTH very unpleasant characters—" (Chapter 4).

20. Bentham even wrote *A Plan for an Universal and Perpetual Peace, published posthumously as a part of his Principles of International Law*. Despite his rather fierce critique of the utilitarian doctrine (1992, 129–33; 2004, 37–40), Walzer himself seems to concede in a footnote that utilitarian arguments and rights arguments are not completely dissimilar (1992, 156; see also Orend 2000, 120; S. Lee 2004, 247).

21. Although Hutcheson still held that "the dignity, or moral importance of persons, may compensate numbers" (*Treatise* II.III.viii), and Mill thought it better "to be a human being dissatisfied than a pig satisfied, better to be Socrates dissatisfied than a fool satisfied" (1987b, 281). This idea of Mill that higher forms of pleasure are of more worth than lower ones is incompatible with the calculating

of utility Bentham proposed (Bentham *Principles* IV.v; see also Rawls *A Theory of Justice* §8n2).

22. According to Mill, "in the golden rule of Jesus of Nazareth, we read the complete spirit of the ethics of utility" (1987b, 288).

23. It is not only a psychological impossibility, though, but also a sociological one: John Dewey concluded (with some disappointment), in a defense of an ethic with a consequentialist side, that "theoretical approvals that run counter to strong social tendencies tend to become purely nominal" (1989, 259).

24. Although he does not mention him, Bentham would probably hold that Cicero's work stems from "the principle of sympathy and antipathy," one of the principles adverse to utilitarianism. It is not really a principle, though, writes Bentham:

> A great multitude of people are continually talking about the Law of Nature; and then they go on giving you their sentiments about what is right and what is wrong: and these sentiments, you are to understand, are so many chapters and sections of the Law of Nature (*An Introduction to the Principles of Morals and Legislation* II.xix).

Another rival system is the ascetic principle, and its adherents go as far "as to think it meritorious to fall in love with pain. Even this, we see, is at bottom but the principle of utility misapplied" (*Principles* II.ix).

25. According to economist Wesley C. Mitchell

> Social science nowadays aims to give an intelligent account of social processes, to promote the understanding of social facts. While we may value such "science" mainly for its practical serviceability, we profess to distinguish sharply between our explanations of what is and our schemes of what ought to be. In Bentham's world, on the contrary, the felicific calculus yields a social science that is both an account of what is and an account of what ought to be (1974, 170).

In fact, *An Introduction to the Principles of Morals and Legislation* opens with the statement that

> Nature has placed mankind under the governance of two sovereign masters, *pain* and *pleasure*. It is for them alone to point out what we ought to do, as well as to determine what we shall do. On the one hand the standard of right and wrong, on the other hand the chain of causes and effects, are fastened to their seats.

26. According to Mill expert Allan Ryan it was "essential for Mill to be able to justify punishment, with its attendant notions of blame, guilt, and responsibility, since Utilitarian ethics depend very closely on the idea that moral rules, like laws, are essentially backed by sanctions" (1970, 112).

27. Mandeville suggested that our common sense morality is in fact quite utilitarian, at least in this aspect: "when we pronounce actions good or evil, we only regard the hurt or benefit the society receives from them, and not the person who commits them" (*Fable* vol. I 274). Also for Hume, as will be remembered, what was considered virtuous and what was useful (with both notions being more or less equal to what is praised and what is praiseworthy) often boiled down to essentially the same thing, namely acting in the public interest. There is in theory therefore some convergence between consequentialism and that what some authors expect from advancing virtues, that is, good outcomes. In practice there is an important difference between consequentialism and virtue ethics in this aspect: virtues in general aim at good outcomes for the members of a particular community, whereas consequentialism is about giving equal weight to the interests of all parties involved. Also, insofar as we promote virtues because of its positive pay offs most virtue ethicists will hesitate to call it virtue ethics in the first place. Promoting certain virtues because they are beneficial to others amounts to what is sometimes (although admittedly not very often) described as character consequentialism.

28. That armed forces socialize their employees thoroughly into the organization (and, possibly even more so, into their own service) contributes to the strong organizational loyalty of military personnel. That military personnel is predominantly trained in house, whereas doctors and legal professionals receive most of their formal professional training before entering their job (the oldest profession, the clergy, possibly forms an exception), makes this socialization into the organization, instead of into a profession, easier. As a consequence, there are organizational values (in many forces still service specific), but not really any values of the military profession. The values and standards of other professions are universal, in the sense that they are not confined to the institution the professional works for; they have largely originated in universities and professional associations. These latter institutions are also principally responsible for the professional's socialization, where normally (i.e., for non-professionals) the employing organization takes care of that task (Mintzberg 1983, 192). Although some have for these reasons maintained that the military profession is ill suited to develop into a "true" profession (see for instance Van Doorn 1975), most authors today see officership as a profession nonetheless (see for instance Burk 2002).

29. The medical oath stipulates that doctors should work in the interest of their patients; there is no mention of parties outside the doctor-patient relationship, such as hospitals or governments. The military oath stresses loyalty to, for instance, a head of state, constitution, or republic and people. The people at the receiving end are not included. This means that a doctor in the military serves in his capacity as a physician a different client than in his role as a member of the armed forces; for non-medical military personnel the client is the state or the people, not the local population. For civilian medical personnel, the patient is the

client, and no one else. Similarly, the value lists of armed forces mainly mention values (such as courage, loyalty, discipline, and obedience) that further military effectiveness and the interests of the soldiers themselves, their fellow-soldiers, and the military organization (Robinson 2007a). Armed forces are for instance less hesitant than most ethicists about the beneficial properties of loyalty; they consider it a cardinal virtue, and often include it in their lists of values (Robinson 2007a). And clearly, militaries mean loyalty to the organization when they include loyalty as a value. This is in line with how other values are defined: they also mainly relate to colleagues. In comparison, the values of the medical profession give precedence to the patient and the doctor-patient relationship: doctors should always work in the interests of the patient; refrain from prescribing treatment known to be harmful; and respect the patient's dignity. In addition, military codes of conduct often aim at safeguarding military personnel against pestering, sexual intimidation, and discrimination. These codes regulate the conduct of soldiers towards each other, not their conduct towards those they are to protect. Codes of conduct for doctors emphasize the interests of third parties, namely the patients. Practitioners of medicine have their own worldwide association, the World Medical Association, with its own International Code of Medical Ethics, which goes into great detail about the duties of a physician to his or her patients, but says little about duties towards colleagues.

30. In such cases, military medical personnel "have to balance the medical needs of their patients, who happen to be detainees, with their military duty to their employer" (Clark 2006, 570; see also Miles 2006). Other professionals working in large organizations also experience problems of dual loyalties. For instance, in recent years anthropologists working for the military have come to fear that their knowledge could be used for, for instance, identifying targets, and the American Anthropological Association Executive Board stated on October 31, 2007 that "such use of fieldwork-derived information would violate the stipulations in the AAA Code of Ethics that those studied not be harmed" (the statement can be found at http://www.aaanet.org/about/policies/statements /human-terrain-system-statement.cfm). Yet, it seems that the dual loyalties experienced by military medical personnel are particularly testing. Medical ethicist Peter A. Clark writes:

> Military medical personnel, especially in a time of war, are faced with the most ethically difficult dual loyalty of doing what is in the best interest of their patient and doing what is in the best interest of their government and fellow soldiers. This conflict has existed for as long as we have fought wars. It is the most difficult because it is the state or the military exerting the pressure on the medical professional (2006, 571).

31. Advising on the prisoner's physical limitations enables the interrogator to use, for instance, sleep deprivation without causing lasting harm. In Guantanamo Bay, writes Clark, some doctors have been guilty of overlooking, not

reporting, advising, and even assisting in the abuse of detainees (2006, 577). Different dilemmas arise when healthcare is provided to bolster the support for a military mission. In recent years military personnel took part in projects aimed at building goodwill by providing medical care to the local population. This can lead to tensions for medical personnel, thinking that they should provide care independently of "what is in it for us." Finally, in the medical rules of eligibility used in some of today's conflicts the interests of own military personnel outweigh the interests of local nationals, who for instance only get care for injuries that are threatening to life, limb, or eyesight. In order to keep enough capacity for own personnel, every so often military medical personnel will not help locals in need of medical attention. The question is how bad a thing that is. Most military colleagues of military doctors and nurses, considering military effectiveness most important, will think it is not, while their medical colleagues from the civilian world, with their own oaths and codes in mind, will probably beg to differ, holding that military medical personnel should act from a strictly impartial ethos. Basically, military medical personnel have the choice between following the military line by strictly going by the rules, or taking a more lenient view on these rules (they can for instance exaggerate wounds), and thus acting upon their medical professional ethic.

32. Since military necessity is a matter of interpretation, there is some reason for worry (see also Slim 2007, 174). One could therefore argue that is necessary to have civilian oversight by means of "a commission with membership that includes an adequate number of civilian health professionals skilled in ethical issues and human rights" (London et al. 2006, 388). This commission should provide "the needed balance in determining what kind of military necessity justifies deviating from the norms of ethical medical practice" (London et al. 2006, 388). The plan of Benatar and Upshur for a "totally independent" medical ethics tribunal, which ought to decide when dilemmas occur, boils down to the same thing: only principles of public health should guide the tribunal's deliberations (2008, 2166).

33. The WMA states that "medical ethics in times of armed conflict is identical to medical ethics in times of peace." This means that "if, in performing their professional duty, physicians have conflicting loyalties, their primary obligation is to their patients." The International Code of Medical Ethics of the WMA specifies that "a physician shall owe his patients complete loyalty and all the resources of his science." The WMA policy can be found at http://www.wma.net /en/30publications/10policies/a20/index.html.

34. The military ethic has a collectivist outlook (Huntington 1964, 79; Toner 1992), and traditionally stresses the supremacy of society over the individual. Moreover, military men and women seem to share a rather pessimistic and conservative outlook on human nature, seeing man as essentially selfish and weak (Huntington 1964, 63). That probably explains why honor still finds a fertile ground in the military: it is seen as an incentive to overcome the inherent weaknesses of man and as a check to the "softening" influence of a society (Janowitz

1960, 248). But today the tasks of militaries have widened in scope, and most militaries have to deal with more than just opposing forces: military personnel have to take the interests of others, rather than just the organization and colleagues, into account (Olsthoorn 2010). Behind many moral questions military personnel face today is the conflict between loyalty to a group—one's colleagues or organization—on the one hand and a more universal ethic on the other, and often the interests of colleagues and the organization win through. But undue force protection and negative views of outsiders are in the longer run detrimental to what today's missions try to achieve.

35. Another case in point: 27 Israeli pilots wrote in September 2003 a letter to the Israeli air force chief, stating that they would no longer conduct missions above Palestinian territory that endangered civilians. The air force fired the nine pilots who were still on active duty.

36. The interview is part of the *Samuel Proctor Oral History Program* of the University of Florida and can be found at http://www.uflib.ufl.edu/ufdc/?b=UF 00005614&v=00001. The case of Rockwood has been used at the U.S. Naval Academy, though not necessarily as an example to follow (Pierce 2002).

37. On closer inspection, Freud continues, a stranger "has more claim to my hostility and even my hatred. He seems not to have the least trace of love for me and shows me not the slightest consideration" (1961, 67). Although it is "possible to bind together a considerable number of people in love," according to Freud this can only be done as long "as there are other people left over to receive the manifestations of their aggressiveness" (1961, 72).

38. At the same time Hume acknowledged that "the heart takes not part entirely with those general notions, nor regulates all its love and hatred, by the universal, abstract differences of vice and virtue, without regard to self, or the persons with whom we are more intimately connected" (*An Enquiry Concerning the Principles of Morals* V.ii).

Chapter 4. Internalizing Honor: Integrity

1. According to G. F. Jones, "the sense of personal integrity or inner voice, did not become widespread before the middle of the eighteenth century" (cited in F. H. Stewart 1994, 40).

2. But Rousseau takes sides with the Stoics in more than that aspect alone: Richard Vernon, for instance, speaks of Rousseau's "evident debt to Stoic writers (. . .) perhaps most especially to Seneca. The critique of sophistication, vanity, and luxury; the loss of original 'humanity' under the weight of artifice; the corrupting consequences of slavery; the identification of reason with the capacity of autonomy; the appeal to 'man, of whatever country you are': all these are Stoic themes" (1986, 40). According to Peter Gay, "the key to Emile is the Stoic injunction that man must live according to nature; it was Rousseau's genius to harness this idea, derived from Seneca, to the idea of human development" (1979, 542).

Diderot wrote about "Jean-Jacques, who recalls Seneca to us at a hundred points, and who does not owe Cicero a line" (cited in Roche 1974, 19). Françoise and Pierre Richard, editors of *Emile* for Garnier, called Seneca, Marcus Aurelius, and Epictetus—all Stoic, all Roman—the "vrais inspirateurs de Jean-Jacques" (1964, p. v note d). But Levine argues (writing about *Emile*) that

> in the classical view, community is not the supersession of atomic individualism, for atomic individualism is itself inconceivable. Man is essentially and always a *political animal*; and community—far from being a human contrivance, a covenant, for the realization of *self*-determination—is natural, indeed inevitable, for such political animals as we are. Private virtue, as discussed in *Emile*, is an absurdity, as is the very ideal of self-determination. Rousseau's classicism is thus deceptive (1976, 196).

3. According to William A. Galston,

> for Rousseau, the central phenomenon is pride, the desire for reputation or the esteem of others, which is the prime motive for the development of both the social virtues and of the natural faculties (the arts and the sciences). In his account, pride is responsible for the greater part of human misery, of unnecessary endeavor, and of unnatural needs; it operates, moreover largely in opposition to genuine social morality (1975, 96).

Gay adds that "Rousseau, in his two Discourses, was inclined to hold pride responsible for civilization with all its glaring flaws" (1979, 192). Rousseau's stance on pride was, according to Gay, just an example of the general sentiment among thinkers of the Enlightenment: "This much seemed evident: pride appeared in some egregious forms—conceit, vanity, lust for power—and in these forms it had done good only, if at all, unintentionally or by indirection" (1979, 192).

4. In addition, Rousseau recommended "that, by honours and public rewards, all the patriotic virtues should be glorified, that citizens should constantly be kept occupied with the fatherland." This as part of "the art of ennobling souls and of turning them into an instrument more powerful than gold" (*Considerations on the Government of Poland*). Rousseau, like other Romantics, contributed to the idea of national honor that was a topic of the previous chapter.

5. "The romantics devoted much of their energy to deploring the state of contemporary society, and its trends as they perceived them. This accounts for a great deal of their popularity: woe and calamity have always had a ready market" (Gordon 1991, 268).

6. The late eighteenth century German philosopher Johann Gottlieb Fichte asked us to turn our gaze away from our surroundings us and to look inside ourselves instead (cited in Furst 1969, 58).

7. According to Sennett, nowadays "the real self is the self of motivations and impulses; it is the active self. But it is not active in society; instead a passive 'me' exists there" (1977, 331).

8. But it echoes not only in in the humanistic psychology of Maslow and Fromm. Albert Ellis, the founder of *Rational Emotive Therapy*, thinks for instance that healthy people "refuse to measure their intrinsic worth by their extrinsic achievements or by what other people think of them. They frankly choose to accept themselves unconditionally, and try to completely avoid rating themselves" (Ellis and Dryden 1987, 19). Essentially, "the stoic viewpoint which stated that people are disturbed not by things but their view of things, became the foundation of RET," while its "theory of human value is similar to the Christian viewpoint of condemning the sin but forgiving the sinner" (Ellis and Dryden 1987, 2–3).

9. But opposing modern individualism there is still the conservative view: "'Man was born free' (said Rousseau, with his faith in natural goodness of man) 'but is everywhere in chains.' 'In chains, and so he ought to be,' replies the thoughtful conservative, defending the good and wise and necessary chains of rooted tradition and historic continuity, upon which depend the civil liberties" (Viereck 1965, 158). According to Burke, Rousseau's "doctrines, on the whole, are so inapplicable to real life and manners, that we never can dream of drawing from them any rule for laws or conduct" (1969, 267).

10. Opposing this view is the idea that "the modeling of conduct through the examples of others" can have a positive role in moral education based on virtue ethics (Carr and Steutel 1999, 253).

11. Edmund Burke met Rousseau in England:

> As I had good opportunities of knowing his proceedings almost from day to day, he left no doubt on my mind that he entertained no principle either to influence his heart, or to guide his understanding but *vanity*. With this vice he was possessed to a degree little short of madness. (1967, 263).

Burke therefore called Rousseau "the philosopher of vanity" (cited in Mansfield 1987, 689).

12. Although Richard Sennett sees a somewhat similar problem with authenticity. Nowadays, "expression is made contingent upon authentic feeling, but one is always plunged into the narcistic problem of never being able to crystallize what is authentic in one's feeling" (1977, 259). According to Pocock, "classical man tends to assume that he has an identity and to inquire what can be done with it (. . .). Romantic man tends to assume that his identity requires to be asserted or discovered" (1971, 275).

13. Allan Bloom, however, is rather critical of this idea of an unique manner:

> The respectable and accessible nobility of man is to be found not in the quest for or discovery of the good life, but in creating one's own "life-style," of which there is not just one but many possible, none comparable to another. He who has a "life-style" is in competition with, and hence inferior to, no one, and because he has one he can command his own esteem and that of others (1987).

14. Anna Karenina's suicide is in keeping with the ideas of Rousseau, who wrote in *Emile* that "opinion is the grave of virtue among men" (1991, 365), but that this is different for women. Rousseau thought that, the world being what it is, opinion is for them in fact the throne of virtue; something that is ordained "by the very law of nature." So, "when a woman acts well, she has accomplished only half of her task, and what is thought of her is no less important to her than what she actually is" (1991, 364).

15. According to Boyd, "Julien's secret admiration for Napoleon has less to do with the latter's authoritarian means, nationalistic excesses, or lionization of the theory of the great man than with the fact that the age of Bonaparte was a time of unfettered social mobility" (2005, 374). It was for a reason that Napoleon opened the officer ranks of the post-revolutionary army to the lower classes: in Tolstoy's *War and Peace* prince Andrew quotes Napoleon as having said about the French aristocrats: "I showed them the path to glory, but they did not follow it (. . .), I opened my antechambers and they crowded in" (Part 1, Chapter 5).

16. But according to Walzer it is not

> aristocratic honor that everyman is after. As the struggle has broadened, so the social good at issue is infinitely diversified, and its names are multiplied. *Honor, respect, esteem, praise, prestige, status, reputation, dignity, rank, regard, admiration, worth, distinction, deference, homage, appreciation, glory, fame, celebrity:* the words represent an accumulation over time and were originally used in different social settings and for different purposes (1983, 252).

17. "One would like to say: whatever is going to seem right to me is right. And that only means that here we can't talk about 'right'" (*Philosophical Investigations* §258). Elsewhere in the *Investigations* he writes: "And hence also 'obeying a rule' is a practice. And to think one is obeying a rule is not to obey a rule. Hence it is not possible to obey a rule 'privately': otherwise thinking one was obeying a rule would be the same thing as obeying it." (*Investigations* §202; see also Kripke 1982, 3; Johnston 1993, 211–20).

18. This quote from *On Liberty* suggests that Hayek was not entirely fair to Mill when he wrote that

> a hundred years ago, in the stricter moral atmosphere of the Victorian era, when at the same time coercion by the state was at a minimum, John Stuart Mill directed his heaviest attack against such 'moral coercion.' In this he probably overstated the case for liberty. (. . .) Whether or not we wish to call coercion those milder forms pressure that society applies to nonconformists, there can be little doubt that these moral rules and conventions that possess less binding power than the law have an important and even indispensable role to perform and probably do as much to facilitate life in society as do the strict rules of law. (. . .) On the whole, those conventions and norms of social intercourse and individual conduct do not constitute a

serious infringement of individual liberty but secure a certain minimum of uniformity of conduct that assists individual efforts more than it impedes them (1990, 146–7).

19. Freud thought that many people lack a super-ego, and "allow themselves to do any bad thing which promises them enjoyment, so long as they are sure that the authority will not know anything about it or cannot blame them for it; they are afraid only of being found out" (1961, 86).

20. Although the word courage is no longer synonymous with virtue as it was in pre-Socratic times (see also Plutarch *Coriolanus* 1), most of us will feel they have a fairly accurate idea of what courage is. Yet, one of the oldest attempts to grasp its essence, Plato's *Laches*, ends in disappointment, for "we have not discovered what courage is" (199e). One of the more recent texts on courage actually *begins* with a similar statement: William Ian Miller writes at the start of his *The Mystery of Courage* that he has "no single theory, for none I have seen, nor none I can come up with, will work" (2000, 14).

21. Notwithstanding these differences, the two forms of courage sometimes come together. The German soldier who refused to fight for Hitler, presented as an example of moral courage by one author, was certainly also physically courageous: he would be beheaded (Toner 2000, 115, 189n17).

22. Against this position is the psychologist's finding that someone can be fearful of one thing and not of another, and that it is more sensible to speak of courageous acts than of courageous persons, suggesting that the presence or absence of one form of courage in a person does not say much about the measure of the other form (see for instance Rachman 1990).

23. According to military historian John Lynn, the repeated failure of the Arabic militaries during the second half of the twentieth century was a consequence of the Arabic shame culture, which made that officers tended to conceal or downplay losses. For instance, on 5 June 1967 (the first day of the Six-Day War) the Egyptian President Nasser only learned late in the afternoon that the Israeli air force had destroyed his air force in the early morning (2003, 281–315).

24. Modern military sociology points to the importance of honor and the concern for one's reputation among colleagues as motivations for physical courage. Only five percent of the enlisted U.S. men in the Second World War named idealistic reasons as incentives for courage (Stouffer 1949, 108, 150); they mentioned religion, the wish to end the war, and group cohesion more often. According to S. L. A. Marshall, that latter factor was the most powerful. Soldiers "do not aspire to a hero's role, but they are equally unwilling that they should be considered the least worthy among those present (. . .) personal honor is the one thing valued more than life itself by the majority of men" (1947, 149). Other authors have argued that social cohesion, not indoctrination by Nazi propaganda, had made *Wehrmacht* soldiers effective in the Second World War (Shils and Janowitz 1948, 280–315). But most of these studies are rather dated, and their methodology

and conclusions are increasingly debated (see for instance Segal and Kestnbaum 2002, 445–6; Ben-Shalom, Lehrer, and Ben-Ari, 2005). Marshall, for example, supposedly drew some of his conclusions beforehand, and later fabricated the evidence to support them (Gat 2001, 302n98). The *Wehrmacht* study was criticized for believing German prisoners of war on their word when they stated that they were not motivated by the Nazi-ideology (Segal and Kestnbaum 2002, 445–6). Also, according to most research social cohesion has no clear correlation with performance, and a high level of social cohesion ("clubbiness") can even have adverse effects if the norms of the group do not align with the goals of the organization (MacCoun et al 2006, 647). These Second World War studies have nonetheless been very influential in the military, and authors from a military background still refer to Marshall's study (see for instance Wong et al. 2003, 2; Daddis 2004, 27; Horn 2004, 14). Regarding the question what in truth motivates soldiers, there is "an ever-changing mixture of social, moral, pragmatic and psychological theory. Rather than being universal truths about how men fight, these are themselves historical material in their own right" (Wessely 2006, 286).

25. Aristotle thought that seemingly courageous acts that spring from impulses like anger or revenge (the motives of the Homeric heroes), or the concern for reputation (or any other expedient motive), do not deserve that predicate. Especially the salaried soldier (which would be a mercenary in Aristotle's days) did not have his approval. But also the citizen soldier, although he comes closer to being courageous than the soldier who fights for money and attaches more value to his own safety than to his good name (*Nicomachean Ethics* 1116b), falls short of true courage since he is mainly motivated by his preference for death over disgrace; his object is to avoid dishonor. Aristotle's definition of courage is clearly that of a philosopher, and possibly aimed at bringing courage within the philosopher's reach (Miller 2000, 50). It certainly takes it outside the reach of most others; sticking to the requirement that a courageous act should spring from a love of virtue would probably deny that predicate to most acts that now go under that name.

26. Also, we would not want to deny all German soldiers who fought in World War II the label courageous, although their actions clearly lacked a noble cause. Evidently, they were mere instruments of an evil regime (compare Toner 2000, 113–14). But most of us would not wish to call the 9/11 terrorists courageous men. The moral difference between the terrorist and the German soldier is pretty straightforward, though: the former deliberately chose to serve an immoral cause, the latter often much less so (for a different view, see McMahan 2009). Susan Sontag received a lot of criticism for her remark that "if the word 'cowardly' is to be used, it might be more aptly applied to those who kill from beyond the range of retaliation, high in the sky, than to those willing to die themselves in order to kill others" (2001). Sontag termed courage a "morally neutral" virtue (2001).

27. Social cohesion can foster anything from overly warrior-like behavior to too much force protection, but perhaps not conduct that is beneficial to

outsiders. In 1993, for instance, Canadian airborne soldiers from 2 Commando, known for its strong in-group loyalty, beat to death a Somali teenager who had tried to access the Canadian camp—and kept silent about it. A reconstruction for court showed that about 16 unit members must have heard the screaming, but did nothing to stop their colleagues. Canada disbanded its elite airborne regiment because of this incident (see for the role of group bonding in this incident Winslow 1999). In that same year, a Belgian paratrooper urinated on a dead Somali civilian, two of his colleagues held a Somali civilian over an open fire. In both cases it was attempted to conceal the events. An U.S. Army report showed that marines in Iraq were more likely to behave unethically, and less willing to report a colleague who acted improperly, than army soldiers. For instance, only 40 percent of the marines were willing to report a unit member who injured or killed an innocent noncombatant, while 55 percent of the army soldiers were prepared to do so (Mental Health Advisory Team 2006). That difference is probably due to group ties among marines being stronger than among average military personnel. According to Westhusing, regimental honor "tends to pervert and transfigure both greatness of mind and extended benevolence, but especially extended benevolence" (2003, 207). Nonetheless, that incidents as described here come closer to being really incidents (albeit sometimes very serious ones) than was the case in the wars of the past, when cruelty was more structural. In general, wars are nowadays fought with more restraint, which suggests that *jus in bello* and military ethics are not contradictions in terms (see also Pinker 2011).

28. Appiah sees a middle way, though. According to Appiah, "a person with integrity will care that she lives up to her ideals. But (. . .) it is the concern for respect that connects living well with our place in a social world. Honor takes integrity public" (2010, 179).

29. In *Lord of the Flies* William Golding describes how once civilized 12-year-olds, stuck on an otherwise uninhabited island, turn savages when they hide their face behind Indian-like warpaint. The concealing paint brought "liberation into savagery" (Chapter 11).

Chapter 5. Denying Honor: Respect and Humiliation

1. According to Christina Tarnapolsky, "pride and shame can work in a non-zero-sum game in those regimes where respect and dignity are considered basic goods to which all citizens are entitled" (2010, 183).

2. The virtue of justice is the obvious exception; Aristotle deemed it the most complete virtue because the best is not he "who practices virtue toward himself, but who practices it toward others, for that is a hard thing to achieve" (*Nicomachean Ethics* 1030a).

3. Some of those who demand respect quite vehemently nowadays seem especially sensitive about being disrespected, and this might be more about old

honor than about the modern notion of respect. Spierenburg thinks that "our understanding of today's gang cultures can be enhanced by the study of the culture of violence and honor in distant societies in the past" (1998, 26). According to Bowman, honor survives in a "degraded form" in gangs and hip-hop culture (2006, 7). In the conclusion of his book Bowman links gang culture to a topic of the next sections of this chapter, writing about "the degraded or primitive models of masculine honor offered by gang culture on the one hand or terrorism on the other" (2006, 323; see also Pinker 2011, 148).

4. According to some authors honor and loyalty are even becoming more important in much of the Muslim world. According to anthropologist Akbar Ahmed,

> the failure to create a just and compassionate society leads people to fall back to ideas of tribal honor and revenge. Divisions in society deepen on the basis of blood and custom. Killing and conflict are encouraged. The honor of the group and—if it is attacked—the need to take revenge become more important than worshiping God in peace and engendering compassion in society (2004, 6).

In the view of another author, Arab society today is characterized by strong group loyalties and exaggerated forms of shame (Lynn 2003, 313)—which, incidentally, also points to a close relationship between honor and loyalty. This sensitivity to honor and shame is probably not a matter of religion: honor and shame might be alien to Christianity, but they are not markedly important in the Koran either. Although many have noted that honor and shame play an important role in most societies where Islam is dominant, this is something that predates the rise of this religion (see for instance Bowman 2006, 19, 26; Firestone 1999, 30–1).

5. Today, political Islamists sometimes harbor views of the West that are just as simplified as the pictures many Christians over the ages have held of Islam. In their view, the U.S., as the leader of the West, resembles Rome in its later, degenerate and demoralized stage (Buruma and Margalit 2004, 126). The ideologue of the Muslim Brotherhood Sayyid Qutb, for instance, wrote about the noisy materialism and, in his view, ill-advised sexual freedom he witnessed travelling in the U.S. in 1948–50 (see for instance Qutb 2006). A view that resembles that of some conservative Western authors, who worry that in larger society moral standards are rapidly fading away. As we have seen, similar fears were already present in the work of Cicero and Sallust.

6. Apparently, "Islamists juxtapose this perception of the death-fearing infidel with the readiness to die that is said to prevail among the true Muslim" (Moghadam 2003, 71). As a Taliban fighter remarked, "they love Pepsi-Cola, but we love death" (Buruma and Margalit 2004, 49). According to Osama bin Laden Muslim fighters in Somalia were surprised to learn that the U.S. soldier was just a "paper tiger," easier to defeat than the Soviet Union in Afghanistan (bin Laden 1998; see also Bowman 2006, 22).

7. The example is of course debatable (and has been extensively debated in moral philosophy and military ethics alike; see for instance Nagel 1972; Murphy 1973), and that is illustrative of the complexities attached to drawing a line between what can be excusable on rare occasions, and what under no circumstances. For instance, debates on the "justifiableness" of torture seem to center around that same distinction between excusable (and hence not justified) and not excusable (Davis 2005), although the Bush government tried to lend some legitimacy (and thus justifiableness) to "torture lite" and "enhanced interrogation."

8. But some go a bit further than that, maintains Walzer in *Arguing about War*; whereas not many people are justifying terrorism, some go beyond merely looking for explanations, and are finding excuses as well. They suggest for instance that under certain circumstances terrorism can be pardonable as a "last resort." Although terrorism is almost universally condemned, writes Walzer, this practice of finding excuses is not, and its wrongfulness, which lies in the fact that it "undercuts our knowledge of the evil," has to be argued (2004, 52).

9. Osama bin Laden "seized on the notion of honor," blaming corrupt rulers supported by the West "for robbing the Muslims of their honor and dignity," and suggesting violence as the only solution (Ahmed 2004, 57–9). Bin Laden himself said in his 7 October 2001 videotape—in defense of the 9/11 attacks—that Muslims had suffered humiliation by the West for almost eighty years, i.e., since the defeat of the Ottoman sultanate in 1918 (Lewis 2003, p. i). A year later he declared in a *Letter to America* (2002) that the governments of the Arabic countries are agents of America, and that they humiliate their subjects.

10. Some Muslims, writes Islamologist Bassam Tibi, "have a worldview that entitles them to dominate." In reality, "they are dominated by others, to whom they feel—thanks to their divine revelation—superior" (2002, 61). Dominique Moïsi writes rather sweeping about the Muslim world's "culture of humiliation," as opposed to the West's "culture of fear," and Asia's "culture of hope" (2007). Stern holds that people who join religious terrorist groups "start out feeling humiliated, enraged that they are viewed by some Other as second class" (2004b, 281–2). What complicates matters here is that one party feels humiliated, but probably without any intent to humiliate on the side of the other party, in this case Western civilization. But as we have noted, intent to humiliate is not a condition for humiliation to arise. The West's foreign policies, position in the world, military presence abroad, etc., can therefore be a cause of humiliation without the West having any intention of doing so. What complicates things even further here is that the position in the world held by Islamic societies, seen as humiliating by Islamists, is, as some observers have stated, partly of their own doing, or to be more precise: of the doing of their malfunctioning governments (see for instance Lewis 2003).

11. Furthered by humiliation or not, terrorism itself amounts to humiliation with a big H, as its perpetrator denies "the peoplehood and humanity of the groups among whom he or she finds victims" (Walzer 2004, 59). But this

same perpetrator will consider it a humiliation with a small h—the deflation of the pretension to be invulnerable (Saurette 2006, 518). As a form of "expressive violence," terrorism is all about shame (Coker 2008, 117). Especially the 9/11 attacks were interpreted as a humiliation of the West. "Bin Laden realised that many were pleased to see the US wounded and humiliated," writes Burke (2005b). At least one author sees a subsequent "policy of counter-humiliation" by the U.S. and its allies (Saurette 2006, 518–21).

12. Words and deeds that are perceived as disrespectful, and that are widely aired in the media, could impose risks on Western military personnel deployed around the world. Danish troops in Afghanistan had become a more important target because of the publication of the cartoons in *Jyllands-Posten*.

13. After the film *Innocence of Muslims* led to worldwide unrest, the speaker of the European parliament, Martin Schulz, was criticized for giving in too easily after issuing a press statement in which he strongly condemned "not only the content but also the distribution of such a movie, which is humiliating the feelings of a lot of people all over the world." Fear of terrorist reprisals, and the recent memory of the Danish cartoon crisis two years earlier, formed in 2008 the rationale behind the public appeal the Dutch prime minister made to Member of Parliament Geert Wilders not to circulate his critical film on Islam, as the government feared that Wilders was going to desecrate the Qur'an in it. When *Fitna* was released in 2008, the government distanced itself from its contents because it served "no purpose other than to cause offence." The government's reaction differed from the course the Denmark chose in the Danish cartoon crisis; the Danish government saw no reason to interfere if the cartoons were within the limits of the law. Wilders' film eventually led to protests around the world, but not as violent as some had feared. Reactions among Dutch Muslims were moderate, and Wilders complimented them for keeping their cool better than the government. The Dutch government at first glance overreacted. But without hindsight, it is difficult to say if a bolder line had been better. The reaction of the Dutch government has to be seen against the background of the murder of Dutch filmmaker Theo van Gogh, killed in 2004 because of his critical Islam film. Pinned to his chest was a letter to the writer of the script of that film, Ayaan Hirsi Ali (at that time Dutch Member of Parliament and a friend of Wilders), blaming her for terrorizing Islam.

14. According to F. H. Stewart, "honor is a matter of deeds, not just of words" (1994, 3). In his novel *Shame* Rushdie writes: "Looking at smoking cities on my television screen, I see groups of young people running through the streets, the shame burning on their brows and setting fire to shops, police shields, cars" (1983, 117).

15. Later there were stories of rape of Iraqi women by other Iraqis—crimes that were seen as a result of the failure of coalition troops to provide the Iraqis with a reasonably secure environment (Fontan 2006, 223). In an attempt to justify kidnappings and beheadings to the Muslim audience Abu Musab al-Zarqawi, for

instance, picked "one of the single most emotive issues in the Islamic world: the supposed imprisonment, and abuse, of Muslim women by non-Muslim men" (Burke 2004b).

16. We have seen in a previous section that humiliation can occur without an intention to humiliate, but in a previous chapter we have noted that intentions do not matter a lot to those at the receiving end. To the extent that unintended humiliation is the result of a lack of knowledge of local sensitivities, good quality intercultural training, if not already a part of predeployment training, can enhance cultural awareness, and make military personnel more conscious of local sensitivities.

17. Montaigne already pointed out that torture yields unreliable information: "For why should pain make me confess what is true rather than force me to say what is not true?" (*On Conscience*).

18. Social psychologist Philip Zimbardo argues in his book on Abu Ghraib that, on a lower level, the hopeless situation the guards found themselves in (understaffed in an overcrowded prison, with daily mortar and rocket attacks, and pressure from above to break prisoners who were said to be responsible for attacks on U.S. troops outside) made disaster almost unavoidable (2007, 324-443; for a different view, see Mastroianni 2011). Although most people tend to take a dispositional view, a situational view (basically also the view taken by those who seek to explain terrorism) might therefore be more in place (Zimbardo 2007, 6). According to Richard A. Gabriel, the possession of a virtue is a disposition to behave well, but this disposition does not guarantee that someone will behave ethically (1982, 8–9, 150, 152). In Zimbardo's famous Stanford prison experiment of 1971 a team of researchers divided a group of undergraduates in two teams, one playing the role of prisoners, the other that of guards. Within days the latter got so absorbed in their roles that the experiment had to be stopped because they started humiliating prisoners in ways that were very reminiscent of the images that would come out of Abu Ghraib years later (Zimbardo 2007, 328). Roman Krol, one of the U.S. intelligence men convicted and demoted as a result of the Abu Ghraib scandal, later related (in the documentary *Standard Operating Procedure*) how he was sentenced to "eight months in jail for pouring water on somebody, and throwing a Nerf ball at somebody. That's humiliating. People laugh at that." In the end, he was "more humiliated by that sentence than actually punished."

19. According to military historian John Keegan, there is still "no substitute for honor as a medium of enforcing decency on the battlefield, never has been and never will be. There are no judges, more to the point, no policemen at the place where death is done in combat" (cited in Ignatieff 1997, 118). Although part of this warrior code is codified in the Geneva Conventions to make it less particularistic, according to Michael Ignatieff the "decisive restraint on inhuman practices on the battlefield lies within the warrior himself" (1997, 118). According to Nancy Sherman,

Honor, especially in its Homeric mode, where it is linked with machismo and the glory of decoration—still the archetype for many in the military today—can be a misplaced warrior virtue. But it needn't be. It can produce a willingness to take risks to protect those who are not themselves trained to take risks (2010).

Honor can also protect the soldiers from psychological injuries. Military ethicist Shannon E. French thinks that "when there is no battlefield, and warriors fight murderers, they may be tempted to become the mirror image of the evil they hoped to destroy. Their only protection is their code of honor" (2003, 241). So although Walzer has argued that "honor and chivalry seem to play only a small part in contemporary combat," supposedly because, here also, "popular passion overcame aristocratic honor" (1992, 35), the picture regarding honor in today's militaries is in reality not that bleak. In fact, Walzer himself also thinks that "some sense of military honor is still the creed of the professional soldier" (1992, 35). What is true is that, in line with Tocqueville's description of democratic honor, the idea of the officer-gentleman now relates to standards of behavior, not to descent.

20. The U.S. Army describes respect as, among other things, "trusting that all people have done their jobs and fulfilled their duty." This definition limits respect to colleagues as it emphasizes that the Army is a team, and to oneself as it also mentions self-respect as a "vital ingredient." An article in *Military Review* on respect as a value for the U.S. Army does not mention the need to respect outsiders in any way (H. Keller 2006). Interestingly, the modern notion of dignity is an important value in medical ethics, whereas honor, its more exclusive forerunner, is more often to be found on the value lists of militaries.

21. According to Albert Bandura, "there are many social and psychological maneuvers by which moral self-sanctions can be disengaged from inhumane conduct" (1999, 194). They include moral justification (it is for a good cause), advantageous comparison (the other side behaves worse), the displacement and diffusion of responsibility (basically the problem of the many hands—something that has gotten a new relevance with the emergence of network-centric warfare), the dehumanization of enemy forces during wartime, and the use of euphemisms such as collateral damage, servicing the target (Bandura 1999, 195–203), surgical strike, neutralizing assets (Coady 2008, 132) and, in recent years, torture lite and enhanced interrogation (Wolfendale 2009, 53–4). Zimbardo showed that many of these maneuvers played a role in the Abu Ghraib abuse, although here, as is the case with terrorism, a search for causes "does not negate the responsibility of these MPs, nor their guilt; explanation and understanding do not excuse such misdeeds" (2007, 445).

22. Some hold that dehumanization has been a policy in the Israeli-occupied territories: in the conclusions of the report of the United Nations Fact Finding Mission on the Gaza Conflict, the much debated Goldstone report (about Israel's Operation Cast Lead in 2008–9), we read that there appears

to have been an assault on the dignity of the people. This was seen not only in the use of human shields and unlawful detentions sometimes in unacceptable conditions, but also in the vandalizing of houses when occupied and the way in which people were treated when their houses were entered. The graffiti on the walls, the obscenities and often racist slogans, all constituted an overall image of humiliation and dehumanization of the Palestinian population (United Nations Human Rights Council 2009, 407).

23. As Hugo Slim put it in *Killing Civilians*, seeing people primarily as members of an enemy group is probably easiest "from an air force bomber or a computer screen that is miles away from the individuals one is killing" (2007, 175). To be effective, civilian immunity "requires that armed people find a fundamental *identification* with those called civilians and not an excessive *distinction* from them" (2007, 34).

24. That is certainly the case when there is at the remotes someone who thinks that his job is "like a video game. It can get a little bloodthirsty. But it's fucking cool" (P. W. Singer 2009, 332).

25. The Goldstone report points to that relation between respect and basic human rights. During Israel's Operation Cast Lead

> numerous civilians who came into contact with the Israeli armed forces during the military operation recounted shocking stories of humiliation that would certainly be in stark contravention of the principle of respect for human dignity, which forms the core of all human rights and fundamental freedoms (United Nations Human Rights Council 2009, 232).

26. Anthropologist Clifford Geertz points out that writing in too general terms will ignore the differences between the various creeds of Islam (and Islamism), and the different cultures and peoples that are among its believers (2003). Likewise, "the hundreds of groups, cells, movements, even individuals, lumped together under the rubric 'Islamic Terrorism' is enormously diverse" (Burke 2004a, 24).

27. Although the United States is supposedly a society in which "traditional ideas of honor are irrelevant or rejected," writes Ahmed, former U.S. president Bush "clearly linked honor and the need to redeem it through revenge" in his statements after the attacks of September 11, 2001 (2004, 60).

Conclusion

1. According to Galston, a realistic political philosophy should base itself on the principle that "preventing the worst is the first duty of political leaders, and striving for far-reaching social improvement makes sense only when doing so does not significantly increase the odds that some previous abated evil will reappear" (2010, 394). Yet, according to Dunn, a more prudent political philosophy

"would be profoundly lacking both in philosophical *éclat* and in the capacity to inspire emotion, being grounded as it is not in a giddy rapture at the moral splendours of human liberty and autonomy" (1985, 168; see also Hayek 1990, 56, 60).

2. Hume wrote that in each

> system of morality, which I have hitherto met with, I have always remarked, that the author proceeds for some time in the ordinary way of reasoning, and establishes the being of a God, or makes observations concerning human affairs; when of a sudden I am surprised to find, that instead of the usual copulations of propositions, *is* and *is not*, I meet with no proposition that is not connected with an *ought* or *ought not* (*Treatise* III.i.i).

The fact that bothered Hume most was that the "change is imperceptible; but is, however, of the last consequence. For as this *ought*, or *ought not*, expresses some new relation or affirmation, 'tis necessary that it should be observed and explained" (III.i.i). Hume "assumed that the basic division in the fields of knowledge is that between physical and moral subjects. (. . .) Moral subjects are what we, for lack of better terms, probably would call, 'the humanities' and the 'social sciences'" (J. B. Stewart 1963, 10). But today "the fact-value distinction is taken as a given by almost everyone today, no matter whether they are behavioral scientists or committed revolutionaries" (Bloom 1980, 118).

References

Adkins, A. W. H. (1960) *Merit and Responsibility: a Study in Greek Values* (Oxford: Oxford Clarendon Press).

Ahmed, A. S. (2004) *Islam under Siege: Living Dangerously in a Post-Honor World* (Cambridge: Polity Press).

Alexander, L. and M. Moore (2008) Deontological Ethics, in: E. N. Zalta (ed.) *The Stanford Encyclopedia of Philosophy (Fall 2010 Edition)*. Available at: http://plato.stanford.edu/archives/fall2008/entries/ethics-deontological/.

Anscombe, G. E. M. (1961) War and Murder, in: W. Stein (ed.) *Nuclear Weapons: A Catholic Response*, pp. 43–62 (London: Burns & Oates).

Appiah, A. K. (2010) *The Honor Code* (New York: W.W. Norton).

Aquinas, T. (2006) *Summa Theologiae: Questions on God* (Cambridge: Cambridge University Press).

Arendt, H. (1958) *The Human Condition* (Chicago: Chicago University Press).

Aristotle (1962) *Nicomachean Ethics* (Indianapolis: The Bobbs Merrill Company).

Atkinson, R. F. (1969) Hume on "Is" and "Ought": A Reply to Mr MacIntyre, in: W. D. Hudson (ed.) *The Is/Ought Question*, pp. 51–8 (London: MacMillan).

Bacon, F. (1985) *The Essays* (Harmondsworth: Penguin Books).

Ball, T. (1998) Conceptual History and the History of Political Thought, in: I. Hampsher-Monk, K. Tilmans, and F. van Vree (eds) *History of Concepts: Comparative Perspectives*, pp. 75–86 (Amsterdam: Amsterdam University Press).

Bandura, A. (1999) Moral Disengagement in the Perpetration of Inhumanities, *Personality and Social Psychology Review*, 3(3), pp. 193–209.

Bargewell, E. A. (2007) "Simple Failures" and "Disastrous Results," *Washington Post*, April 21.

Barton, C. A. (2001) *Roman Honor: The Fire in the Bones* (Berkeley: University of California Press).

Barry, B. (1973) *The Liberal Theory of Justice: A Critical Examination of the Principal Doctrines in A Theory of Justice by John Rawls* (Oxford: Clarendon Press).

Barry, B. (1989) *Theories of Justice* (London: Harvester-Wheatsheaf).

Barry, B. (1995) *Justice as Impartiality* (Oxford: Oxford Clarendon Press).

Becker, G. S. (1976) *The Economic Approach to Human Behavior* (Chicago: Chicago University Press).

Becker, G. S. (1996) *Accounting for Tastes* (Cambridge: Harvard University Press).

Benatar, S. R. and R. E. G. Upshur (2008) Dual Loyalty of Physicians in the Military and in Civilian Life, *American Journal of Public Health*, 98(12), pp. 2161–7.

Benedict, R. (1967) *The Chrysantium and the Sword: Patterns of Japanese Culture* (London: Routledge & Kegan Paul).

Ben-Shalom, U., Z. Lehrer, and E. Ben-Ari (2005) Cohesion During Military Operations: A Field Study on Combat Units in the Al-Aqsa Intifada, *Armed Forces & Society*, 32(1), pp. 63–79.

Bentham, J. (1996) *An Introduction to the Principles of Morals and Legislation* (Oxford: Clarendon Press).

Bergen, P. and M. Lind (2007) A Matter of Pride: Why We Can't Buy Off the Next Osama bin Laden, *Democracy*, issue 3.

Berger, P. (1984) On the Obsolescence of the Concept of Honour, in: M. J. Sandel (ed.) *Liberalism and its Critics*, pp. 149–58 (Oxford: Basil Blackwell).

Bloom, A. (1980) The Study of Texts, in: M. Richter (ed.) *Political Theory and Political Education*, pp. 113–38 (Princeton: Princeton University Press).

Bloom, A. (1987) *The Closing of the American Mind* (New York: Simon and Schuster).

Bloom, A. (1990) *Giants and Dwarfs Essays 1960-1990* (New York: Simon and Schuster).

Borowitz, A. (2005) *Terrorism for Self-Glorification: The Herostratos Syndrome* (Kent and London: Kent State University Press).

Bourke, J. (2005) *Fear: A Cultural History* (London: Virago Press).

Bowman, J. (2006) *Honor: A History* (New York: Encounter Books).

Boyd, R. (2005) Politesse and Public Opinion in Stendhal's *Red and Black*, *European Journal of Political Theory*, 4(4), pp. 367–92.

Braudy L. (1986) *The Frenzy of Renown: Fame & Its History* (Oxford: Oxford University Press).

Braudy L. (2003) *From Chivalry to Terrorism: War and the Changing Nature of Masculinity* (New York: Alfred A. Knopf).

Buchanan, J. M. and G. Tullock (1967) *The Calculus of Consent* (Ann Arbor: University of Michigan Press).

Burk, J. (2002) Expertise, Jurisdiction, and Legitimacy of the Military Profession, in: D. M. Snider and G. L. Watkins (eds) *The Future of the Army Profession*, pp. 19–38 (New York: McGraw-Hill/Primis Custom Publishing).

Burke, E. (1967) *Reflections on the Revolution in France: Letter to a Member of the National Assembly* (London: Everyman's Library).

Burke, J. (2004a) *Al Qaeda: The True Story of the Radical Islam* (London: Penguin Books).

Burke, J. (2004b) Zarqawi Has Method in his Madness, *The Observer*, September 26.

Burke, J. (2004c) What Exactly Does al-Qaeda Want?, *The Observer*, March 21.

Burke, J. (2004d) One Man's Resistance: "Why I Turned Against America," *The Observer*, September 12.

Burke, J. (2005a) Seven Ways to Stop the Terror, *The Observer*, August 7.

Burke, J. (2005b) Who Did It—And What Was Their Motive?, *The Observer*, July 10.

Buruma, I. and A. Margalit (2004) *Occidentalism: The West in the Eyes of Its Enemies* (New York: Penguin Books).

Button, M. (2005) "A Monkish Kind of Virtue"? For and against Humility, *Political Theory*, 33(6), pp. 840–68.

Caesar (1986) *De Bello Gallico* (Cambridge: Loeb Classical Library).

Cairns, D. (1993) *Aidos: the Psychology and Ethics of Honour and Shame in Ancient Greek Literature* (Oxford: Oxford Clarendon Press).

Carr, D. and J. W. Steutel (1999) *Virtue Ethics and Moral Education* (London: Routledge).

Carroll, L. (1994) *Alice's Adventures in Wonderland* (London: Penguin Popular Classics).

Carroll, L. (2007) *Through the Looking Glass* (London: Penguin Popular Classics).

Carruthers, S. L. (2011) *The Media at War* (Basingstoke: Palgrave Macmillan).

Carter, S. L. (1996) *Integrity* (New York: Harper Perennial).

Castro, C. A. (2006) Military Courage, in: T. W. Britt, C. A. Castro, and A. B. Adler (eds) *Military Life: The Psychology of Serving in Peace and Combat*, vol. 4, pp. 60–78 (Westport: Praeger).

Challans, T. L. (2007) *Awakening Warrior: Revolution in the Ethics of Warfare* (Albany: State University of New York Press).

Cicero (1913) *De Officiis* (Cambridge: Loeb Classical Library).

Cicero (1914) *De Finibus* (Cambridge: Loeb Classical Library).

Cicero (1923) *Pro Archia* (Cambridge: Loeb Classical Library).

Cicero (1927) *Tusculanae Disputationes* (Cambridge: Loeb Classical Library).

Cicero (1928) *De Re Publica* (Cambridge: Loeb Classical Library).

Cicero (1976) *Pro Murena* (Cambridge: Loeb Classical Library).

Cicero (1984) *Pro Publio Quinctio* (Cambridge: Loeb Classical Library).

Clark, P. A. (2006) Medical Ethics at Guantanamo Bay and Abu Ghraib: The Problem of Dual Loyalty, *The Journal of Law, Medicine & Ethics*, 34(3), pp. 570–80.

Coady, C. A. J. (2008) *Morality and Political Violence* (Cambridge: Cambridge University Press).

Coker, C. (2008) *Ethics and War in the 21st Century* (London: Routledge).

Coleman, S. (2009) The Problems of Duty and Loyalty, *Journal of Military Ethics*, 8(2), pp. 105–15.

Condren, C. (1985) *The Status and Appraisal of Classical Texts: An Essay on Political Theory, its Inheritance, and the History of Ideas* (Princeton: Princeton University Press).

Conrad, J. (1993) *Lord Jim* (Hertfordshire: Wordsworth Classics).

Conrad, J. (2007) 'Some Reflections on the Loss of the Titanic,' in: *The Portable Conrad*, pp. 635–46 (London: Penguin)

Cook M. L. (2002) Army Professionalism: Service to What Ends?, in: D. M. Snider and G. L. Watkins (eds) *The Future of the Army Profession*, pp. 337–54 (New York: McGraw-Hill/Primis Custom Publishing).

Cook, M. L. (2004) *The Moral Warrior: Ethics and Service in the U.S. Military* (Albany: State University of New York Press).

Cooley, C. H. (1922) *Human Nature and the Social Order* (New York: Charles Scribner).

Couser, G. T. (1989) *Altered Egos* (Oxford: Oxford University Press).

Cowen, T. and D. Sutter (1997) Politics and the Pursuit of Fame, *Public Choice*, 93(1/2).

Cox, D., M. La Caze, and M. P. Levine (2003) *Integrity and the Fragile Self* (Aldershot: Ashgate).

Creveld, M. van (2008) *The Culture of War* (New York: Presidio Press/Ballantine Books).

Daddis, G. A. (2004) Understanding Fear's Effect on Unit Effectiveness, *Military Review*, July-August, pp. 22–7.

Dadkhah, L. M. (2008) Close Air Support and Civilian Casualties in Afghanistan, *Small Wars Journal*. Available at http://smallwarsjournal.com/blog/journal/docs-temp/160-dadkhah.pdf.

Dahl, R.A. (1991) *Modern Political Analysis* (Englewood Cliffs: Prentice Hall).

Darwall, S. L. (2006) *The Second-Person Standpoint: Morality, Respect, and Accountability* (Cambridge: Harvard University Press).

Darwin, C. (1965) *The Expression of Emotions in Man and Animals* (Chicago & London: University of Chicago Press).

Davis, M. (2005) The Moral Justifiability of Torture and other Cruel, Inhuman, or Degrading Treatment, *International Journal of Applied Philosophy*, 19(2), pp. 161–78.

Defoe, D. (1975) *Robinson Crusoe* (London: Everyman's Library).

Demetriou, D. (2013) Honor War Theory: Romance or Reality?, *Philosophical Papers*, 42(3), pp. 285–313.

Dewey, J. (1989) *The Later Works* vol. 7 (Carbondale and Edwardsville: Southern Illinois University Press).

Dillon, R. S. (2008) Respect, in: E. N. Zalta (ed.) *The Stanford Encyclopedia of Philosophy (Fall 2008 Edition)*. Available at http://plato.stanford.edu/archives/fall2008/entries/respect/.

Dodds, E. R. (1951) *The Greeks and the Irrational* (Berkeley: University of California Press).

Dollard, J. (1944) *Fear in Battle* (Washington DC: The Infantry Journal).

Doorn, J. A. A. van (1975) *The Soldier and Social Change* (London: Sage Publications).

Douglas, M. (1987) *How Institutions Think* (London: Routledge & Kegan Paul).

Downs, A. (1957) *An Economic Theory of Democracy* (New York: Harper & Row).

Dual Loyalty Working Group (2002) *Dual Loyalty and Human Rights in Health Professional Practice: Proposed Guidelines and Institutional Mechanisms* (Washington: Physicians for Human Rights).

Dunn, J. (1985) *Rethinking Modern Political Theory: Essays 1979-1983*, Cambridge: Cambridge University Press.

Durkheim, E. (1964) *The Division of Labor in Society* (New York: Free Press of Glencoe).

Easton, D. (1965) *A Framework for Political Analysis* (Englewood Cliffs: Prentice Hall).

Elias, N. (1965) *The Established and the Outsiders* (London: Cass).

Ellis, A. and W. Dryden (1987) *The Practise of Rational Emotive Theory* (New York: Springer Publishing Company).

Ellison, R. W. (2001) *Invisible Man* (London: Penguin Classics).

Elshtain, J. B. (2007) Terrorism, Regime Change, and Just War: Reflections on Michael Walzer, *Journal of Military Ethics*, 6(2), pp. 131–7.

Elster, J. (2005) Motivations and Beliefs in Suicide Missions, in: D. Gambetta (ed.) *Making Sense of Suicide Missions*, pp. 233–58 (Oxford: Oxford University Press).

Erasmus, D. (1922) *Erasmus in Praise of Folly: With Portrait, Life of Erasmus, and his Epistle to Sir Thomas More* (New York: Peter Eckler Publishing Co.).

Eshleman, A. (2009) Moral Responsibility, in: E. N. Zalta (ed.) *The Stanford Encyclopedia of Philosophy (Winter 2009 Edition)*. Available at http://plato.stanford.edu/archives/win2009/entries/moral-responsibility/.

Etzioni, A. (1995) *The Spirit of Community* (London: Fontana Press).

Euben, J. P. (1990) *The Tragedy of Political Theory: The Road Not Taken* (Princeton: Princeton University Press).

Ewin, R. E. (1992) Loyalty and Virtues, *Philosophical Quarterly*, 42(169), pp. 403–19.

Ferguson, A. (1978) *An Essay on the History of Civil Society* (Edinburgh: Edinburgh University Press).

Fiala, A. (2005) A Critique of Exceptions: Torture, Terrorism, and the Lesser Evil Argument, *International Journal of Applied Philosophy*, 20(1), pp. 127–42.

Fiala, A. (2010) Pacifism, in: E. N. Zalta (ed.) *The Stanford Encyclopedia of Philosophy (Fall 2010 Edition)*. Available at http://plato.stanford.edu/archives/fall2010/entries/pacifism/.

Fine, R. (1986) *Narcissism, the Self, and Society* (New York: Columbia University Press).

Finley, M. I. (1993) *The World of Odysseus* (London: Penguin Books).

Firestone, R. (1999) *Jihad: The Origin of Holy War in Islam* (Oxford: Oxford University Press).

Fletcher, G. P. (1993) *Loyalty: An Essay on the Morality of Relationships* (New York: Oxford University Press).

Fontan, V. (2006) Polarization Between Occupier and Occupied in Post-Saddam Iraq: Colonial Humiliation and the Formation of Political Violence, *Terrorism and Political Violence*, (18)2, pp. 217–38.

Foot, P. (2002) *Virtues and Vices and Other Essays in Moral Philosophy* (Oxford: Clarendon Press).

Forbes, D. (1975) *Hume's Philosophical Politics* (Cambridge: Cambridge University Press).

Forman-Barzilai, F. (2005) Sympathy in Space(s) Adam Smith on Proximity, *Political Theory*, 33(2), pp. 189–217.

Fossum, M. A. and M. J. Mason (1966) *Facing Shame* (London: Norton).

French, S. E. (2003) *The Code of the Warrior* (Lanham: Rowman & Littlefield).

Freud, S. (1961) *Civilization and Its Discontents* (New York: Norton).

Friedman, M. (1960) *Essays in Positive Economics* (Chicago and London: Phoenix Books).

Friedman, M. and R. Friedman (1980) *Free to Choose: a Personal Statement* (Princeton: Princeton University Press).

Friedman, T. L. (2003) The Humiliation Factor, *New York Times*, November 9.

Fromm, E. (1949) *Man for Himself* (London: Routledge and Kegan Paul).

Fukuyama, F. (1993) *The End of History and the Last Man* (New York: Avon Books). Fukuyama, F. (1995) *Trust* (New York: Free Press).

Furst, L. (1969) *Romanticism in Perspective* (London: MacMillan).

Gabriel, R. A. (1982) *To Serve with Honor: A Treatise on Military Ethics and the Way of the Soldier* (Westport: Greenwood Press).

Galston, W. A. (1975) *Kant and the Problem of History* (Chicago: University of Chicago Press).

Galston, W. A. (2010) *Realism in Political Theory*, European Journal of Political Theory, 9(4), pp. 385–411.

Gat, A. (2001) *A History of Military Thought* (Oxford: Oxford University Press).

Gay, P. (1973, 1979) *The Enlightenment: An Interpretation*, 2 vols (London: Wildwood House).

Geertz, C. (2003) Which Way to Mecca? *The New York Review of Books*, June 10.

Giddens, A. (1991) *Modernity and Self-Identity* (Cambridge: Polity Press).

Godwin, W. (1793) *An Enquiry Concerning Political Justice, and Its Influence on General Virtue and Happiness* (London: G. G. J. and J. Robinson).

Goffman, E. (1958) *The Presentation of Self in Everyday Life* (Edinburgh: University of Edinburgh).

Goldhagen, D. J. (2007) The Humiliation Myth: Humiliation Doesn't Explain Terrorism; the Spread of Political Islam Does. A Response to Peter Bergen and Michael Lind, *Democracy*, issue 4.

Golding, W. (1954) *Lord of the Flies* (London: Faber).

Goodin, R. E. (1995) *Utilitarianism as a Public Philosophy* (Cambridge: Cambridge University Press).

Gordon, S. (1991) *The History and Philosophy of Social Science* (London and New York: Routledge).

Grant, R. W. (1997) *Hypocrisy and Integrity: Machiavelli, Rousseau, and the Ethics of Politics* (Chicago: University of Chicago Press).

Gross, M. L. (2006) *Bioethics and Armed Conflict: Moral Dilemmas of Medicine and War* (Cambridge: MIT Press).

Gunnell, J. G. (1986) *Between Philosophy and Politics: The Alienation of Political Theory* (Amherst: University of Massachusetts Press).

Hague Centre for Strategic Studies, The (2008) *Eyes Wide Shut? The Impact of Embedded Journalism on Dutch Newspaper Coverage of Afghanistan* (The Hague: HCSS).

Hanley, R. P. (2008) Commerce and Corruption: Rousseau's Diagnosis and Adam Smith's Cure, *European Journal of Political Theory*, 7(2), pp. 137–58.

Hanley, R. P. (2011) David Hume and the "Politics of Humanity," *Political Theory*, 39(2), pp. 205–33.

Hanson, V. D. (1989) *The Western Way of War* (Oxford: Oxford University Press).

Hanson, V. D. (2002) *Carnage and Culture* (New York: Anchor Books).

Hayek, F. A. von (1985) *New Studies in Philosophy: Politics, Economics and the History of Ideas* (Chicago: University of Chicago Press).

Hayek, F. A. von (1990) *The Constitution of Liberty* (London: Routledge & Kegan Paul).

Heinze, E. A. (2005) Commonsense Morality and the Consequentialist Ethics of Humanitarian Intervention, *Journal of Military Ethics*, 4(3), pp. 168–82.

Held, V. (2008) *How Terrorism is Wrong: Morality and Political Violence* (Oxford: Oxford University Press).

Herman, B. (1981) On the Value of Acting from the Motive of Duty, *The Philosophical Review*, 90(3), pp. 359–82.

Hersh, S. M. (2004) The Gray Zone: How a Secret Pentagon Program Came to Abu Ghraib, *The New Yorker*, May 24, pp. 38–44.

Hill, R. S. (1987) David Hume, in: L. Strauss and J. Cropsey (eds) *History of Political Philosophy* (Chicago: Chicago University Press).

Himmelfarb, G. (1974) *On Liberty and Liberalism: The Case of John Stuart Mill* (New York: Alfred A. Knopf).

Hirschman, A. O. (1970) *Exit, Voice, and Loyalty: Responses to Decline in Firms, Organizations, and States* (Cambridge: Harvard University Press).

Hobbes, T. (1988) *Leviathan* (London: Penguin Books).

Hollis, M. (1994) *The Philosophy of Social Science: An Introduction* (Cambridge: Cambridge University Press).

Holmes, S. (1993) *The Anatomy of Antiliberalism* (Cambridge: Harvard University Press).

Horn, B. (2004) The Worm Revisited: An Examination of Fear and Courage in Combat, *Canadian Military Journal*, Summer, pp. 5–16.

Howe, E. G. (1986) Ethical Issues Regarding Mixed Agency of Military Physicians, *Social Science & Medicine*, 23(8), pp. 803–15.

Huizinga, J. (1982) *Herfsttij der Middeleeuwen* [*The Waning of the Middle Ages*] (Groningen: Wolters-Noordhoff).

Human Rights Watch (2008) *"Troops in Contact": Airstrikes and Civilian Deaths in Afghanistan* (New York: Human Rights Watch).

Hume, D. (1969) *A Treatise of Human Nature* (London: Penguin Books).

Hume, D. (1987) *Essays: Moral, Political and Literary* (Indianapolis: Liberty Fund).

Hume, D. (1998) *An Enquiry Concerning the Principles of Morals* (Oxford: Oxford University Press).

Hume, D. (1999) *An Enquiry Concerning Human Understanding* (Oxford: Oxford University Press).

Huntington, S. P. (1964) *The Soldier and the State: The Theory and Politics of Civil-Military Relations* (Cambridge: Harvard University Press).

Huntington, S. P. (1996) *The Clash of Civilizations and the Remaking of World Order* (New York: Simon & Schuster).

Hutcheson, F. (1994) *Philosophical Writings* (London: Everyman).

Ignatieff, M. (1997) *The Warrior's Honor* (New York: Metropolitan Books).

Janowitz, M. (1960) *The Professional Soldier* (Glencoe: Free Press).

Johnson Bagby, L. M. (2009) *Thomas Hobbes: Turning Point for Honor* (Lanham: Lexington Books).

Johnson, L. M. (2012) *Locke and Rousseau: Two Enlightenment Responses to Honor* (Lanham: Lexington Books).

Johnston, P. (1993) *Rethinking the Inner* (London: Routledge).

Jones, P. (1982) *Hume's Sentiments: Their Ciceronian and French Context* (Edinburgh: Edinburgh University Press).

Kant, I. (1968) *Grundlegung zur Metaphysik der Sitten* [*Groundwork of the Metaphysic of Morals*] (Frankfurt am Main: Suhrkamp).

Kant, I. (2003) *To Perpetual Peace: A Philosophical Sketch* (Indianapolis: Hackett Publishing).

Kaplan, R. D. (2002) *Warrior Politics: Why Leadership Demands a Pagan Ethos* (New York: Random House).

Kasher, A. and Yadlin, A. (2005) Military Ethics of Fighting Terror: An Israeli Perspective, *Journal of Military Ethics*, (4)1, pp. 3–32.

Kasher, A. and Yadlin, A. (2009) Israel and the Rules of War: An Exchange, *The New York Review of Books*, (56)10.

Kaufman, G. (1989) *The Psychology of Shame* (New York: Springer Publishing Company).

Kaurin, P. (2006) *Identity, Loyalty and Combat Effectiveness: A Cautionary Tale*, JSCOPE paper. Available at http://isme.tamu.edu/JSCOPE06/Kaurin06.html.

Keegan, J. (1976) *The Face of Battle* (London: Pimlico).

Keller, H. (2001) An Exploration of Respect in Army Leadership, *Military Review*, 81(1), pp. 66–76.

Keller, S. (2007) *The Limits of Loyalty* (Cambridge: Cambridge University Press).

Kerkhof, A. J. (1992) *De Mens is een Angstig Dier: Adam Smith's Theorie van de Morele Gevoelens* [*Man is a Fearful Animal: Adam Smith's Theory of Moral Feelings*] (Meppel: Boom).

Kinneging, A. A. M. (1994) *Aristocracy, Antiquity, and History*, doctoral dissertation, Leiden University.

Kohlberg, L. (1981) *Essays on Moral Development, vol. 1 The Philosophy of Moral Development: Moral Stages and the Idea of Justice* (San Francisco: Harper and Row).

Kohlberg, L. (1984) *Essays on Moral Development, vol. 2 The Psychology of Moral Development* (San Francisco: Harper and Row).

Kolm, S.-C. (1996) *Modern Theories of Justice* (Cambridge: MIT Press).

Krause, S. R. (2002) *Liberalism with Honor* (Harvard: Harvard University Press).

Kripke, S. (1982) *Wittgenstein on Rules and Private Language: An Elementary Exposition* (Oxford: Blackwell).

Laden, O. bin (1998) Interview by ABC's John Miller, May. Available at http://www.pbs.org/wgbh/pages/frontline/shows/binladen/who/interview.html.

Laden, O. bin (2002) Letter to America, *The Observer*, November 24.

Larmore, C. E. (1987) *Patterns of Moral Complexity* (Cambridge: Cambridge University Press).

Lasch, C. (1979) *Haven in a Heartless World* (New York: Basic Books).

LaVaque-Manty, M. (2006) Dueling for Equality: Masculine Honor and the Modern Politics of Dignity, *Political Theory*, 34(6), pp. 715–40.

Lee, P. (2012) Remoteness, Risk and Aircrew Ethos, *Air Power Review*, 15(1), pp. 1–19.

Lee, S. (2004) Double Effect, Double Intention, and Asymmetric Warfare, *Journal of Military Ethics*, (3)3, pp. 233–51.

Lewis, B. (1990) The Roots of Muslim Rage, *The Atlantic*, September.

Lewis, B. (2003) *The Crisis of Islam: Holy War and Unholy Terror* (London: Weidenfeld & Nicolson).

Leys, R. (2009) *From Guilt to Shame: Auschwitz and After* (Princeton, N.J: Princeton University Press).

Lin, P., G. Bekey, and K. Abney (2008), *Autonomous Military Robotics: Risk, Ethics, and Design* (San Luis Obispo: California Polytechnic State University).

Lindsay-Hartz, J., J. de Rivera, and M. F. Mascolo (1995) Differentiating Guilt and Shame and Their Effects on Motivation, in: J. P. Tangney and K. W. Fischer (eds) *Self-Conscious Emotions: The Psychology of Shame, Guilt, Embarrassment, and Pride*, pp. 274–300 (New York: Guilford Press).

Locke, J. (1975) *An Essay Concerning Human Understanding* (Oxford: Clarendon Press).

Locke, J. (1989) *Some Thoughts Concerning Education* (Oxford: Clarendon Press).

London, L., L. Rubenstein, L. Baldwin-Ragaven, and A. van Es (2006) Dual Loyalty among Military Health Professionals: Human Rights and Ethics in Times of Armed Conflict, *Cambridge Quarterly of Healthcare Ethics*, 15(4), pp. 381–91.

Long, A. A. (2008) The Concept of the Cosmopolitan in Greek & Roman Thought, *Dædalus*, 137(3), pp. 50–8.

Louw, P. E. The 'War Against Terrorism' A Public Relations Challenge for the Pentagon, *Gazette: The International Journal For Communication Studies*, 65(3), pp. 211–30.

Lucretius (1924) *De Rerum Natura* (Cambridge: Loeb Classical Library).

Lynd, H. M. (1958) *On Shame and the Search for Identity* (London: Routledge & Kegan Paul).

Lynn, J. A. (2003) *Battle: A History of Combat and Culture* (Boulder: Westview Press).

MacCoun, R. J., E. Kier, and A. Belkin (2006) Does Social Cohesion Determine Motivation in Combat? An Old Question with an Old Answer, *Armed Forces & Society*, 32(4), pp. 646–54.

MacIntyre, A. (1969) Hume on "Is" and "Ought," in: W. D. Hudson (ed.) *The Is/Ought Question*, pp. 35–50 (London: MacMillan).

MacIntyre, A. (1985) *After Virtue* (London: Ducksworth).

McIntyre, A. (2009) Doctrine of Double Effect, in: E. N. Zalta (ed.) *The Stanford Encyclopedia of Philosophy (Fall 2009 Edition)*. Available at: http://plato.stanford.edu/archives/fall2009/entries/double-effect/.

MacKendrick, P. (1989) *The Philosophical Books of Cicero* (London: Ducksworth).

McMahan, J. (1994) Revising the Doctrine of Double Effect, *The Journal of Applied Philosophy* (11)2, pp. 201–12.

McMahan, J. (2009) *Killing in War* (Oxford: Clarendon Press).

McPherson, L. K. (2007) Is Terrorism Distinctively Wrong? *Ethics*, (117)3, pp. 524–46.

Madison, J., A. Hamilton, J. Jay, and I. Kramnick (1987) *The Federalist Papers* (Harmondsworth: Penguin Books).

Mandeville, B. (1971) *An Enquiry into the Origin of Honour and the Usefulness of Christianity in War* (London: Cass).

Mandeville, B. (1988) *The Fable of the Bees: or Private Vices, Publick Benefits* (Indianapolis: Liberty Fund).

Mansfield (1987) Hume, in: L. Strauss and J. Cropsey (eds) *History of Political Philosophy*, (Chicago: Chicago University Press).

Margalit, A. (1996) *The Decent Society* (Cambridge: Harvard University Press).

Marshall, S. L. A. (1947) *Men against Fire* (New York: William Morrow & Company).

Mastroianni, G. R. (2011) The Person-Situation Debate: Implications for Military Leadership and Civilian-Military Relations, *Journal of Military Ethics*, 10(1), pp. 2–16.

Mendus, S. (2002) *Impartiality in Moral and Political Philosophy* (Oxford: Oxford University Press).

Mental Health Advisory Team IV (2006) *Operation Iraqi Freedom 05-07 Final Report*. Available at http://i.a.cnn.net/cnn/2007/images/05/04/mhat.iv.report.pdf.

Miles, S. H. (2006) *Oath Betrayed: Torture, Medical Complicity, and the War on Terror* (New York: Random House).

Mill, J. S. (1987a) Whewell on Moral Philosophy, in: J. S. Mill and J. Bentham, *Utilitarianism and Other Essays*, pp. 228–70 (London: Penguin Books).

Mill, J. S. (1987b) Utilitarianism, in: J. S. Mill and J. Bentham, *Utilitarianism and Other Essays*, pp. 272–338 (London: Penguin Books).

Mill, J. S. (1993) On Liberty, in: J. S. Mill, *Utilitarianism, On Liberty, Considerations on Representative Government*, pp. 69–185 (London: Everyman's Library).

Miller, I. (1993) *Humiliation* (Ithaca: Cornell University Press).

Miller, I. (2000) *The Mystery of Courage* (Cambridge: Harvard University Press).

Mintzberg, H. (1983) *Structure in Fives* (Englewood Cliffs: Prentice-Hall).

Mitchell, W. C. (1974) Bentham's Felicific Calculus, in: B. Parekh (ed.) *Jeremy Bentham: Ten Critical Essays*, pp. 168–86 (London: Cas).

Moghadam, A. (2003) Palestinian Suicide Terrorism in the Second Intifada: Motivations and Organizational Aspects, *Studies in Conflict and Terrorism*, 26(2), pp. 65–92.

Moïsi, D. (2007) The Clash of Emotions, *Foreign Affairs*, 86(1), pp. 8–12.

Moller, A. C. and E. L. Deci (2010) Interpersonal Control, Dehumanization, and Violence: A Self-Determination Theory Perspective, *Group Processes and Intergroup Relations*, 13(1), pp. 41–53.

Montaigne, M. (1965) *Essays* (London: Dent).

Montesquieu, M. (1989) *The Spirit of the Laws* (Cambridge: Cambridge University Press).

Moore, J. (2002) Utility and Humanity: The Quest for the Honestum in Cicero, Hutcheson, and Hume, *Utilitas*, 14(3), pp. 365–86.

Murphy, J. G. (1973) The Killing of the Innocent, *The Monist*, 57(4), 527–50.

Nafziger, G. F. and M. W. Walton (2003) *Islam at War: A History* (Westport: Praeger).

Nagel, T. (1972) War and Massacre, *Philosophy and Public Affairs*, 1(2), pp. 123–44.

Nagel, T. (1986) *The View from Nowhere* (New York: Oxford University Press).

Nye, R. (1998) The End of the Modern French Duel, in: P.C. Spierenburg (ed.) *Men and Violence: Gender, Honor, and Rituals in Modern Europe and America*, pp. 82–95 (Columbus: Ohio State University Press).

Olsthoorn, P. (2010) *Military Ethics and Virtues: An Interdisciplinary Approach for the 21st Century* (London: Routledge).

O'Neill, B. (1999) *Honor, Symbols, and War* (Ann Arbor: University of Michigan Press).

Oprisko, R. L. (2012) *Honor: A Phenomenology* (New York: Routledge).

Orend, B. (2000) *Michael Walzer on War and Justice* (Cardiff: University of Wales Press).

Osiel, M. J. (1999) *Obeying Orders: Atrocity, Military Discipline & the Law of War* (New Brunswick and London: Transaction Publishers).

Ossowska, M. (1971) *Social Determinants of Moral Ideas* (London: Routledge & Kegan Paul).

Øverland, G. (2011) High Fliers: Who Should Bear the Risk of Humanitarian Intervention? in: J. Wolfendale and P. Tripodi (eds) *New Wars and New Soldiers: Military Ethics in the Contemporary World*, pp. 68–86 (Farnham: Ashgate).

Pape, R. A. (2005) *Dying to Win* (New York: Random House).

Parfit, D. (1987) *Reasons and Persons* (Oxford: Oxford University Press).

Pattyn, B. (1997) To Recommence Where Rorty Leaves Off: On Loyalty and Identification, *Ethical Perspectives*, 4(3), pp. 171–9.

Peristiany, J. G. and J. Pitt-Rivers (1992) *Honor and Grace in Anthropology* (Cambridge: Cambridge University Press).

Peters, T. J. and R. H. Waterman (1982) *In Search of Excellence* (New York: Harper and Row).

Picq, A. du (1947) *Battle Studies* (Harrisburg: Military Publishing Company).

Pierce, A. C. (2002) Captain Lawrence Rockwood in Haiti, *Journal of Military Ethics*, 1(1), pp. 53–4.

Pillar, P. R. (2009) Who's Afraid of a Terrorist Haven?, *Washington Post*, September 16.

Pinker, S. (2011) *The Better Angels of Our Nature: Why Violence Has Declined* (New York: Viking).

Pitt-Rivers, J. (1974) Honour and Social Status, in: J. G. Peristiany (ed.) *Honour and Shame: The Values of Mediterranean Society*, pp. 19–78 (Chicago: Midway Reprint).

Plato (1951) *The Symposium* (London: Penguin Books).

Plato (1973) *Laches and Charmides* (Indianapolis: Bobbs-Merrill).

Plato (1987) *The Republic* (London: Penguin Books).

Plato (1988) *The Laws of Plato* (Chicago: University of Chicago Press).

Plaw, A. (2010) Upholding the Principle of Distinction in Counter-Terrorist Operations: A Dialogue, *Journal of Military Ethics*, (9)1, pp. 3–22.

Plutarch (1965) *Makers of Rome* (Harmondsworth: Penguin Books).

Pocock, J. G.A. (1962) The History of Political Thought: A Methodological Enquiry, in: P. Laslett and W. G. Runciman (eds) *Philosophy, Politics and Society: Second Series*, pp.183–202 (Oxford: Basil Blackwell).

Pocock, J. G. A. (1971) *Politics, Language, and Time* (New York: Atheneum).

Pocock, J. G. A. (1980) Political Ideas as Historical Events: Political Philosophers as Historical Actors, in: M. Richter (ed.) *Political Theory and Political Education*, pp. 139–58 (Princeton: Princeton University Press).

Porter, H. (1888) The Philosophy of Courage, *The Century*, 36(2).

Primoratz, I. (2004) *Terrorism: The Philosophical Issues* (Basingstoke and New York: Palgrave Macmillan).

Primoratz, I. (2008) Patriotism and Morality: Mapping the Terrain, *Journal of Moral Philosophy*, 5(2), pp. 204–26.

Princen, P. (1995) *Een Kwestie van Kiezen [A Matter of Choice]* (Den Haag: Uitgeverij BZZTôH).

Quinn, W. (1989) Actions, Intentions, and Consequences: The Doctrine of Double Effect, *Philosophy and Public Affairs*, 18(4), pp. 334–51.

Qutb, S. (2006) *Milestones* (Birmingham: Maktabah).

Rachman, S. J. (1990) *Fear and Courage* (New York: W.H. Freeman and Company).

Raphael, D. D. (2007) *The Impartial Spectator: Adam Smith's Moral Philosophy* (Oxford: Oxford University Press).

Rawls, J. (1971) *A Theory of Justice* (Oxford: Oxford University Press).

Rawls, J. (1993) *Political Liberalism* (New York: Columbia University Press).

Rawls, J. (1999) *The Law of Peoples* (Cambridge: Harvard University Press).

Raz, J. (1995) *Ethics in the Public Domain: Essays in the Morality of Law and Politics* (Oxford: Oxford Clarendon Press).

Rest, J. R. (1986) *Moral Development: Advances in Research and Theory* (New York: Praeger).

Riesman, D. (1950) *The Lonely Crowd* (New Haven: Yale University Press).

Robinson, P. (2007a) Ethics Training and Development in the Military, *Parameters*, Spring, pp. 22–36.

Robinson, P. (2007b) The Way of the Warrior, *Spectator*, June 13.

Robinson, P. (2009) Integrity and Selective Conscientious Objection, *Journal of Military Ethics*, 8(1), 34–47.

Roche, K. F. (1974) *Rousseau Stoic & Romantic* (London: Methuen).

Rorty, R. (1997) Justice as a Larger Loyalty, *Ethical Perspectives*, 4(3), pp. 139–51.

Rousseau, J.-J. (1953) *The Confessions* (London: Penguin Books).

Rousseau, J.-J. (1960) *Lettre à M. d'Alembert* (New York: Cornell University Press).

Rousseau, J.-J. (1964) *Emile ou de l'Education* (Paris: Garnier).

Rousseau, J.-J. (1991) *The Social Contract and Discourses* (London: Everyman Classics).

Rousseau, J.-J. (1991) *Emile* (London: Penguin Books).

Royce, J. (1995) *The Philosophy of Loyalty* (Nashville: Vanderbilt University Press).

Runciman, W. G. (1969) *Social Science and Political Theory* (Cambridge: Cambridge University Press).

Rushdie, S. (1993) *Shame* (London: Johnatan Cape).

Ryan, A. (1970) *The Philosophy of John Stuart Mill* (London: MacMillan).

Sabl, A. (2006) Noble Infirmity, *Political Theory*, 34(5), pp. 542–68.

Sallust (1963) *The Jugurthine War/The Conspiracy of Cataline* (London: Penguin Books).

Sandel, M. J. (1982) *Liberalism and the Limits of Justice* (Cambridge: Cambridge University Press).

Sartre, J.-P. (2001) The Wretched of the Earth, in: *Colonialism and Neocolonialism*, pp. 75–86 (London: Routledge).

Saurette, P. (2006) You Dissin Me? Humiliation and Post 9/11 Global Politics, *Review of International Studies*, 32(3), pp. 495–522.

Saxonhouse, A. W. (1993) Texts and Canons: The Status of the "Great Books," in: A.W. Finifter (ed.) *The State of the Art*, pp. 3–27 (Washington: American Political Science Association).

Scanlon, T. M. (1998) *What We Owe to Each Other* (Cambridge: Belknap Press of Harvard University Press).

Scanlon, T. M. (2008) *Moral Dimensions: Permissibility, Meaning, Blame* (Harvard University Press).

Schneider, C. D. (1977) *Shame, Exposure, and Privacy* (Boston: Beacon Press).

Segal, D. R. and M. Kestnbaum (2002) Professional Closure in the Military Labor Market, in: D. M. Snider and G. L. Watkins (eds) *The Future of the Army Profession*, pp. 441–58 (Boston: McGraw-Hill).

Sen, A. (2009) *The Idea of Justice* (Cambridge: Belknap Press of Harvard University Press).

Seneca (1917) *Epistles* (Cambridge: Loeb Classical Library).

Sennett, R. (1977) *The Fall of Public Man* (Cambridge: Cambridge University Press).

Sennett, R. (2003) *Respect in a World of Inequality* (New York: W. W. Norton).

Sensen, O. (2011) Human Dignity in Historical Perspective: The Contemporary and Traditional Paradigms, *European Journal of Political Theory*, (10)1, pp. 71–91.

Sessions, W. L. (2010) *Honor for Us: A Philosophical Analysis, Interpretation and Defense* (New York: Continuum).

Shaw, M. (2005) *The New Western Way of War* (Cambridge: Polity Press).

Sherman, N. (2010) The Guilt They Carry: Wounds of Iraq and Afghanistan, *Dissent*, Spring, pp. 80–2.

Shils, E. and M. Janowitz (1948) Cohesion and Disintegration in the Wehrmacht in World War II, *Public Opinion Quarterly*, 12(2), pp. 280–315.

Shue, H. (2006) Torture in Dreamland: Disposing of the Ticking Bomb, *Case Western Reserve Journal of International Law*, 37(2/3), pp. 231–40.

Singer, B. (2004) Montesquieu, Adam Smith and the Discovery of the Social, *Journal of Classical Sociology*, 4(1) pp. 31–57.

Singer, P. (1972) Famine, Affluence, and Morality, *Philosophy and Public Affairs*, 1(1), pp. 229–43.

Singer, P. (1997) The Drowning Child and the Expanding Circle, *New Internationalist*, 289, pp. 28–30.

Singer, P. W. (2009) *Wired For War: The Robotics Revolution and Conflict in the Twenty-First Century* (New York: Penguin Books).

Skinner, B. F. (1971) *Beyond Freedom and Dignity* (New York: Alfred A. Knopf).

Skinner, Q. (1978) *The Foundations of Modern Political Thought*, vol. I. (Cambridge: Cambridge University Press).

Skinner, Q. (1988) Meaning and Understanding in the History of Ideas, in: Q. Skinner and J. Tully (eds) *Meaning and Context: Quentin Skinner and his Critics*, pp. 29–67 (Princeton: Princeton University Press).

Slim, H. (2007) *Killing Civilians: Method, Madness and Morality in War* (London: Hurst & Company).

Smith, A. (1961) *An Inquiry into the Nature and Causes of the Wealth of Nations* (London: Methuen).

Smith, A. (1976) *The Theory of Moral Sentiments* (Oxford: Oxford Clarendon Press).

Smith, E. R., and D. M. Mackie (2000) *Social Psychology* (Philadelphia: Psychology Press).

Snow, N. E. (2009) How Ethical Theory Can Improve Practice: Lessons from Abu Ghraib, *Ethical Theory & Moral Practice*, 12(5), pp. 555–68.

Sontag, S. (2001) Talk of the Town, *The New Yorker*, September 24.

Spencer, H. (1982) *The Man versus the State: With Six Essays on Government, Society, and Freedom* (Indianapolis: Liberty Fund).

Spierenburg, P. C. (1998) Masculinity, Violence, and Honor: An Introduction, in: P.C. Spierenburg (ed.) *Men and Violence: Gender, Honor, and Rituals in Modern Europe and America*, pp. 1–29 (Columbus: Ohio State University Press).

Stendhal (1997) *Red and the Black* (New York: Random House).

Stern J. (2003) Terrorism's New Mecca, *The Globe and Mail*, November 28.

Stern, J. (2004a) Explaining the Addiction to Jihad, *The Daily Star (Lebanon)*, February 5.

Stern, J. (2004b) *Terror in the Name of God: Why Religious Militants Kill* (New York: Harper Collins).

Stern, J. (2004c) Beneath Bombast and Bombs, a Caldron of Humiliation, *Los Angeles Times*, June 6.

Stern, J. (2004d) Holy Avengers, *Financial Times*, June 12.

Stern, J. (2006a) Jihad—A Global Fad, *Boston Globe*, August 1.

Stern, J. (2006b) Al Qaeda, American Style, *New York Times*, July 15.

Stern, J. (2010) Mind over Martyr, *Foreign Affairs Magazine*, January/February 2010.

Stevenson, R. L. (1994) *The Strange Case of Dr Jekyll and Mr Hyde* (London: Penguin Books).

Stewart, F. H. (1994) *Honor* (Chicago: University of Chicago Press).

Stewart J. B. (1963) *The Moral and Political Philosophy of David Hume* (New York: Columbia University Press).

Stouffer, S. (1949) *The American Soldier*, vol. II. (Princeton: Princeton University Press).

Strachan-Davidson, J. L. (1894) *Cicero and the Fall of the Roman Republic* (New York: G.P. Putnam's Sons).

Sturrock, J. (1993) *The Language of Autobiography* (Cambridge: Cambridge University Press).

Tarcov, N. (1984) *Locke's Education for Liberty* (Chicago: University of Chicago Press).

Tarnopolsky, C. H. (2010) *Prudes, Perverts, and Tyrants: Plato's Gorgias and the Politics of Shame* (Princeton: Princeton University Press).

Taylor, C. (1980) The Philosophy of the Social Sciences, in: M. Richter (ed.) *Political Theory and Political Education*, pp. 76–93 (Princeton: Princeton University Press).

Taylor, C. (1992a) *Sources of the Self: The Making of the Modern Identity* (Cambridge: Cambridge University Press).

Taylor, C. (1992b) *The Ethics of Authenticity* (Cambridge: Harvard University Press).

Taylor, C. (1994) The Politics of Recognition, in: A. Gutmann (ed.) *Multiculturalism: Examining the Politics of Recognition*, pp. 25–74 (Princeton: Princeton University Press).

Thompson, M. and B. Ghosh (2009) The CIA's Silent War in Pakistan, *Time*, June 1.

Thucydides (1972) *History of the Peloponnesian War* (Harmondsworth: Penguin Books).

Tibi, B. (2002) *The Challenge of Fundamentalism* (Berkeley: University of California Press).

Tocqueville, A. de (1969) *Democracy in America* (New York: Harper & Row).

Tolstoy, L. (1938) *War and Peace* (New York: Heritage Press).

Tolstoy, L. (1939) *Anna Karenina* (New York: Random House).

Toner, J. H. (1992) *The American Military Ethic: A Meditation* (New York: Praeger).

Toner, J. H. (2000) *Morals under the Gun: The Cardinal Virtues, Military Ethics, and American Society* (Lexington: University Press of Kentucky).

Tönnies, F. (1955) *Community and Association* (London: Routledge & Kegan Paul).

Trilling, L. (1972) *Sincerity and Authenticity* (London: Oxford University Press).

Truman, D. B. (1968) The Impact on Political Science of the Revolution in the Behavioral Sciences, in: M. Brodbeck (ed.) *Readings in the Philosophy of the Social Sciences*, pp. 541–60 (New York: Macmillan).

U.S. Senate Committee on Armed Services (2008) *Senate Armed Services Committee Inquiry into the Treatment of Detainees in U.S. Custody* (Washington DC: U.S. Senate Committee on Armed Services).

United Nations Human Rights Council (2009) *United Nations Fact Finding Mission on the Gaza Conflict* (Geneva: United Nations Human Rights Council). Available at http://www2.ohchr.org/english/bodies/hrcouncil/docs/12session/A-HRC-12-48.pdf.

United Nations Assistance Mission in Afghanistan (2012) *Annual Report on Protection of Civilians in Armed Conflict, 2011* (Kabul: United Nations Assistance Mission to Afghanistan). Available at http://www.unhcr.org/ref world/pdfid/4f2fa7572.pdf.

Veblen, T. (1970) *The Theory of the Leisure Class* (London: Unwin Books).

Vernon R. (1986) *Citizenship and Order: Studies in French Political Thought* (Toronto and London: Toronto University Press).

Viereck, P. (1965) *Conservatism Revisited* (New York: Free Press).

Wakin, M. M. (2000) *Integrity First: Reflections of a Military Philosopher* (Lanham: Lexington Books).

Walzer, M. (1983) *Spheres of Justice: a Defense of Pluralism and Equality* (New York: Basic Books).

Walzer, M. (1992) *Just and Unjust Wars* (New York: Basic Books).

Walzer, M. (1994) *Thick and Thin: Moral Argument at Home and Abroad* (Notre Dame: Notre Dame Press).

Walzer, M. (2004) *Arguing about War* (New Haven and London: Yale University Press).

Walzer, M. (2009) Responsibility and Proportionality in State and Nonstate Wars, *Parameters: US Army War College Quarterly*, (39)1, pp. 40–52.

Walzer, M. and Margalit, A. (2009) Israel: Civilians & Combatants, *The New York Review of Books* (56)8.

Weber, M. (1978) Politik als Beruf (Politics as a Vocation), in: W. G. Runciman (ed.) *Selections in Translation* (Cambridge: Cambridge University Press).

Wells, H. G. (2005) *The Invisible Man* (London: Penguin Classics).

Welsh, A. (2008) *What is Honor? A Question of Moral Imperatives* (New Haven: Yale University Press).

Wessely, S. (2006) Twentieth-century Theories on Combat Motivation and Breakdown, *Journal of Contemporary History*, 41(2), pp. 268–86.

Westacott, E. (2006) The Rights and Wrongs of Rudeness, *International Journal of Applied Philosophy* (20)1, pp. 1–22.

Westhusing, T. (2003) A Beguiling Military Virtue: Honor, *Journal of Military Ethics*, 2(3), pp. 195–212.

Wheeler, M. O. (1973) Loyalty, Honor, and the Modern Military, *Air University Review*, May-June.

Williams, B. (1973) A Critique of Utilitarianism, in: J. J. C. Smart and B. Williams (eds) *Utilitarianism; For and Against*, pp. 77–150 (Cambridge: Cambridge University Press).

Williams, B. (1993) *Shame and Necessity* (Berkeley: University of California Press).

Williams, R. (1983) *Rousseau and Romantic Autobiography* (Oxford: Oxford University Press).

Winch, D. (1978) *Adam Smith's Politics* (Cambridge: Cambridge University Press).

Winslow, D. (1999) Rites of Passage and Group Bonding in the Canadian Airborne, *Armed Forces & Society*, 25(3), pp. 429–57.

Wittgenstein, L. (1967) *Philosophische Untersuchungen* (Suhrkamp: Frankfurt am Main).

Wittgenstein, L. (1997) *Philosophical Investigations* (Oxford: Basil Blackwell).

Wolfendale, J. (2009) The Myth of Torture Lite, *Ethics & International Affairs*, 23(1), pp. 47–61.

Wong, L., T. A. Kolditz, R. A. Millen, and T. M. Potter (2003) *Why They Fight: Combat Motivation in the Iraq War* (Carlisle Barracks: Strategic Studies Institute, U.S. Army War College).

Wrage, S. (2002) Captain Lawrence Rockwood in Haiti, *Journal of Military Ethics*, 1(1), pp. 45–52.

Wyatt-Brown, B. (2005) The Ethic of Honor in National Crises: The Civil War, Vietnam, Iraq, and the Southern Factor, *The Journal of the Historical Society*, 5(4), pp. 431–60.

Zimbardo, P. G. (2007) *The Lucifer Effect: Understanding How Good People Turn Evil* (New York: Random House).

Index

Abu Ghraib, 74, 89, 125, 149–51, 190, 191
Achilles, 53, 137
Agamemnon, 53
altruism, 7, 12, 38, 61, 64, 157
ambition, 16, 18, 23–5, 52, 56, 70, 94, 134
Appiah, Kwame Anthony, 4, 11, 41, 57, 58, 127, 134, 136, 186
Arendt, Hannah, 21, 26, 164
authenticity, 2–3, 70, 117–8, 129, 159, 182
autobiography, 47, 108, 114–5, 121
autonomy, 2–3, 6–7, 10–11, 17, 56, 62–3, 66–70, 129, 156, 170, 180, 193

Baader-Meinhof Group, 116–7
Bacon, Francis, 27, 52
Bandura, Albert, 151–2, 191
Barry, Brian, 44, 66, 92
battle, 21, 27, 99, 126, 162, 171
Becker, Gary, 59–61, 69, 167
Bentham, Jeremy, 43, 46, 51, 69, 91, 93–5, 133, 175–6
Berger, Peter, 3, 70, 136, 161
Bin Laden, Osama, 147–8, 187, 188, 189
Bloom, Allan, 61, 164, 170, 182, 193
blushing, 137, 163
Bowman, James, 4, 51, 73, 75, 114, 140, 146, 187
Burke, Edmund, 114, 124, 166, 182
Burke, Jason, 140–1, 143–4, 147, 149, 153, 189–90, 192

Caesar, 17, 22, 23, 25, 53, 136
Caine, Sebastian, 6, 51, 167
Cairns, Douglas, 9
Calley, Lieutenant, 125
Carroll, Lewis, 170, 175
Catiline, 17, 22–3, 136
Cato Major, 125
Cato Minor, 125, 18

censure, 6, 20, 35–6, 37, 69, 112, 168–9
chivalry, 26–7, 191
Christianity, 26–7, 38, 39
class, 32, 53, 57, 73, 156, 183
cohesion, 128, 184–5
colonialism, 73, 138
communitarianism, 79, 118, 169, 170
conformism, 104, 116, 123, 129, 183
Conrad, Joseph, 1–4, 59, 74, 78, 83, 96, 107, 115–6, 118
conscience, 6–7, 9, 11–2, 50, 63, 70, 100, 108–10, 113, 124, 137, 156
conscientious objectors, 74, 75
consequentialism, 84–6, 89–90, 95, 169, 173, 176, 199
Cooley, Charles, 7, 49, 55, 56, 63, 169
Coriolanus, 22–3, 136
cosmopolitism, 92, 95–7
Costa Concordia, 10
courage, 1, 2, 6, 15, 30, 40, 62, 65, 106, 107, 114, 125–8, 131–3, 151, 162, 178, 184–5
Crusoe, Robinson, 121, 122–3
Cynics, 18, 137

Dahl, Robert, 60, 168
Darby, Joe, 74–77, 79, 100, 125
darkness, 2, 6, 52, 130
Demetriou, Daniel, 151
dignitas, 26, 29, 135–8
dignity, 1, 7, 14, 29, 64, 70, 124, 134–8, 144–5, 148, 151–4, 156, 170, 175, 178, 183, 186, 188, 191–2
dishonor, 23, 32, 53, 57, 75, 94, 141, 155, 163, 171
Dodds, Eric, 63
double effect, 82–4, 89, 131, 172–3
Douro, sinking of the, 78
Downs, Anthony, 60
dual loyalty, 97–9, 178

dueling, 4, 10, 11, 30, 57, 64, 155, 167
Dunn, John, 157, 192
Durkheim, Emile, 30
duty-based ethics, 9, 68, 85, 89, 133, 174

education, 15, 35, 40–1, 42, 45, 50, 56,
    66–7, 98, 103, 144, 166, 182
Elias, Norbert, 152–3
Ellison, Ralph, 54, 130, 138
Emile (from Rousseau's *Emile*), 110, 120,
    122
emulation, 47, 52, 101, 109
Enlightenment, 4, 32, 181
Epicureanism, 18–21, 26, 32, 61–2, 68–70,
    91, 156, 162–3, 166
Erasmus, 41–2, 109
Etzioni, Amitai, 124, 169
examples, role of, 23, 113, 182

fame, 2, 17–8, 20–25, 46–7, 62, 64, 94, 109,
    115, 125, 155, 168, 183
Fénelon, François (Archbishop of Cambray),
    87, 92, 122
Ferguson, Adam, 51
feudalism, 32, 156
flattery, 24, 40–1
Fletcher, George, 75, 78, 81, 89
Fontan, Victoria, 149–50, 189
Freud, Sigmund, 33, 67, 101, 110, 180
Friedman, Milton, 59–60, 167
Friedman, Thomas, 142–3, 149
Fromm, Erich, 112, 124, 182
Fukuyama, Francis, 31, 65, 168, 170

Galston, William, 26, 103, 157, 181
Gay, Peter, 32–3, 48, 110, 162, 180, 181
Genet, Jean, 116
Gesinnungsethik, 90, 131
glory, 15, 17, 18, 20–7, 30–1, 40–2, 46–7,
    49–50, 52–3, 55, 62, 109, 114, 154, 183
Godwin, William, 87, 92, 102, 122, 127
Goffman, Erving, 63, 169
Goodin, Robert, 90–1, 93
Griffin, 6, 51, 54, 167
Gross, Michael, 99–100
Guantanamo Bay Detention Camp, 149,
    151, 178
guilt, 3, 9, 63, 137, 139, 151, 156, 167–8,
    176; difference with shame, 9; guilt
    culture, 3, 63, 168
Gyges, 5, 6, 20, 51, 54, 105, 110, 130, 167

Haditha killings, 89, 151
Hayek, Friedrich, 162, 166, 168

Hersh, Seymour, 149
Hobbes, Thomas, 28, 32, 33, 36, 39, 62, 69,
    70, 161–3
Homer, 27, 56, 167
honor, as something artificial, 3, 12, 36–7,
    130; as a check on conduct, 23, 38,
    51–2, 110, 112, 124; cultural honor, 140;
    difference with dignity, 7, 134, 135–6,
    191; external, 5, 7–8, 11–3, 51, 55, 71,
    158–9; as not being found out, 6, 11, 13,
    38, 51, 56, 72, 105; two functions, 9–10,
    19–20, 71; honor groups, 5, 13, 72, 73,
    75, 78–81, 89, 92–93, 95, 97–98, 103,
    125, 127–9, 131, 143, 152, 155, 158;
    internalized, 8, 11, 34, 55–6, 72, 129,
    158, 159, 162; literature on, 4; modern
    view on, 11; reflexive honor, 140, 146,
    153; as a reward, 9–10, 12, 15, 18, 22,
    24–5, 27, 55, 58, 69, 81, 129, 159, 181;
    between states, 153–4; of thieves, 57,
    131; in war, 5, 15, 30–1, 39–40, 53, 73,
    127–8, 151, 153–4, 162, 171, 190–1
Human Rights Watch, 80–1, 88
Hume, David, 5, 10, 31, 33–4, 42–51,
    54, 56, 63–4, 66, 68, 69, 70, 92–3, 95,
    102, 108–111, 115, 124, 133, 157, 163,
    165–6, 167, 168–9, 170, 177, 180, 193
humiliation, 5, 125, 134, 137–53, 159,
    188–9, 190, 192; difference between
    normative and psychological, 137–8,
    146, 153
humility, 16, 27, 39, 152
Huntington, Samuel, 143, 153
Hutcheson, Francis, 33, 91, 175
hypocrisy, 131

impartial spectator, 48, 50, 55–6, 96, 102,
    110, 129, 168
infamy, 58, 94
inner-directedness, 113
integrity, definitions of, 105–7; and honor,
    11, 13, 158–9; and Romanticism, 108,
    112; and subjectivity, 13, 128, 130, 133,
    159; and uniqueness, 107–8, 111–2, 115,
    117–8
intentions, 2, 26, 38, 55, 81–6, 89–90, 93–4,
    128, 131, 146, 172–5, 188, 190
invisibility, 5, 54, 105, 130, 138
is/ought distinction, 157
Islam, 139, 142–7, 153, 187–90, 192

Jim, from *Lord Jim*, 1–5, 8–10, 59, 78, 82,
    83, 96, 107, 111–2, 115–6
judicious spectator, 42, 44, 102

Just War Theory, 82–3, 88, 90, 173
justice, 5–7, 10, 15, 44–5, 57, 64–8, 71, 76, 78–80, 93, 105, 107, 131–3, 186

Kaiten, 127
Kant, Immanuel, 31, 63–4, 66–71, 86, 92, 110, 113, 133–5, 156, 160
Karenina, Anna, 119, 183
Kinneging, Andreas, 156, 165
knaves, 44, 70
Kohlberg, Lawrence, 67–8, 71, 95, 174
Krause, Sharon, 4, 11
Kurtz, 116–7

Levin, Konstantin, 118, 120
Lewis, Bernard, 142–3, 147
Lindh, John Walker, 75
Locke, John, 5–7, 12, 32, 34–6, 40–2, 50, 57, 67, 70, 96, 108, 110, 111, 126, 140
losing face, 5, 6, 62, 67, 169
loyalty, not the opposite of disloyalty, 77; to a group, 13, 77–80, 81, 82, 101, 105, 107, 128, 130–1, 134, 153, 158, 180, 186, 187; literature on, 75; to loyalty, 104; to a principle, 13, 77–9, 82, 101, 104, 105–6, 130–1, 158; professional, 13, 97–101, 128–9, 158; a virtue or not, 13, 75–6; in war, 80–9, 128, 180, 186
Lucretia, 127
Lucretius, 18, 32, 162

Machiavelli, Niccolò, 33, 62
MacIntyre, Alasdair, 62, 63–4, 112, 169
magnanimity, 16, 20, 134
Mandeville, Bernard, 12, 36, 36–43, 45, 48, 50–1, 53, 56, 63, 68–9, 88, 109, 119, 124, 127, 133, 140, 152, 164, 168, 167, 177
Margalit, Avishai, 27, 66, 116, 136–9, 143, 145–7, 153, 187
marines, 32, 88, 151, 86
Marlow, Charles, 2, 4, 6, 96, 112, 115–7, 137–8, 151
medical ethics, 98–100, 178, 179, 191
Mendus, Susan, 71, 102
Middle Ages, 26–7
Mill, John Stuart, 5, 32, 43, 51, 60, 64, 66, 69, 93–5, 97, 123–4, 155, 158, 167–8, 175–6, 183
Miller, William Ian, 66, 76, 125, 126, 138, 139, 140–1, 184
models to follow, need for, 23, 104, 120–1, 159, 182
Montaigne, Michel de, 54, 55, 62, 163, 190

Montesquieu, Charles, 28–9, 109, 124
Montgomery, Field Marshall Bernard, 53
moral courage, 56, 124–8, 132–3, 184
moral development, 3, 12, 56, 65–8, 71, 95
motivational realism, 157
My Lai, 89, 100, 101, 125, 128, 171

Nagel, Thomas, 82, 102
Napoleon, 120, 165, 183
nationalism, 73, 103

obligations to strangers, 79–80, 86–9, 92, 107
obscurity, 17, 52, 54, 109, 158
occidentalism, 139, 143
Oprisko, Robert, 4, 11
other-directedness, 112–3, 117, 124

pacifism, 82, 84, 90, 131, 172–3
Patna, 1, 6, 8, 10, 116, 130, 160
patriotism, 73, 87, 181
Patusan, 2, 10, 74, 82, 96, 123, 127
peer pressure, 3, 6, 68
Phalanx, 15, 162
Philip, Zimbardo, 151, 190, 191
Piaget, Jean, 66, 68
Picq, Colonel Ardant Du, 15, 62
Pinker, Steven, 57, 153
Pitt-Rivers, Julian, 3, 8, 11, 39, 53, 55, 161
Plato, 5, 15–7, 28–9, 51, 62, 69, 75, 105, 106, 125, 126, 155, 164, 184
Plutarch, 12, 17, 22, 23, 25, 121, 125, 184
Pocock, John, 33–4, 60, 164, 182
politicians, 23, 36, 41, 44–5, 74, 80, 82, 86, 89, 90, 97, 103, 106, 131, 147, 154
Pompey, 23, 125, 156
pride 8, 9, 27, 36, 39, 40–1, 46, 114, 94, 145
Princen, Poncke, 74–5, 79, 100
private sphere, 28, 90
public opinion, 29, 30, 80, 108, 124, 129, 170
public sphere, 81–2, 90, 102, 103, 131

Qutb, Sayyid, 144, 187

Rawls, John, 9–10, 58, 64–8, 71, 90, 96, 116–8, 135–6, 153, 170, 175–6
Raz, Joseph, 135
recognition, 4–5, 11–2, 20, 22–3, 26, 31, 53–4, 58, 62, 64, 66, 70, 115, 120–1, 128, 134, 156, 170
Renaissance, 27

respect, 11, 13–4, 52, 53–4, 62, 64, 70–1,
    131–6, 139, 146, 149, 151, 152, 153, 154,
    155, 156, 159–60, 183, 186–7, 191, 192
revenge, 47, 141, 146, 155, 174, 185, 187
Riesman, David, 112–3, 124, 169
Robinson, Paul, 151, 178
Rockwood, Captain Lawrence, 100, 101,
    128, 180
Roman Republic, 25, 26, 125, 136, 162
Romanticism, 108, 112, 115, 118, 139, 181,
    182
Rome, 15, 19, 25, 32, 187
Rorty, Richard, 78–81
Rotterdam, 41
Rousseau, Jean-Jacques, 66, 69, 108–10,
    112, 114–6, 118–122, 139, 180–1, 182,
    183
Royce, Josiah, 77–8, 83, 104
rule following, 50, 121–2
Rumsfeld, Donald, 74, 150
Rushdie, Salman, 189

Sallust, 12, 15, 17, 25, 28, 31, 125, 187
Sandel, Michael, 64
Sarte, Jean-Paul, 63, 116, 145
Scanlon, Thomas, 83–5, 94, 103
Self-esteem, 26, 66, 135–7, 140, 146
Self-respect, 7, 65–6, 134–7, 145–6, 149,
    191
Seneca, 18, 39, 51, 108, 162, 180–1
Sennet, Richard, 55, 112–3, 149, 152, 181,
    182
Sessions, William Lad, 4, 11, 98
shame, 3, 5–6, 9, 15–6, 19, 22, 35, 40–1,
    45, 53, 56, 63–65, 94, 112, 114, 116,
    125, 127–8, 135, 137, 139–40, 148–9,
    151–2, 156, 161–3, 166–9, 184, 186–7,
    189; difference with guilt, 9; shame
    culture, 3, 56, 63, 127, 139, 148–9, 167,
    184
sincerity, 38, 117, 129
Singer, Peter, 86–78
Skinner, B.F., 63, 169
Skinner, Quentin, 3, 27–8, 33–4, 60, 164
Smith, Adam, 5, 8, 10, 11, 30–1, 34, 38,
    42, 48–51, 52–6, 58, 61–2, 62–4, 70, 90,
    95–6, 102, 108, 110–11, 113–4, 124,
    129, 130, 157, 158, 159, 163, 166, 167,
    168–9, 170
social stratification, 32, 156
Socrates, 25, 126, 163, 164, 175
Sorel, Julien, 120–1, 137, 138, 183
Spierenburg, Pieter, 8, 31, 58, 73, 161, 167,
    170, 187

status, 58–9, 62, 65–6, 134, 135, 138–9,
    156, 170, 183,
Stauffenberg, Claus Schenk von, 101, 128
Stendhal, 5, 120–1, 124, 137–8
Stern, Jessica, 143–6, 148, 150, 188
Stewart, Frank Henderson, 8, 134, 159, 161,
    162, 189
Stoicism, 12, 18–21, 24, 26–8, 32, 38–9, 40,
    43, 45–6, 48, 52, 54–5, 62–4, 66, 68–70,
    92, 95–6, 108–9, 113, 129, 156, 162–3,
    166, 180–1, 182

Tarcov, Nathan, 35, 140
Taylor, Charles, 17–8, 28, 59–61, 64, 111,
    114, 118, 121, 130
terrorism, 14, 83, 141–9, 153, 187, 188–9,
    190, 191, 192
Thompson, Hugh, 100, 101, 125, 128
Thucydides, 153–4, 162
Tocqueville, Alexis de, 28–32, 51, 57, 61,
    119–20, 123–4, 156, 158, 191
Tolstoy, Leo, 118–20, 183
Trilling, Lionel, 117–8, 210

utilitarianism, 13, 43, 60, 82, 85–7, 89–99,
    103, 122, 175, 176, 177

vanity, 16, 26, 28, 36, 39, 42, 45–6, 50, 52,
    61, 69, 94, 109–10, 114–5, 121, 166,
    180, 181, 182
Veblen, Thorstein, 58–61
Verhoeven, Paul, 5, 51
virtue, 2, 6, 9–11, 13, 15–22, 24–5, 27–8,
    30–2, 36–9, 41–4, 46–7, 49, 51, 53, 55,
    57, 62–5, 69, 70, 73, 75–6, 78–9, 81,
    84–5, 88, 89–90, 93–4, 105–111, 116–7,
    122, 124, 128–34, 155–7, 159, 163, 164,
    165, 169, 174, 175, 177, 178, 180, 181,
    182, 183, 184, 185, 186, 190, 191
virtue ethics, 9, 84–5, 89, 133, 174, 177,
    182

Weber, Max, 90, 131
Wells, H.G., 5, 51, 54
Welsh, Alexander, 4, 8
West Point honor code and credo, 11
whistleblowers, 74–7, 101, 125–6, 128
Williams, Bernard, 56, 64, 68, 82, 90, 122,
    167
Wittgenstein, Ludwig, 122
World Medical Association, 99–100, 179
Wronski, Andrej, 119

Zawahiri, Ayman, 144–5, 148